Sherlock Holmes
for the 21st Century

SHERLOCK HOLMES FOR THE 21ST CENTURY

Essays on New Adaptations

Edited by
Lynnette Porter

McFarland & Company, Inc., Publishers
Jefferson, North Carolina, and London

LIBRARY OF CONGRESS CATALOGUING-IN-PUBLICATION DATA

Sherlock Holmes for the 21st century : essays on new adaptations /
edited by Lynnette Porter.
    p.   cm.
Includes bibliographical references and index.

ISBN 978-0-7864-6840-9
softcover : acid free paper ∞

1. Sherlock Holmes films — History and criticism.   2. Sherlock
Holmes television programs — History and criticism.   3. Doyle
[sic], Arthur Conan, Sir, 1859–1930 — Characters — Sherlock
Holmes.   4. Doyle [sic], Arthur Conan, Sir, 1859–1930 — Film
adapatations.   5. Holmes, Sherlock (Fictitious character)
6. Holmes, Sherlock (Fictitious character) in mass media.
I. Porter, Lynnette R., 1957–   II. Title: Sherlock Holmes for
the twenty-first century.
PN1995.9.S5S54 2012
791.43'651—dc22   2012026506

BRITISH LIBRARY CATALOGUING DATA ARE AVAILABLE

On the cover: Benedict Cumberbatch in *Sherlock*, 2010
(© BBC/Hartswood Films/Photofest); *inset* Robert Downey, Jr.,
in *Sherlock Holmes*, 2009 (© Warner Bros./Photofest);

Manufactured in the United States of America

McFarland & Company, Inc., Publishers
  Box 611, Jefferson, North Carolina 28640
  www.mcfarlandpub.com

Table of Contents

Introduction
In Search of the Real Sherlock Holmes

London could have dubbed the first week of December 2011 as Sherlock Holmes Week, or possibly Holmescoming Week. The BBC television hit *Sherlock* held its second season's premiere at the British Film Institute (BFI) on Wednesday night, and the cast of Warner Bros.' *Sherlock Holmes: A Game of Shadows* walked the red carpet at its Leicester Square premiere the next. Both events attracted fans from around the world who wanted to glimpse in person the actors now famous for playing Sherlock Holmes and John Watson on screen.

BFI tickets sold out faster than for any previous event, and fans unable to get tickets queued hours ahead of the screening to see if tickets might be returned. The BFI screening started the BBC's countdown to the second season, which kicked off 2012 programming with the highly anticipated episode, "A Scandal in Belgravia." The BBC representative introducing the episode commented on the number of fans attending from around the world. (I was one of them.)

During the screening, the audience cheered, applauded, and "awww"ed as they responded to Sherlock's dialogue or surprising plot twists. Although *Sherlock's* John Watson (Martin Freeman) was off in New Zealand filming another iconic role, Bilbo Baggins in Peter Jackson's *The Hobbit* films, Benedict Cumberbatch, who plays Sherlock Holmes, attended the screening — sitting among more than 400 fans in the crowded BFI Theatre 1. He, along with series' creators Steven Moffat and Mark Gatiss, guest star Lara Pulver (Irene Adler), and moderator Caitlin Moran, discussed the new series and answered a few questions from the audience. Afterward, Cumberbatch politely posed for photos or signed autographs for everyone who waited for him at the theater door.

At the Empire Theatre on Leicester Square, fans lined up hours before the evening premiere of *A Game of Shadows* and waited in the increasingly stormy weather for the stars to arrive. Robert Downey, Jr., and Jude Law, the film franchise's Holmes and Watson, quickly signed autographs amid bursts of digital flashes, but the majority of their time on and off the red carpet was spent with the press. From my (dry) vantage point beneath the Empire's marquee, I watched the duo hug and mug for the press. They clearly are in demand and know how to emphasize their on-camera chemistry and off-camera friendship to help sell the film. Despite the inclement weather, many fans (such as the father standing next to me) had taken off work or (like his daughter) skipped classes to wait beside the red carpet. When the teenager who had stood for nearly eight hours to see Downey finally received an autograph, she could barely contain her joy. Her smile, her father admitted, made the trip to London and the miserable afternoon of waiting worth all the trouble.

If my two evenings spent with other Holmes fans are any indication, the early 21st century is indeed a fine time to be Sherlock Holmes — or to portray him on television or film. These adaptations of Sir Arthur Conan Doyle's stories may be only the latest in a long line, but they indicate how well the characters have thrived since their introduction more than a century ago.

The Most Recent Adaptations

Although the BBC's *Sherlock* and Guy Ritchie's *Sherlock Holmes* film franchise generate the majority of press, they are far from the only recent adaptations winning the detective new fans, whether Holmes is modern or traditionally Victorian, close to canon or far afield in interpretation. Whereas Moffat and Gatiss' *Sherlock* brings the consulting detective into modern London, it surprisingly is more faithful to canon than some adaptations set in the Victorian era, and details from Conan Doyle's stories are cleverly worked into the episodes. Interest in a modern Holmes, and the British series' critical and popular success, spawned an American adaptation in early 2012; CBS commissioned a pilot for a new television series, *Elementary,* in which Sherlock Holmes is a modern detective living in New York. The casting proved interesting, as well as designed to legally separate itself from the BBC's modernized Holmes, especially through a different vision for the role of Watson. CBS' Sherlock Holmes is Jonny Lee Miller, who, ironically, also shared the roles of Victor Frankenstein and the Creature with the BBC's Sherlock, Benedict Cumberbatch; they alternated roles in Danny Boyle's adaptation of *Frankenstein* at London's National Theatre early in 2011. In the CBS adaptation, British Holmes moves to New York City for drug rehabilitation. The former Scotland Yard consultant soon meets his "sober companion" Joan Watson (Lucy Liu), a surgeon who lost her license after a patient died (Bricker).

Long before CBS decided whether the pilot would be turned into a television series, *Elementary* generated plenty of media and fan attention for its modern take on Holmes, the Americanization of an iconic British character, and casting, but the attention was not all positive. *Sherlock's* producer, Sue Vertue, told *The Independent,* "Let's hope their pilot script has stayed further away from our Sherlock than their casting choice," and added, "We have been in touch with CBS and informed them that we will be looking at their finished pilot very closely for any infringement of our rights" (Sherwin). *The Huffington Post* worried that *Elementary* "appears to be little more than a patently transparent attempt to cash in on a recognizable name" (Prudom). In late March 2012, fans eagerly analyzed photographs from the first days' filming in Manhattan to see what the newest Holmes would look like. CBS' Holmes, like his BBC counterpart, wears a scarf tied around his neck and often carries a phone in hand, but his coat is far from cape-like. Liu's Watson seems to be far more fashionable than Freeman's Watson (Larkin), but like Holmes and Watson anywhere and everywhere, they are caught up in their own world when they converse about a case. On either side of the pond, modern Holmes seems to be increasingly irresistible and newsworthy.

Taking a more traditional approach to setting, Guy Ritchie's films remain true to Conan Doyle's Victorian time frame but present Holmes as an action hero whose antics stray much farther from canon than the BBC's *Sherlock* but not so far from the original as *Elementary's* creators apparently envision their Holmes and Watson. Although "action hero" Holmes may not be exactly what Conan Doyle created, the films' flashy style and subtext-laden bromance between Holmes and Watson are box office gold.

Not to be outdone by film or television, print media also celebrate Sherlock Holmes with a plethora of new publications, most notably one not only sanctioned but commissioned by the Arthur Conan Doyle Estate. Anthony Horowitz's *The House of Silk,* published internationally in November 2011, retains the Victorian setting and many elements of a traditional Conan Doyle story, but this time Watson's reminiscences have been written long after Holmes' real death. Watson details a final adventure, one so scandalous that the good doctor has the manuscript sealed for one hundred years. Fortunately for readers, the scandal involving the House of Silk can now be revealed.

Even pastiches (short stories written in the style of Conan Doyle) have received remarkable acclaim. Fantasy writer Neil Gaiman's award-nominated or -winning stories involving Sherlock Holmes and John Watson place the duo in a different genre (science fiction) than the mystery or detective story. However, the great detective is easily recognizable, even when he is living in the London of an alternate universe or studying the remarkable properties of mutant bees in China.

The adaptations analyzed in this book are by no means the only Sherlocks new to popular culture in the past few years. In addition to the sanctioned novel, dozens of new Sherlock Holmes novels and stories continue to be published annually, now that many original works are in the public domain and authors can take their turn in furthering the great detective's adventures according to their own interests or agendas. Companies such as Infinity Publishing, Pegasus, and Titan offer the public several new titles each year.

Victorian Holmes also is a comic book character. In DC Comics' "Victorian Undead" series, he even battles zombies. Dynamite Comics chose to pay homage to the original stories, and Image Comics bases its series on Moriarty (Price). In December 2011, Bluewater Comics launched a Victorian heroes series featuring, each in his own comic book, Sherlock Holmes and Alan Quartermain. The press release proudly states that "[i]n contrast to the heroes currently aided with high tech pcs, weaponry and all types of clever gadgets, Sherlock Holmes and Allan Quartermain fought evil only armed with their wits and an unbelievable intention," clearly separating the comic book from other recent adaptations (Bluewater Productions).

Not to be outdone by other media, videogames have their own version of Sherlock Holmes. "The Testament of Sherlock Holmes," which debuted early in 2012, offers players a "dark ambiance" and "strong story centered on a controversial hero with obscure motives" ("Testament"). Frogwares developed the game for multiple platforms: Xbox 360, PlayStation 3, and PC. Video teasers released on the game's website intrigued viewers in late 2011 with glimpses of yet another Sherlock Holmes. In the first trailer, Dr. Watson denounces Holmes for deceiving him for years and betraying their friendship. Although the role-playing game promises gamers a crime-detection and clue-following experience, the scenario again emphasizes the Holmes-Watson friendship and, as also shown in the BBC's second season of *Sherlock*, illustrate stresses in the characters' bond.

Some fans want to do more than passively watch or read about the adventures of Holmes and Watson. For those who want to role play beyond the virtual reality of videogames, cinematic tourism may provide the experience they seek. Movie and television filming locations in the U.K., as well as London-based museums, restaurants, and hotels, offer Holmesians (or Sherlockians) the opportunity to see where and how their favorite characters (or the actors playing them) live and work.

With so many adaptations of Sherlock Holmes available, in the past few years in particular, which ones have gained the greatest public favor, and why? An attempt to debate the issue of which Holmes is "best" took place in early November 2011. The online discussion, called the Great Sherlock Holmes Debate, allowed teams to choose a side and offer key points about which Holmes is best and why. Holmes scholars, members of Sherlock Holmes societies, and webmasters of fan sites joined debate teams. The online event, publicized on websites and social media sites like Facebook, attracted an international crowd. The results? The pre-debate vote, based on presentations published online, was firmly in favor of BBC Sherlock (52 votes), with the Warner Bros. Holmes coming in last with 3 votes. "Traditional" Holmes (the original Conan Doyle character) received 9 votes, an equal number to those who remained undecided about which version is best. After the live debate, BBC Sherlock still came out on top (38 votes), but more judges (30) were undecided after hearing additional evidence about traditional, BBC, and Warner Bros. Sherlocks. The traditionalists retained 5 votes, but poor Warner Bros. Holmes received no votes in this final tally (Sherlockology). Whether modernization, references to canon, or the number of Benedict Cumberbatch fans helped change voters' minds, the BBC adaptation certainly is in vogue, but traditional Holmes remains a valuable reason for the detective's current popularity.

Whether an adaptation for a non-print medium, an attempt to re-create Conan Doyle's prose style, or part of role or game playing, Sherlock Holmes is perhaps the most popular he has ever been, especially to an international audience. To understand the current global popularity of so many adaptations presented through so many media, Holmes' place in British literature and popular culture must be discussed as the foundation for his resurgence in popularity.

Sherlock Holmes in the 19th and 20th Centuries

For more than a century, Sherlock Holmes has been a significant character in British literature and a cultural icon. The original stories by Sir Arthur Conan Doyle were first published as magazine serials beginning in 1887 with "A Study in Scarlet" in *Beeton's Christmas Annual* but gained greater popularity when the stories were regularly published in *Strand Magazine* beginning four years later. Novels soon joined the stories, the last tale being published in 1927. Sherlock Holmes' adventures have never gone out of print, and in the 21st century, several new editions have appeared ("Sherlock Holmes").

A first, previously unpublished novel, *The Narrative of John Smith*, written by Sir Arthur Conan Doyle was published in September 2011 (Saunders), a move to help satisfy the author's fans' desire for more. The Sherlock Holmes stories have been translated into at least 60 languages (Thompson). Now another generation of readers around the world is turning to the original texts for the first time, largely because of their renewed presence on cinema and television screens and online. In November 2011, BBC Books began publishing new television tie-in editions, first with *A Study in Scarlet* and *The Adventures of Sherlock Holmes*; the introductions were written by, respectively, *Sherlock* co-creators Steven Moffat and Mark Gatiss.

The audience for Sherlock Holmes stories is broader than ever. Readers who grew up with the stories often remain purists who do not like anyone messing around with canon; they often are the backbone of societies like the Baker Street Irregulars, a by-invitation-only society founded in 1934, or the Sherlock Holmes Society of London, which, since 1951, encourages anyone interested in Holmes to attend regular meetings. Such societies can be found around the world; they are especially prevalent in Canada, the United States, Japan, and, of course, all across the U.K.

Then there are readers who are fans of the printed stories but who also grew up in Britain with several television series and movies (from the 1930s onward, with the popular Granada television series generating renewed interest in Holmes). Other countries (e.g., the U.S., with a syndicated series in the 1950s) also have enjoyed television or film adventures based on the original Holmes and Watson.

Especially in his home nation, Holmes has played an important role in popular culture after the conclusion of Conan Doyle's stories, which continue to be republished in new editions. As author Peter Haining (43) notes in *The Television Sherlock Holmes,* when "Holmes and Watson made their television debut on the little screen, it soon proved to be just one further step in the development of the Legend of Sherlock Holmes, because he had already been adapted for the stage, screen and radio and proved hugely popular on both sides of the Atlantic." Holmes continued on film and television throughout the 20th century, primarily in the U.K. but also in adventures filmed in other countries, including Russia and the U.S. The table on the opposite page lists the most often documented examples of Holmes' television popularity in the previous century (Haining 93–7), but other adaptations have been made in other countries (e.g., Turkey, Greece, Denmark, Spain, Japan).

Television productions by companies based in the U.K., U.S., Russia, or Germany developed individual television movies or limited-run series as well as full-fledged television series. Sometimes the casting seemed designed purely to bring new viewers to a Holmes story, such as Leonard Nimoy (*Star Trek*'s Spock) as Holmes in 1975's *The Interior Motive*. The most popular casting of television in the 20th century has to be that of Granada Television's *The Adventures of Sherlock Holmes,* which debuted in 1984. Jeremy Brett became Holmes for a generation growing up on the televised stories. The cast included David Burke as Watson, with Rosalie Williams as Mrs. Hudson and Eric Porter as Professor Moriarty.

A Sherlock Holmes exhibit at the British Film Museum in London devotes a room to Victorian Holmes and Watson. As with many similar recre-

Table 1. Best-Known Sherlock Holmes International Adaptations, 1930s–1980s

Year	Title	Country and/or Network
1937	*The Three Garridebs*	U.S./NBC
1949	*The Adventures of the Speckled Band*	U.S.
1951	*The Man with the Twisted Lip*	U.K.
	The Mazarin Stone	U.K./BBC
	Sherlock Holmes	U.K./BBC
1953	*The Black Baronet*	U.S./CBS
1954	*Sherlock Holmes*	France/Guild Films
1964	*The Speckled Band*	U.K./BBC
1965	*Sherlock Holmes*	U.K./BBC
1968	*The Cases of Sherlock Holmes*	U.K./BBC
	Sherlock Holmes and the Deadly Necklace	Germany/Constantin Film Verlieg
1972	*The Longing of Sherlock Holmes*	Czechoslovakia/Czech Films aD
	The Hound of the Baskervilles	U.S./ABC
1974	*Doctor Watson and the Darkwater Hall Mystery*	U.K./BBC
1975	*The Interior Motive*	U.S./Kentucky Educational TV
1976	*The Return of the World's Greatest Detective*	U.S./NBC
	Sherlock Holmes in New York	U.S./NBC
1980	*Sherlock Holmes and Doctor Watson*	U.S./Filmways (distributor), U.S. production (Sheldon Leonard Productions), Polish production (Telewizja Polska)
1981	*Sherlock Holmes*	U.S./HBO
1982	*The Hound of the Baskervilles*	U.K./BBC
	Sherlock Holmes and Doctor Watson	Russia/Lenfilms
1983	*Sherlock Holmes*	U.K./Mapleton Films
1984	*The Masks of Death*	U.K./Tyburn Productions
	The Adventures of Sherlock Holmes	U.K./Granada

ations across London of the sitting room at 221B Baker Street, this one features a hearth resplendent with paraphernalia relating to the Conan Doyle stories. In the hallway outside the exhibit, photographs of key actors in the role (e.g., Jeremy Brett, Peter Cushing, Basil Rathbone) illustrate the continuing presence of Sherlock Holmes in British cinematic history and popular culture. A timeline, from wall to wall (its information edited and updated in the table on the following two pages), documents the Holmes stories made and shown in the U.K., whether on television or film.

Although many Conan Doyle stories are represented, *The Hound of the*

Table 2. Actors in Sherlock Holmes
Adaptations Made in the U.K., 1905–2012

Year	Adaptation Title	Actor Playing Sherlock Holmes
1905	The Adventures of Sherlock Holmes	Maurice Costello
1913	Sherlock Holmes Solves the Sign of Four	Harry Benham
1914	A Study in Scarlet	James Bragington
1916	Valley of Fear	William Gillette
1922	Sherlock Holmes	John Barrymore
1929	The Return of Sherlock Holmes	Clive Brook
1931	The Speckled Band	Raymond Massey
	The Sleeping Cardinal	Arthur Wontner
1932	The Hound of the Baskervilles	Clive Brook
1933	A Study in Scarlet	Reginald Owen
1939	The Hound of the Baskervilles	Basil Rathbone
	The Adventures of Sherlock Holmes	Basil Rathbone
1942	Sherlock Holmes and the Voice of Terror	Basil Rathbone
1944	The Spider Woman	Basil Rathbone
	The Scarlet Claw	Basil Rathbone
	The Pearl of Death	Basil Rathbone
	The House of Fear	Basil Rathbone
1945	The Woman in Green	Basil Rathbone
	Pursuit to Algiers	Basil Rathbone
1946	Terror by Night	Basil Rathbone
	Dressed to Kill	Basil Rathbone
1951	The Man Who Disappeared	John Longden
1955	The Adventures of Sherlock Holmes	Ronald Howard
1959	The Hound of the Baskervilles	Peter Cushing
1962	Sherlock Holmes and the Deadly Necklace	Christopher Lee
1965	A Study in Terror	John Neville
1968	Sherlock Holmes	Peter Cushing
1970	The Private Life of Sherlock Holmes	Robert Stephens
1972	The Hound of the Baskervilles	Stewart Granger
1975	The Adventures of Sherlock Holmes' Smarter Brother	Douglas Wilmer
1976	Sherlock Holmes in New York	Roger Moore
	The Seven Percent Solution	Nicol Williamson
1977	Silver Blaze	Christopher Plummer
	The Strange Case of the End of the World as We Know It	John Cleese
1978	The Hound of the Baskervilles	Peter Cook
1979	Murder by Decree	Christopher Plummer
1980	Sherlock Holmes and Doctor Watson	Geoffrey Whitehead
1981	Sherlock Holmes	Frank Langella

Year	Adaptation Title	Actor Playing Sherlock Holmes
1982	*Sherlock Holmes*	Paul Guers
	The Hound of the Baskervilles	Tom Baker
1983	*The Hound of the Baskervilles*	Ian Richardson
	The Sign of Four	Ian Richardson
	The Baker Boys	Roger Ostine
1984	*The Masks of Death*	Peter Cushing
	The Adventures of Sherlock Holmes	Jeremy Brett
1985	*Young Sherlock Holmes*	Nicholas Rowe
1987	*The Return of Sherlock Holmes*	Jeremy Brett
	The Sign of Four	Jeremy Brett
1988	*Without a Clue*	Michael Caine
	The Hound of the Baskervilles	Jeremy Brett
1990	*Hands of a Murderer*	Edward Woodward
1991	*The Crucifer of Blood*	Charlton Heston
	Incident at Victoria Falls	Christopher Lee
1992	*Sherlock Holmes and the Leading Lady*	Christopher Lee
1993	*The Hound of London*	Patrick McNee
	The Casebook of Sherlock Holmes	Jeremy Brett
1994	*Sherlock Holmes Returns*	Anthony Higgins
	The Memoirs of Sherlock Holmes	Jeremy Brett
1999	*Sherlock Holmes in the 22nd Century*	Jason Gray-Stanford
2000	*Sherlock Holmes TV Film Series*	Matt Frewer
2002	*The Hound of the Baskervilles*	Richard Roxburgh
	Sherlock	James d'Arcy
2005	*Sherlock Holmes and the Case of the Silk Stocking*	Rupert Everett
2007	*I Am Bob*	Humphrey Ker
	The Baker Street Irregulars	Jonathan Pryce
2008	*Batman: The Brave and the Bold*	Ian Buchanan (voiceover)
2009	*Sherlock Holmes*	Robert Downey, Jr.
2010	*Sherlock*	Benedict Cumberbatch
2010	*Sherlock Holmes*	Ben Syder
2011	*Sherlock Holmes 2: A Game of Shadows*	Robert Downey, Jr.
2012	*Sherlock*	Benedict Cumberbatch
	Elementary	Jonny Lee Miller

Baskervilles by far is the most often adapted for screen, a choice continued in 2012 by Moffat and Gatiss for the BBC's television series, *Sherlock* (this time called "The Hounds of Baskerville"). As Table 2 shows, just as favorite stories have been re-interpreted in numerous adaptations, some actors have been favored in the role of Holmes, playing the character two or more times during their career.

Among the 21st century adaptations, however, none gained nearly the notoriety or popularity of the films, series, and books arriving on scene beginning in 2009. The Guy Ritchie–directed *Sherlock Holmes* earned $209 million internationally at the box office and became the record holder for the highest-grossing film opening on Christmas Day, with a $24.6 million one-day total (Subers). The BBC's *Sherlock* won awards or nominations for its writing, production values, and acting (e.g., BAFTAs, BAFTA Cymru awards, an Emmy nomination), not only at home but abroad. The hype surrounding film or television premieres guarantees that the name Sherlock Holmes remains in the media year round.

The many different Sherlock Holmeses have been accepted and absorbed into popular culture in typical cult-fandom fashion. Not only are the official movie, DVD, and television websites frequently visited by fans eagerly awaiting news of the next round of stories, but the number of fan sites has grown exponentially. Of course, there have always been fan sites for Sherlock Holmes by societies studying and revering the original literary texts. Newer fan sites, however, are as likely to be devoted to a film, television series, relationship pairing (not exclusively Holmes-Watson), or actor as they are to be limited to Holmes himself. Fan fiction incorporates topics of interest to fans, who interpret the characters shown on film or television in their own way. Fans' adaptations of adaptations increasingly lead Holmes further astray from Conan Doyle's description. When fans today think of or write about "Sherlock Holmes," whom do they envision?

The plethora of Sherlocks in the 21st century warrants further examination from a variety of perspectives. Just who are they, and why are they so popular now? What do these adaptations indicate about the nature of popular culture and audiences' need for Sherlock Holmes? How does John Watson help readers or viewers understand Sherlock Holmes, and how does Watson's changing role fit with societal expectations of relationships between men?

The following chapters present several scholars' analyses of the great detective. The authors discuss Sherlock Holmes as a technology-savvy modern man (e.g., a digital native), an action hero, a traditional hero according to definitions established by Thomas Carlyle or Joseph Campbell, or an anti-hero. The impact of the Victorian era on recent adaptations reflects modern interest in the original stories as well as the demand to make old stories relevant to 21st century audiences; some chapters compare modern versions of Sherlock Holmes with the character's Victorian origins. Other authors discuss the nature of adaptation and its effects on popular culture, including Holmes' influence on other television characters and series. Fan fiction and online fandom are two areas of current interest, but so too is cinematic tourism.

The Guy Ritchie films (*Sherlock Holmes*, 2009; *Sherlock Holmes: A Game of Shadows,* 2011); the BBC television series *Sherlock* (2010–present); the Anthony Horowitz novel, *The House of Silk* (2011); and Neil Gaiman's short stories, "A Study in Emerald" (2004) and "The Case of Death and Honey" (2011) are the best loved, most profitable, and most representative of the many new Sherlock Holmes stories so far this century. Many of the following chapters compare television and film versions, but Horowitz's novel and Gaiman's pastiches are analyzed as well. These adaptations deserve "forensic" analysis before we can deduce just exactly who Sherlock Holmes is in the 21st century and why he continues to maintain such a hold over fans around the world.

WORKS CITED

"The Baker Street Irregulars." Sherlockian.Net. n.d. Web. 12 June 2011. <http://www.sherlockian.net/societies/index.html>.

Bluewater Productions. "Sherlock Holmes and Alan Quartermain Head to Bluewater Productions." Comicnews. 20 Dec. 2011. Web. 29 Dec. 2011. <http://comic-news.ansipedi.com/sherlock-holmes-and-allan-quartermain-head-to-bluewater-productions/>.

Bricker, Tierney. "Lucy Liu to Star in CBS' Sherlock Holmes Pilot, *Elementary.*" E!Online. 27 Feb. 2012. Web. 3 Mar. 2012. <http://www.eonline.com/news/watch_with_kristin/ lucy_liu_star_in_cbs_sherlock_holmes/297299>.

British Film Museum. London. Sherlock Holmes exhibit. 24 May 2011.

Haining, Peter. *The Television Sherlock Holmes* (rev. ed.). London: Virgin Books, 1991. Print.

Larkin, Mike. "An Elementary Mistake? Lucy Liu Joins Jonny Lee Miller on the Set of Latest Sherlock Holmes Adaptation." *Mail Online.* 21 Mar. 2012. Web. 21 Mar. 2012. <http://www.dailymail.co.uk/tvshowbiz/article-2118565/Lucy-Liu-joins-Jonny-Lee-Miller-set-latest-Sherlock-Holmes-adaptation.html?ito=feeds-newsxml>.

Price, Matthew. "Sherlock Holmes Solves Mysteries in Comics, Too." Nerdage. 16 Dec. 2011. Web. 29 Dec. 2011. <http://blog.newsok.com/nerdage/2011/12/16/sherlock-holmes-solves-mysteries-in-comics-too/>.

Prudom, Laura. "*Elementary* Aims to Update Sherlock Holmes with Dated Ideas: Is CBS Afraid to Go Gay?" *The Huffington Post.* 29 Feb. 2012. Web. 3 Mar. 2012. <http://www.huffingtonpost.com/laura-prudom/elementary-cbs_b_1311340.html>.

Saunders, Emma. "First Conan Doyle Novel to be Published." BBC News. 6 June 2011. Web. 12 June 2011. <http://www.bbc.co.uk/news/entertainment-arts-13667508>.

"Sherlock Holmes." MysteryNet.com. 12 June 2011. Web. 29 Dec. 2011. < http://www.mysterynet.com/holmes/>.

The Sherlock Holmes Society of London. n.d. Web. 12 June 2011. <http://www.sherlock-holmes.org.uk/>.

Sherlockology. "The GSHD Results Are In!" 11 Nov. 2011. Web. 29 Dec. 2011. <http://www.slideshare.net/greatsherlockholmesdebate/final-vote-the-great-sherlock-holmes-debate>.

Sherwin, Adam. "Jonny Lee Miller to Play Sherlock Holmes in US Series." *The Independent.* 15 Feb. 2012. Web. 3 Mar. 2012. <http://www.independent.co.uk/arts-entertainment/tv/news/jonny-lee-miller-to-play-sherlock-holmes-in-us-series-6939158.html>.

Subers, Ray. "End-of-Run Report: Case Closed on 'Sherlock Holmes.'" Box Office Mojo. 5 May 2010. Web. 12 June 2011. <http://www2.boxofficemojo.com/news/ ?id=2758&p=.htm>.

"The Testament of Sherlock Holmes: Sherlock Shows His True Face in Video." 21 Dec. 2011. Web. 29 Dec. 2011. <http://www.sherlockholmes-thegame.com/index.php?rub=news-infos&id=26>.

"The Testament of Sherlock Holmes." Teaser #1. 20 Nov. 2011. Web. 29 Dec. 2011. <http://www.sherlockholmes-thegame.com/index.php?rub=media>.

Thompson, Dawn. "The Game Is Afoot at the Vincent House." *The Messenger.* 14 Apr. 2008. Web. 29 Dec. 2011. <http://www.messengernews.net/page/content.detail/id/ 504812.html?nav=5010>.

1

The Noble Bachelor and the Crooked Man

Subtext and Sexuality in the BBC's *Sherlock*[1]

Carlen Lavigne

> Watson: I'm glad no one saw that.
> Holmes: Mm?
> Watson: You, ripping my clothes off in a darkened swimming pool. People might talk.
> Holmes: People do little else.
>
> — *"The Great Game,"* Sherlock

The BBC's *Sherlock* (2010–present) makes no attempt to hide the potential homoeroticism innate in the relationship between Holmes and Watson; gay references constitute a running gag throughout the first and second seasons. From the first inspection of 221B Baker Street, when Mrs. Hudson enquires genially whether the two men will require the second bedroom, characters consistently and openly question the nature of the partnership between Holmes and Watson — noted bachelors who live together, work together, exchange frequent meaningful glances, and obviously share a deep and satisfying rapport. Of course, when Sergeant Sally Donovan suggests, "Opposites attract" ("The Blind Banker"), this is intended for humorous effect; Holmes and Watson, we are to understand, are certainly *not* gay, as Watson's frequent protests and Holmes' declared asexuality are meant to reinforce. The series brings its queer subtexts to the surface only to disavow them; as such, its dogged preservation of heteronormative paradigms hardly constitutes adventurous television. At the same time, however, *Sherlock* demonstrates a playful willingness to highlight and explore its own "bromance" tropes, creating a persistent, open tease of queer possibilities.

The idea that Holmes and Watson might be "more than friends" is not new; indeed, according to the plainly-titled and admirably thorough *Gay Sherlock Holmes* blog, the two characters (in their various novel/television/film incarnations) have publicly been the subjects of gay erotic imagining for some time, as evidenced by works such as *The Sexual Adventures of Sherlock Holmes* (a 1971 novel by Larry Townsend) and *The American Adventures of Surelick Holmes* (a 1975 pornographic film). Shades of homoeroticism may also be found in Guy Ritchie's *Sherlock Holmes* (2009), which has reinvigorated Holmes' popularity in film at the same time as the BBC series has reimagined Holmes on television. Ritchie's 2009 outing provoked controversy when star Robert Downey, Jr., told MTV that Holmes and Watson were "two men who happen to be roommates who wrestle a lot and share a bed" (Carroll par. 9); while the gay references in the film are not so pronounced as the BBC *Sherlock*'s direct discussions of Holmes' sexual (non)proclivities, and the film provides heterosexual love interests for both male leads, the narrative focuses repeatedly on Holmes' jealousy over Watson's impending nuptials. Gay jokes abound ("Don't get excited," warns Holmes, reaching toward Watson's waist; later, a sardonic Watson tells a hungover Holmes, "You look gorgeous"). In separate scenes from the 2011 sequel *Sherlock Holmes: A Game of Shadows*, we see Holmes dressing (poorly) in drag, grappling intimately with Watson, and asking Watson to dance, as the film's subtext transitions to open satire. "Bromance" is becoming a standard part of the contemporary Holmes mythos.

Holmes and Watson are additionally the heroes of innumerable slash fiction stories — amateur fan-authored works that feature favorite characters in non-canonical and often graphic same-sex relationships. Holmes/Watson slash may be found most currently on Fanfiction.net, or LiveJournal communities such as 221b_recs, but also in archival fanzines such as *Pæan to Priapus II* (1990, containing Edi N. Burgh's story "Post Scriptum"). Notably, slash fiction's existence is flitting along the edges of mainstream awareness; originating in *Star Trek* fan works pairing Kirk and Spock (Kirk/Spock, or Kirk-"slash"-Spock), such stories, formerly distributed via mimeographed or photocopied fanzine, now spread across thousands of film and TV series fandoms and are freely available on the Internet. Author participation has grown exponentially, as has actor, writer, and producer awareness of such fan-crafted stories, videos, and art. Fan fiction, including its slash subset, has "become a worldwide, public phenomenon reported on in global media and openly acknowledged by cultural producers" (Lo par. 5). The Holmes/Watson relationship is definitely popular with slash writers; as of December 27, 2011, searching specifically for Holmes and Watson romance yields 1,965 results from a total of 6,725 *Sherlock* stories available on Fanfiction.net. An additional 440 slash stories (out of 1,375) are based on the *Sherlock Holmes* movie(s), while 220 (of

2,997) are set in the world of the Arthur Conan Doyle books. Admittedly, slash fiction's same-sex (particularly male/male) eroticism is complicated by the fact that the majority of its authors are heterosexual women (Penley; Jones 80); separate from slash fiction's questionable legitimacy as a queer outlet, however, and most relevant to this chapter's argument, is the open speculation involving Holmes and Watson—the fact that numerous fans have publicly considered (and sometimes graphically illustrated) the possibility of a romantic relationship between the two characters.

Sherlock's writers are explicitly aware of such fan debates. On the commentary track for the first episode, "A Study in Pink," writer/co-creator Steven Moffat notes that Sherlock's sexuality is "supposedly controversial" but expresses surprise, asserting that the topic was "never discussed at all" when the series was created. The accuracy of this statement seems somewhat dubious, as Moffat makes this comment during a scripted scene wherein Watson openly asks Holmes about his sexual orientation. It is likely, rather, that Moffat's intent is to argue that Sherlock's sexuality was not an *issue* among the creators— that is to say, that the writers on the series all agreed on Holmes' asexuality as overtly established within the narratives. Moffat, indeed, argues that the series' true subtext is the story of the platonic Holmes and Watson relationship—"the story of the greatest friendship ever"—and that "although people talk about it being ambiguous or mysterious, the truth is that the books are completely clear. [Holmes] is not interested in [sex] at all. He's interested in what his brain is doing ... the fact is, people say he shows no interest in women, therefore he must be gay. He shows no interest in men, either. That's just not what he does." The ensuing discussion of Holmes' sexual potential (among Moffat, writer/co-creator Mark Gatiss, and producer Sue Vertue) quickly establishes Watson's heterosexuality (Vertue points out that he is married in Doyle's canon) and focuses on Irene Adler (known also as The Woman, from the Doyle story "A Scandal in Bohemia") as a possible canonical love interest whose importance is often read "out of proportion" (Gatiss), or who serves to fill the "endless movie trope of putting Sherlock up against a femme fatale" (Moffat). Indeed, when Adler does subsequently make an appearance (in the Season Two premiere "A Scandal in Belgravia"), her role as sexual temptress could not be more explicit: she is a professional dominatrix who confounds Holmes by presenting herself to him in the nude. But her seduction is unsuccessful, at least physically; Moffat has since ventured that Holmes may be afraid of women ("Hounds" BAFTA Screening). In general, the series creators make it clear that they are aware of allegations that Watson and Holmes could be gay; that they dismiss these allegations, reading Watson as straight and Holmes as dedicatedly asexual; and that *if* Holmes could be perceived as having a love interest, the most obvious choice would be a heterosexual pairing.

Sherlock ultimately makes no canonical commitments regarding Holmes' sexuality; the opinions the writers express on the first season's commentary track seem to belie the questions the series persistently raises. Holmes' fraught relationship with Adler does suggest heterosexual tension. Conversely, however, the potential gay reading of the Holmes/Watson relationship is the joke that will not die; it is referenced in each episode. In "A Study in Pink," both Mrs. Hudson and a restaurant waiter assume that Holmes and Watson are gay; whereas Mrs. Hudson questions the need for a second bedroom, the waiter goes to get a candle for the table because it is more "romantic." In "The Blind Banker," Holmes and Watson briefly discuss Watson's evening plans, specifically Watson's upcoming date with his new employer, Sarah:

HOLMES: I need to get some air. We're going out tonight.
WATSON: Actually, I've got a date.
HOLMES: What?
WATSON: Where two people who like each other go out and have fun?
HOLMES: That's what *I* was suggesting.
WATSON: No, it wasn't. At least, I hope not.

The throughline continues in "The Great Game," when Mrs. Hudson notes Holmes and Watson arguing and responds with a cheerful, "Woo-hoo! Have you two had a little domestic?"—not long before Sally Donovan makes the already-documented comment about opposites attracting. Season Two maintains this trend with similar dialogue from Irene Adler ("A Scandal in Belgravia"), an inn manager ("The Hounds of Baskerville"), and a journalist ("The Reichenbach Fall"); when Holmes and Watson must hold hands to run, handcuffed together in "The Reichenbach Fall," Watson observes, "Now people will definitely talk." Each script contains some reference to the homoerotic possibilities of the Holmes/Watson bond. Of course, all such assumptions are quickly met with Watson's vocal objections—he is swift to defend his hetero street cred, marked most clearly by his frustrated pronouncement to Adler, "Who the hell knows about Sherlock Holmes, but, for the record, if anyone out there still cares, I'm not actually gay" ("A Scandal in Belgravia"). It often seems as though *Sherlock* acknowledges the inevitability of its own homosexual subtext only to deny, even lightly mock, such readings.

Indeed, the homosexual tension potentially buried within their ostensibly homosocial relationship, along with Watson's steady stream of denials, situates Holmes and Watson within a broad category of Western popular culture's "buddy cop" pairings. They are *Lethal Weapon*'s Riggs and Murtaugh, *Hawaii Five-O*'s McGarrett and Dann-o, *Miami Vice*'s Crockett and Tubbs; though Holmes and Watson are British, rather than American, they also share a great deal in common with their fellow crime fighters. Like these other famous partners, they are caught "between the representational poles of homoeroticism and homophobia, in love with their self-displays and at odds with their implications" (Fuchs 195). The buddy cop pattern occurs in narratives that center on a closely bonded platonic relationship between two men who share professional and domestic intimacy, who form two halves of one powerhouse whole, but whose frequent looks and physical proximity must constantly struggle against their own romantic implications. Media texts that concentrate primarily — even myopically — on the close relationship between two men frequently demonstrate enhanced homoerotic possibility (Sparks 356); *Sherlock* falls into this grouping. When Watson snipes, "Girls, calm down," to a bickering Holmes and Lestrade ("The Great Game"), it reinforces and denigrates stereotypes about feminine behavior while also highlighting the fact that *Sherlock* has few prominent women; secondary recurring characters such as Mrs. Hudson or Sally Donovan hardly possess the same narrative agency as Holmes, Watson, or even Lestrade and Mycroft. The series' close focus on the homosocial may explain some of *Sherlock*'s popularity with slash authors; it also necessitates the canonical reiteration of on-screen heteronormativity. Buddy cop narratives frequently include tertiary girlfriends, former wives, or homophobic humor in order to repeatedly (re-)establish the male protagonists' heterosexuality (Fuchs 196); in *Sherlock,* and most specifically in the case of Watson, this pattern holds true. When Watson flirts awkwardly with Mycroft's assistant Anthea ("A Study in Pink," "A Scandal in Belgravia"), asks Sarah on a date ("The Blind Banker"), or chats up an attractive female therapist ("The Hounds of Baskerville"), it reasserts his heterosexuality for the audience. Likewise, when he cracks, "People might talk," or squirms awkwardly on a couch next to an openly gay crime suspect ("The Great Game"), it establishes his resistance to any gay labeling and serves as a (somewhat more genial) callback to *Lethal Weapon*'s uncomfortable jokes about "fags." Watson's heterosexuality, so often reiterated in *Sherlock,* serves as a predictable and well-used buffer against any accusation of queer possibility.

Concurrently, however, *Sherlock* re-inscribes the potential for such readings — particularly in the character of Holmes, who repeatedly ignores allegations that he and Watson might be gay. Watson's comment to Adler, "Who the hell knows about Sherlock Holmes," is telling; while Watson inevitably protests any supposition that he is romantically partnered with Holmes, Holmes himself fails to refute such notions. In "A Study in Pink," he does not react to the assumptions of Mrs. Hudson or the restaurant waiter; when he is asked point-blank about his own orientation, his response is ambiguous:

WATSON: You don't have a girlfriend, then?
HOLMES: Girlfriend? No, not really my area.
WATSON: Mmm. Oh, right. Do you have a boyfriend? Which is fine, by the way.
HOLMES: I know it's fine.

WATSON: So you've got a boyfriend, then.

HOLMES: No.

WATSON: Right, OK. You're unattached. Like me. Fine. Good.

HOLMES: John, um ... I think you should know I consider myself married to my work, and while I'm flattered, I'm really not looking for any —

WATSON: No, I'm ... not asking. No. I'm just saying, it's all fine.

HOLMES: Good. Thank you.

Again, we see Watson asserting his own heterosexuality ("I'm not asking"), but his curiosity (and, presumably, ours) regarding Holmes' orientation remains unsatisfied; Holmes is "married to [his] work," we are to understand, and according to the writers on the commentary track, we should take this disavowal of romance as an indication of the detective's definitive asexuality. On a subtextual level, however, Holmes' ambiguous response leaves the character suspended within a realm of permanent possibility; he is assuredly queer, in the most generic, non-heteronormative sense of the word, and he *could be* gay, straight, bisexual, asexual, or pansexual. He does not commit himself in any way.

Certainly Holmes' primary relationships are with men: his friendship with Watson, his collegiality with Lestrade, his feud with Mycroft, and his rivalry with Moriarty. While he may maintain a soft spot for Mrs. Hudson, she is a sideline mothering presence at best; she has no role in solving mysteries, and her desires and needs are not what motivate him. Apart from Adler's brief, one-sided, and hyper-sexualized flirtation, Holmes also has no on-screen romances; Molly, a morgue employee, is clearly interested in him (she fixes her hair; she puts on lipstick; she asks him to coffee), but Holmes does not reciprocate. In true sociopathic fashion, he only acknowledges Molly when he wants something; he compliments her hair in "The Blind Banker" in order to obtain access to autopsied bodies, but he does not pursue the matter further. Additionally, he not only eschews romance for himself, but he interferes with Watson's first burgeoning courtship; he hijacks Watson and Sarah's "first date" by offering tickets to a circus he is investigating and then tagging along without invitation. Hijinks naturally ensue; it is a wonder, after nearly being impaled in "The Blind Banker," that Sarah is still willing to speak to Watson in "The Great Game." Again, on the surface, one might read Holmes' unapologetic meddling as a symptom of his single-minded focus on the mystery; he uses the circus tickets as a tool to force Watson into further pursuit of the case. The possibility of his possessive jealousy, however, goes unaddressed within the text, thus ensuring that Holmes' sexuality remains undefined.

Furthermore, while Holmes' relationship with Watson — their unquestioning trust and mutual respect, their sharing of domestic space, their willingness to sacrifice for each other — receives central attention in the series, his rivalry with Moriarty also invites — indeed, nearly demands — queer readings. From Moriarty's first greeting to Holmes — "Hello, sexy" ("The Great Game") — their competition takes the form of romantic flirtation. Indeed, the first time Moriarty appears on screen (also in "The Great Game"), he is disguised as a gay man: Jim, a hospital computer tech, whom Molly proudly introduces as her boyfriend in a transparent attempt to make Holmes jealous. Holmes, we are to believe at the time, is not fooled; he sees through Molly's facade in a heartbeat, noting details such as Jim's visible designer underwear band and — most damningly — the manner in which Jim surreptitiously leaves his phone number under Holmes' petri dish. But this is only the first level of Moriarty's deception; according to the episode's later dialogue, we are meant to interpret him as inhabiting the same nebulously undefined sexuality as Holmes. Moriarty himself asserts that he was "playing gay; did you like the little touch with the underwear?" If we take his words at face value, then his gayness was an act of performance, or disguise, masking his innate self.

But the codings of Moriarty's gender and sexuality are fluid; Mark Gatiss states on the commentary track that Moriarty's supervillainy establishes him as "not just a cheap gay joke." Moriarty's flirtations with Holmes are ongoing and overt ("Is that a British army Browning L9A1 in your pocket, or are you just pleased to see me?") — and, notably, Moriarty himself is presented androgynously, either through his high-pitched and therefore feminized voice, or through the multitude of proxy voices he uses to speak. Our first hint of Moriarty comes from the lips of a dying taxi driver ("A Study in Pink"); next, we see him as text on a screen ("The Blind Banker"). In "The Great Game," Moriarty repeatedly attaches bombs to people and forces his victims to phone Holmes, reading Moriarty's texted clues aloud in terrified voices; when we hear that first greeting of "Hello, sexy," it is in the voice of a sobbing woman. "We were made for each other, Sherlock," seduces Moriarty via his human vocoder; Holmes, not denying it, only counters, "Then talk to me in your own voice." He is (and we are) stymied by his counterpart's ever-shifting and androgynous identity. Moriarty speaks through plain text, two women (young and old), a young boy, and a man; while he appears as Jim early in "The Great Game," he does not appear as himself until the episode climax. His flirtation with Holmes is thus maintained through a variety of shifting voices and identities; notably, before he "reveals" his face, the last voice with which he speaks to Holmes is Watson's.

Holmes and Moriarty are a matched pair intellectually — a consulting detective and a consulting criminal — and the narrative tension of "The Great Game" rests in part on whether Holmes will become the same sort of sociopath as Moriarty, one whose enthrallment with the puzzle outweighs (indeed, replaces) all other moral or ethical considerations. The homoeroticism latent in the notion of Holmes and Moriarty as potential puzzle-solving soul mates is exacerbated by Moriarty's consistently seductive language. Watson, irritated at Holmes' callousness, claims outright (if sarcastically) that Holmes and Moriarty are a perfect couple: "I hope you'll be very happy together." It might be easy to read his indignance as jealousy, just as it might be easy to read the same jealousy into Moriarty's kidnapping of Watson at the end of the episode; while Moriarty makes a game of deceiving Molly (she of the unrequited Holmesian crush), he is no real threat to her, because the best way to attack Holmes is obviously by attacking Watson. Moriarty's interference in the Holmes and Watson partnership begs the same scrutiny as Holmes' interference with Watson's date night; he occupies the potential position of the scorned lover, scheming to interfere with any relationships that thwart his own advances toward the object of his affection. Indeed, as Watson serves as Holmes' conscience, it is necessary for Moriarty to destroy Watson if Moriarty and Holmes are ever to work together — Moriarty must clear away the competition, and the push and pull for Holmes' affections thus form the basis for the first season's climax. Holmes must choose a partner: will he stay with Watson, his dependable moral base, or be lured away by Moriarty's seductive mystery? His choice of Watson naturally cues Moriarty's vengeful plotting in Season Two.

The purpose of this chapter is not to argue that Holmes, Watson, and Moriarty *are* gay, bisexual, or (in the cases of Holmes and Moriarty) more nebulously queer, but rather that they *can* be read that way, and that *Sherlock* is particularly open to such readings despite the surface denials presented in Watson's dialogue or the writers' commentary track. Moreover, the scripts demonstrate the writers' explicit awareness of the show's queer themes; we come back to allegations of Holmes/Watson couplehood in every episode, even if only so that Watson can refute the rumors. It is not enough to raise the issue in the pilot; rather, we return to it again and again, never quite letting the *possibility* of homoerotic tension fade — even when it is presented as a joke. The consistent throughline of allegation and denial is exacerbated by Holmes' silence on the subject, by Moriarty's shifting gender and openly flirtatious language, and by the series' tight focus on male/male relationships. Perhaps no text outside of amateur fan productions acknowledges these undercurrents so well as South Korean channel OCN's trailer promos for the series, which consist primarily of moody close-up shots of both Holmes and Watson, along with on-screen written statements such as "Love of the Loveless" and (in Korean) "They need each other." User commentary on the posted trailer's YouTube page reads, "Hahaha this cable channel completely changed the genre of Sherlock to romance" ;) (allofuslost), "This makes me believe South Korea consists solely of slash fans" (capriatidemon) and "what do you mean 'completely changed the genre of Sherlock to romance' was it something else before?" (southkoreagotseoul).

In this context, it seems no coincidence that two early and obvious mistakes Holmes makes in *Sherlock* are based on sexuality. His dissection of Watson's personal history in "A Study in Pink" is spelled out for the audience in fine detail; some examples are Watson's psychosomatic limp (because Watson uses a cane but doesn't experience discomfort when standing) and alcoholic sibling (because Watson's phone is scratched and was a gift from the sibling's partner, now divorcing). The analysis of the phone is based on a similar incident with a pocket watch in the Doyle story "The Sign of Four"; unlike Doyle's version, however, in which Holmes' deductions are flawless, our first sign that *Sherlock*'s Holmes is not invincible is his mistaken assertion that the phone's inscription ("Harry Watson — from Clara XXX") must be to Watson's estranged brother. In fact, we discover, "Harry" is "Harriet," and Watson's lesbian sister has foiled an otherwise perfect deductive trail. With that, the series challenges both Holmes' heteronormative assumptions and our own, marking queer space within the text. Moreover, when "Jim" Moriarty first appears on screen, he successfully distracts Holmes (and the audience) from guessing his true identity by posing as a gay man pretending to be straight; Holmes, fixating immediately on the contradictions between Jim's supposed heterosexual relationship (with Molly) and stereotypically homosexual behaviors, completely misses the much more vital question of Moriarty's archvillain status. Questions of sexuality thus twice prove the undoing of Holmes' vaunted detective skills; this disruption of the great detective's otherwise logical deductive process underscores the persistent and tricky ambiguity of *Sherlock*'s queer themes.

It must be acknowledged that, in terms of U.K. television, the themes themselves are not groundbreaking — certainly other British series, such as the successful *Queer as Folk* (1999) or *Torchwood* (2006–present), have featured overtly queer leads rather than playing subtextual games, while long-running programs like *Brookside* (1982–2003) and *EastEnders* (1985–present) were televising gay relationships on U.K. screens in the 1980s (Barlaam 118). In contrast, *Sherlock*'s problematic treatment of its canonically queer characters — the comic relief provided by openly gay men ("The Great Game," "The Hounds of Baskerville"), or the predictable association of Irene Adler's bisexuality with sexual promiscuity ("A Scandal in Belgravia") — reasserts regrettably common stereotypes and offers little counterpoint to these categorizations. Likewise, the series might rightfully be critiqued for sexist tropes (Syme; Penny) and racist imagery (Penny); though a case might be made for Watson's easy, openminded acceptance of Holmes' undefined sexuality, *Sherlock*'s politics are, at heart, mainly conservative.

Regardless, *Sherlock*'s subtext is worthy of close examination. Holmes and Watson occupy a position of particular cultural importance; as Michael Saler argues, "Holmes was the first character in modern literature to be widely treated as if he were real and his creator fictitious" (600). Sherlock Holmes' adventures on paper, in film, and on television over the last century have inspired widespread fandom, capturing the public imagination in a manner which once caused ardent fans of Doyle's creation to write letters to Holmes (Saler 609). While Internet communications currently make new fan partic- ipation easy, dedicated members of the international Baker Street Irregulars have also met in various locales since 1934 to discuss the adventures of their favorite sleuths (Redmond). Holmes is decidedly mainstream; the Sherlock Holmes figure in his deerstalker hat is an almost universal Western cultural touchstone, possessing a long-lived prominence that characters from *Queer as Folk, Torchwood,* or even *Doctor Who* (from which *Torchwood* sprang) lack. Holmes' iconic status makes *Sherlock*'s open acknowledgment of its own queer possibilities all the more intriguing. Granted, this acknowledgment is lim- ited — it takes the form of a running gag, after all, thus using humor to disarm or rebut any slash potential. It seems, nevertheless, that a Holmes of the 21st century is a Holmes who must deal with 21st century sexual politics; as the homoeroticism inherent in its buddy bromance grows more and more explicit, *Sherlock* consistently calls attention to the flexibility of its own sexual para- digms, never quite allowing such possibilities to fade from view.

WORKS CITED

Barlaam, Silvia. "'There's Nowt as *Queer as Folk*': British and American Televisual Approaches to the Politics of Homosexuality." *American Remakes of British Television: Transformations and Mistranslations.* Eds. Carlen Lavigne and Heather Marcovitch. Lanham, MD: Lex- ington Books, 2011. 117–142. Print.

Carroll, Larry. "Robert Downey, Jr., Jude Law Explore 'Bromance' on 'Sherlock Holmes' Set." MTV.com. 12 Feb. 2009. Web. 27 Dec. 2011.

Fuchs, Cynthia. "The Buddy Politic." *Screening the Male: Exploring Masculinities in Hollywood Cinema.* Eds. Steven Cohan and Ina Rae Hark. New York: Routledge, 1993. 194–210. Print.

Gay Sherlock Holmes. 25 Dec. 2011. Web. 27 Dec. 2011.

"The Hounds of Baskerville." *Sherlock.* BBC. 8 Jan. 2012. Television.

"The Hounds of Baskerville — BAFTA Screening Q&A." *Cumberbatchweb.* 8 Jan. 2012. Web. 16 Jan. 2012.

Jones, S. G. "The Sex Lives of Cult Television Characters." *Screen* 43.1 (2002): 79–90. Print.

Lo, Malinda. "Fan Fiction Comes Out of the Closet." *After Ellen.* 4 Jan. 2006. Web. 27 Dec. 2011.

"OCN's *Sherlock* Trailer 1." *YouTube.* 1 Feb. 2011. Web. 27 Dec. 2011.

"Pæan to Priapus Series." *Oblique Publications.* 2003. Web. 27 Dec. 2011.

Penley, Constance. *NASA/Trek: Popular Science and Sex in America.* New York: Verso, 1997. Print.

Penny, Laurie. "No Shit, Sherlock." *NewStatesman.* 3 Aug. 2010. Web. 16 Jan. 2012.

Redmond, Chris. "Sherlockian.Net: Societies." *The Web Portal About the Great Detective: Sherlockian.Net.* 2009. Web. 27 Dec. 2011.

"The Reichenbach Fall." *Sherlock.* BBC. 15 Jan. 2012. Television.

Saler, Michael. "'Clap If You Believe in Sherlock Holmes': Mass Culture and the Re-Enchantment of Modernity, c.1890–c.1940." *The Historical Journal* 46.3 (2003): 599–622. Print.

"A Scandal in Belgravia." *Sherlock.* BBC. 1 Jan. 2012. Television.

Sherlock. 2010. BBC, 2011. Blu-ray.

Sherlock Holmes. Dir. Guy Ritchie. 2009. Warner Bros., 2010. Blu-ray.

Sherlock Holmes: A Game of Shadows. Dir. Guy Ritchie. Warner Bros, 2011. Film.

Sparks, Richard. "Masculinity and Heroism in the Hollywood 'Blockbuster.'" *British Journal of Criminology* 36.3 (1996): 348–360. Print.

Syme, Holger. "Steven Moffat, *Sherlock,* and Neo-Victorian Sexism." *Disposito: Arguments About Early Modern Things, and Sometimes About Politics.* 2 Jan. 2012. Web. 16 Jan. 2012.

NOTE

1. The title for this chapter is derived from two original Sherlock Holmes stories, "The Adventure of the Noble Bachelor" and "The Adventure of the Crooked Man." With apologies to Sir Arthur Conan Doyle.

2

Sex and the Single Sleuth

ANISSA M. GRAHAM *and*
JENNIFER C. GARLEN

> "Brainy's the new sexy."
> — *Irene Adler, "A Scandal in Belgravia"*

Sir Arthur Conan Doyle never intended for Sherlock Holmes to be a figure of romance. From the opening pages of the first Sherlock Holmes tale, *A Study in Scarlet*, Conan Doyle presents his hero as a creature of science rather than emotion, a man whose enthusiasms run all toward data rather than dates. The reader's initial introduction to the great detective certainly does not encourage a romantic response. As Dr. Watson describes him,

> His very person and appearance were such as to strike the attention of the most casual observer. In height he was rather over six feet, and so excessively lean that he seemed to be considerably taller. His eyes were sharp and piercing, save during those intervals of torpor to which I have alluded; and his thin, hawk-like nose gave his whole expression an air of alertness and decision. His chin, too, had the prominence and squareness which mark the man of determination [Conan Doyle, *A Study in Scarlet* 13].

This thin, hawkish figure is hardly the stuff of women's dreams, and Conan Doyle actively discouraged the idea that Holmes might take up a lover's role. In an 1892 letter to his mentor, Dr. Joseph Bell, Conan Doyle wrote that "Holmes is as inhuman as a Babbage's Calculating Machine, and just about as likely to fall in love" (Letter to Joseph Bell). Conan Doyle, however, was not entirely in control of what Sherlock Holmes would or would not do, as the outcome of the Reichenbach Falls episode amply proved. The public, not his creator, had come to own Holmes, and they had other ideas about the detective's fate and his fortunes with the ladies. Indeed, posterity has declared Sherlock Holmes a positive heartthrob, and the revision of Conan Doyle's lean, clean, thinking machine into the nerd girl's ultimate dreamboat has been going on for quite a long time. The sexualization of Sherlock almost as soon as the first stories went to print, but the cultura of Holmes as a romantic hero has only increased since then, with tne recent adaptations starring Robert Downey, Jr., and Benedict Cumberbatch as testaments to the ways in which popular culture has exerted its influence over the iconic intellectual whom Conan Doyle invented. Today, Sexy Sherlock is almost a given, and his popularity as such suggests the ways in which geek culture has rendered scientific smarts and eccentric habits the hallmarks of a new masculine ideal.

If we only had Conan Doyle's description to rely upon, it is doubtful that Holmes would ever have evolved into a figure of desire. Watson's description of the detective is not likely to have set many Victorian hearts aflutter; however, Sidney Paget's early illustrations for *The Strand* certainly did. Even the most casual Holmes enthusiast can tell the story of how Sidney Paget came to be the illustrator for Conan Doyle's tales. The art editor at *The Strand* originally commissioned Paget's older and better-known brother, Walter, to illustrate the stories; the commission letter, however, accidentally went to Sidney Paget instead. Much of what we believe about the physical appearance of Holmes depends upon Paget's illustrations (Pointer 12). Paget used his handsome brother, Walter, as the model for Holmes' figure, making him much more dashing than the raptor-like gent of Watson's description. While Walter Paget did have a rather prominent nose, this feature was offset by a firm jaw and full mouth, and these qualities combined to create a more approachable and appealing Holmes. Even though the artist used his brother as the physical model for Holmes, he lent the detective his own sartorial style. Sidney was the first to add the iconic deerstalker cap, an item that he often wore himself, to Holmes' wardrobe. Paget's illustrations had a profound influence on later illustrators and performers, for the image of Holmes as slender, intense, and handsome was quite solidly established in the public imagination by the time of the artist's death in 1908.

When Holmes made the move from page to stage, Paget's illustrations carried over into casting choices; the many actors set to impersonate Holmes found themselves at the mercy of the well-cut evening suit or the iconic deerstalker cap. The stage adaptations and their leading men furthered Holmes' transformation into heartthrob material. In 1899, William Gillette, one of America's premier leading men, began appearing in *Sherlock Holmes*, a play written largely by Gillette himself. He collaborated with Sir Arthur Conan Doyle on the project, and in many ways he seemed to suit Conan Doyle's vision of the character perfectly. A description of the first meeting between Conan Doyle and Gillette by biographer John Dickson Carr highlights just how impressive Gillette was as Holmes: "out of [the train], in a long gray cape, stepped the living image of Sherlock Holmes. Not even Sidney Paget had done it so well in a drawing. The clear-cut features, the deep-set eyes, looked out from under a deerstalker cap; even Gillette's age, the middle forties, was right" (qtd. in Riley and McAllister 60). Even Conan Doyle himself, it seems, was not immune to the charms of his creation brought to life.

Some significant changes, however, were inevitable. Gillette, whose successful career depended on his appeal as a romantic lead, wanted to have Holmes fall in love. When he asked Conan Doyle about the possibility of marrying Holmes off, the author sardonically replied: "You can marry him, or murder or do what you like with him" (Eyles 34). The resulting play, based loosely upon "A Scandal in Bohemia" and "The Final Problem," did indeed do what Gillette liked. It was a huge success, and Gillette made use of many of the traditional props mentioned in the canon, including the violin and magnifying glass, to give his Holmes some flair, but the actor's own "clear-cut features" and "deep-set eyes" became focal points for Holmes' sex appeal. Posters promoting the play emphasize these more dashing and seductive qualities. Shown in his dressing gown with meerschaum pipe firmly in his mouth, Gillette seems at once relaxed and filled with potential motion. Even more striking is an image of Holmes embracing the young Alice Faulkner, the play's replacement for Irene Adler. Her curly blonde head rests on Holmes' shoulder, while his head touches hers in an attitude of romantic intimacy. It is an image certain to inspire cooing among the sentimental members of the Holmes audience. Gillette would appear as Holmes off and on for nearly 36 years. Such a long association with a single character is nearly unheard of in the modern era and is due in part to the appeal of Gillette as a passion-inspiring Holmes.

As Holmes has since moved from page to stage to screen, the desirability of the detective has continued to develop, particularly as audiences have become increasingly involved in interpreting and revising the performances to emphasize their own attitudes towards the character and the actors who have played him. Of course, Holmes has enjoyed a long and complex screen career and is, along with Count Dracula, one of the most frequently represented fictional characters in film history. Among the actors who have played Holmes are handsome leading men like John Barrymore, Clive Brooks, Christopher Plummer, and even Roger Moore, as well as Peter Cushing, Christopher Lee, and the lesser known Arthur Wontner, whom some critics hail as the most faithful personification of the character. Basil Rathbone, however, became the first actor to really inhabit the role for a generation of viewers. He first played the great detective in 1939's *The Hound of the Baskervilles*, and in all he made 14 screen appearances as Sherlock Holmes. In addition to his performances as Holmes, Rathbone played suave villains in swashbucklers like *The Adventures of Robin Hood* (1938) and *The Mark of Zorro* (1940), but he had been handsome enough to play romantic leads during the early part of his career. Still, his tall, hawkish figure suited Conan Doyle's description of Holmes, and the image of Rathbone sporting the deerstalker hat and meerschaum pipe would dominate the popular image of the character for many years.

Billy Wilder's 1970 film, *The Private Life of Sherlock Holmes,* serves as something of a counterpoint to the performances of Rathbone. Here the image of Holmes is quite solidly based in a post–sexual revolution world, even if that image might not strictly belong to the time and place of his adventures. As the film's title suggests, the *private* aspects of the life of Sherlock Holmes continue to prove fascinating to both the Holmes aficionado and the casual moviegoer. From the simple detail of his height to the more complex one of his sexual orientation, the *Private Life* Watson is confronted with a Holmes who is not the controlled aesthete he wishes him to be but rather a man of strong appetites. Two brief examples from the film emphasize Holmes as one who desires and one who is desired. In an exchange with Watson, Holmes remarks of a young woman: "I found her body quite rewarding." As the audience processes the potential meanings of such a statement, Holmes adds, "particularly the palm of her right hand." What begins as sexual innuendo ends in the revelation of a clue. Holmes is capable of desire and equally capable of tweaking his audience (Watson and us) about it. Holmes is also the object of desire of not one but two women. The German spy, Ilse Von Hoffmanstahl, masquerades as a woman in search of a missing husband; the missing husband is a ruse, but her desire for Holmes is not. She needs his brain to help her find a rather secret British weapon of war. Additionally, the Russian ballerina, Madame Petrova, wants Holmes for his brain, too, but instead of using that brain to solve a case, she wishes him to supply the genetic material for her child. To stave off the advances of Madame, Holmes tells her that he and Watson are lovers. In that one sequence Wilder has Holmes again tweak the audience's expectations by giving a nod to the rumors that Watson and Holmes are not merely companions but an actual couple. While Holmes' brain apparently drives the desire of these women, Robert Stephens' Holmes is also desired for his looks, for he is, as Peter Bradshaw of *The Guardian* points out in a 2002 review of the film, "splendidly debonair."

If Robert Stephens' Holmes is "splendidly debonair," then Roger Moore's turn as the great detective in the 1976 television movie, *Sherlock Holmes in New York,* ought to have continued that trend. Set in 1901, *Sherlock Holmes in New York* involves a plot to steal the world's gold, using Irene Adler's son as leverage against Holmes' involvement. In keeping with the mores of the period (the Edwardian, not the 1970s), everything about this film is buttoned up and proper, even though Moore was in the early years of his portrayal of that other British icon of sexy masculinity, James Bond. With both the debonair Saint and the overtly sexual James Bond as part of his repertoire, one would think Moore would bring out Holmes' sexual side. Surprisingly, there are no clinches or even a kiss in this film; there is, however, a child, Scott Adler.

Holmes' relationship to Irene's son is hinted at throughout the film. First Holmes reveals in a conversation with Watson that his full name is "William Sherlock Scott Holmes." The possible paternal connection is a bit sketchy because, in choosing one of Holmes' less well known names, Irene has attempted to hide the father's identity. Building on that sketchy connection is a conversation between Irene and Holmes near the end of the film. The audience discovers that Irene and Holmes spent a week together in Montenegro in 1891. Irene was performing in *Rigalleto,* and Holmes was on a walking tour of Southern Europe. They comment on the unlikely nature of their positions, with Holmes expressing surprise at finding Irene so far away from the glittering lights of a metropolis and Irene equally stunned by Holmes' presence outside of London. Also revealed in that conversation is that Irene never remarried after what one presumes is the death of Godfrey Norton, the man she marries at the end of "A Scandal in Bohemia." If Scott were Norton's son, he would most certainly carry his father's name, but he doesn't. His age makes it likely that he was conceived during Irene's time in Montenegro, and therefore one can reasonably assume that Holmes is the father.

While *Sherlock Holmes in New York* never shows a passionate embrace or kiss, Scott is the result of what must have been a passionate affair. As unsatisfying as their restraint is to the viewer, Scott makes it clear that Holmes is not merely desirable but capable as well, capable of giving in to his emotions, capable of giving in to his desires. What Scott's presence also makes clear is the impossibility of a stable "normal" relationship with a man like Holmes. His desire to chase the unknown may be what draws women to Holmes, and his brilliant mind might make them want to have his child to pass on that brilliance, but those features which ignite desire also make Holmes an inappropriate choice for a mate.

Stephens and Moore are, however, one-shot depictions of the great detective, which limits their ability to influence overall perceptions of the character. For many Holmes fans living today, Jeremy Brett is the definitive performer of the role, and Brett also functions as a powerful figure of audience desire. Brett played the character for over a decade, appearing in 41 episodes of the Granada Television series, *The Adventures of Sherlock Holmes.* His performance has become one of the most enduring, and fan devotion to Brett continues to be astounding, even more than 15 years after his death. Internet sites and fan videos on YouTube pay ample tribute to Brett's charisma and sex appeal as Holmes. On Holmesian.net, for example, the question "Is Holmes/Jeremy Brett sexy?" has elicited over a thousand enthusiastic responses. Among the fan-made video tributes are montages set to Justin Timberlake's "Sexyback," ZZ Top's "Sharp Dressed Man," and "I Like the Way" by Bodyrockers. The videos highlight the ways in which viewers read Brett's Holmes as an object of desire, even though the series itself shied away from overt representations of Holmes as a sexual being. In his book, *Bending the Willow: Jeremy Brett as Sherlock Holmes*, David Stuart Davies tries to locate the source of Brett's tremendous appeal:

> There were about Jeremy Brett two elements which aided his personification of Sherlock Holmes on screen. Firstly, there was a dangerous, almost eccentric, edge to his playing which was attractive, and fascinating, but which also created a sense of pleasurable unease in the audience. We could not help but watch his every move, listen with bated breath to his every nuance. Secondly, Brett exuded a fierce sexual ambivalence, ideally suited to the character of Holmes, who moved in that paradoxical Victorian age when lust and primness jostled side by side in the public consciousness. Men were fascinated by Brett's Holmes, a fascination which stirred uncertain emotions within the modern man's breast. Women were less troubled; they admired and lusted after him.

Later incarnations of Holmes have built on the powerful attraction of Brett's portrayal, but the Brett interpretation of Holmes remains extremely popular with fans and is the touchstone against which all subsequent versions of the character must be measured.

The admiration and lust inspired by Brett's portrayal of Holmes find an outlet in the various pastiches that offer the hero's further adventures, often set in the years after his final retirement. Men's novels about the later life of the great detective, like Michael Chabon's *The Final Solution*, tend to avoid sustained romantic plots, but women's pastiches play out the fulfillment of a persistent wish to see Sherlock Holmes paired with an appropriate female counterpart. Sena Jeter Naslund's 1993 novel, *Sherlock in Love*, overtly states its intention to depict the detective in a romantic entanglement, although the affair turns out to be a forbidden, Byronic passion between Holmes and his cross-dressing half-sister. In *The Affair of the Incognito Tenant: A Mystery with Sherlock Holmes*, Lora Roberts imagines a romance between Holmes and a widowed young housekeeper, while Autumn Sabol's *Elementary, My Dear* (2005) plots a time-traveling love triangle among Holmes, Watson, and a 21st century heroine. Perhaps the most successful of this sort of pastiche is the Mary Russell series by Laurie R. King. Beginning with *The Beekeeper's Apprentice*, King's Mary Russell appears first as Holmes' protégé, moves on to being his professional partner, and finally ends up as his wife. King presents her heroine as Holmes' match in every respect; although romantic moments between the two are few and far between, they form an intimate partnership, two halves of an intellectual, adventurous whole. For a series based on Holmes' marriage to a much younger woman, King's novels are remarkably prim, but the most recent Mary Russell novel, *The Language of Bees*, does suggest the extent of Holmes' capacity for passion in a plot that reveals the existence of Holmes' illegitimate child with one-time paramour, Irene Adler.

While King passes over bedroom scenes with her married characters, the wealth of online Holmesian fan fiction reveals the extent to which Holmes devotees long to have the veil lifted on such intimate moments. A review of Fanfiction.net's section for stories based on the Holmes oeuvre uncovers more than 2000 works by authors writing in English and seven other languages. Fan fiction authors are not shy about placing characters in sexually charged situations. While genres for these stories range from drama to mystery, many stories are classified by their authors as romances or as "hurt/comfort" stories. These latter categories frequently climax with the lead characters consummating their relationships. Fan communities organize themselves based on their favorite pairings; the most popular pairings are of Holmes and Watson (a pairing referred to as Shwatsonlock) and of Holmes and Irene Adler, although the pairing of Holmes with his nemesis, Professor Moriarty, seems to be growing in popularity.

All of these earlier revisions and influences have a hand to play in director Guy Ritchie's 2009 film, *Sherlock Holmes*, and its 2011 sequel, *Sherlock Holmes: A Game of Shadows*. In the first film, Ritchie and his screenwriters develop Holmes' sexuality in several directions simultaneously, but the conflicts help to underscore the way in which the sexualization of the great detective has become a major element of his representation. In the first place, the films' creators cast charismatic leading man Robert Downey, Jr., as the title character. Downey is undeniably handsome, and he bears very little physical resemblance to Conan Doyle's original vision. His puckish, bad boy looks make him a credible leading man and a hit with female audiences, but he is not particularly lean, and in both of Ritchie's films he appears more muscular than wiry. Standing only 5 feet 8 inches, Downey is much too short for the lanky Holmes, and his retroussé nose is quite the opposite of the protruding beak described by Conan Doyle. Visually, then, Downey seems very much the opposite of the Holmes character, but much of his actual performance has its origins in the canonical texts. His presentation of Holmes as a skilled fighter comes from original descriptions of the detective as a master of fencing, bare-knuckle fighting, and the martial arts, and Downey's own experience as an action hero makes him well-suited for this kind of work. Downey's reputation as a gifted character actor also fits with the idea of Holmes as a master of disguise, and both films feature scenes in which Downey's hero indulges in comical but effective self-transformation. The actor and the character share personal demons, too, and in this regard the casting of Downey might be a little too accurate for comfort, given the performer's well-known struggles with drug addiction. Such flaws, however, do as much to develop the character's sexual appeal as his strengths; popular culture has amply demonstrated that audiences adore the complicated, rebellious, Byronic type of hero much more than the straight arrow.

In the first film, Holmes' sexuality works in two directions at once. His "bromance" with bosom friend John Watson has strong homosexual undertones, highlighted by Holmes' jealousy when Watson becomes engaged to be married. Downey spent a fair bit of time on the talk show circuit suggesting the romantic nature of the two men's relationship, enough that the holder of the U.S. copyright for the Holmes character threatened to pull the plug on any sequels that might pursue the idea more fully. At the same time, the film presents Holmes as utterly besotted with Irene Adler, whose personal charms and duplicitous nature keep the detective off balance every time she appears. Thus, rather than an asexual human computer, Downey's Holmes is transformed into a bisexual rogue, a man whose taste for adventure includes boudoirs as well as back alleys. The high point of the first film's depiction of Sexy Sherlock comes when Holmes, having been drugged, stripped, and handcuffed to a bed by Irene Adler, appears on screen wearing nothing but a pillow. The idea of a naked Holmes sitting handcuffed on a bed must have had Sir Arthur Conan Doyle spinning in his grave, but it is only the logical endpoint of the cultural revision of the character that has been going on ever since Paget's first illustrations made the hero more attractive than the author had intended.

The sequel, *A Game of Shadows*, puts the majority of its energy into developing the masculine bond between Holmes and Watson, although it stops short of confirming Downey's controversial claims about the two being lovers. Holmes' heterosexual outlet is shut down when Irene Adler is murdered very early in the film, although his emotional attachment to her gets some expression thanks to the token of her blood-stained handkerchief. With Irene dead and Mary pushed out of a moving train by Holmes (albeit to save her life), the boys spend the rest of the picture running, fighting, and grappling with their complex feelings for one another. The homosexual undertones are emphasized by Sherlock's brief appearance in drag, although he ends up looking rather like Tim Curry in *The Rocky Horror Picture Show*, delivering innuendo-laden lines to Watson while shirtless, tussled, and bedecked with eye shadow. Further hints of Sherlock's sexual orientation are provided by the casting of Stephen Fry as his queeny brother, Mycroft, who persistently refers to the hero as "Sherly." Despite the sequel's more provocative suggestions about homosexual desire, the film still depicts both Holmes and Watson as objects of female adoration, with the two handsome actors getting plenty of opportunities to display their physical charms in between action sequences.

Guy Ritchie's films are not the only recent and very visible revisions of Conan Doyle's character. Sherlock Holmes has also turned up in the wildly successful BBC series *Sherlock*, which was co-created by *Doctor Who* writers Steven Moffat and Mark Gatiss. The series stars Benedict Cumberbatch as a modern day version of the great detective, and the first series, which aired in 2010, rapidly became the darling of the BBC season. The series returned for a critically acclaimed second run in 2012 and is already scheduled for a third outing. Although this latest Sherlock states early on in the first series that girlfriends are not among his interests, he is certainly the sort of young man who proves interesting to his audience. Tall, with striking cheekbones and gorgeously tousled hair, Cumberbatch makes for a breathtakingly attractive Holmes, although like Basil Rathbone before him the actor has a look that also lends itself to villains and morally inscrutable characters. Audiences and critics have been quick to pick up on the inherent sexiness of this latest incarnation. In an August 2010 article on *The Guardian/The Observer* online, Polly Vernon enthusiastically admired Cumberbatch's sense of style on the show and offers this striking summary of the hero's history:

> Holmes was created a fashion icon: chic, theatrical, a devotee of a grand silhouette, a fan of a flamboyant accessory. Cumberbatch's version of Holmes' style is entirely appropriate. It's timeless, sleek, minimal, sharp, fastidious, uncompromised, free of any self-conscious quirk intended to offer insight into Holmes' character. It's lean: completely without flounce or fancy, give or take the swirl on the coattails, a swirl which invokes "cape," without having to go as literal as, you know, actually being a cape.

Holmes has now been thoroughly transformed; where Conan Doyle saw a Babbage's Calculating Machine we now see an icon of style, a model for the well-dressed British male, an object of emulation, admiration, and desire. Other media reactions to the first series also reflect the overwhelming appeal of a sexy Sherlock show. Tim Oglethorpe of the *Daily Mail* announced, "Sherlock's Got Sexy!" while another *Guardian* article similarly declared, "Sherlock Makes Sunday Night TV Sexy." The show's overwhelming success in Britain and the United States shows the extent to which viewers are ready to embrace this updated, unabashedly attractive image of the iconic character.

Given the overwhelming sense of the show as "sexy," it was inevitable that *Sherlock* would eventually have to address the sleuth's sexuality in a more overt way, and the series two opener, "A Scandal in Belgravia," does just that. Irene Adler once more appears as "the woman" who goes toe-to-toe and head-to-head with the great detective, although in the updated version she is not only a brilliant criminal but also a seductive, lesbian dominatrix. As the Catwoman to Sherlock's Batman, Irene teases, tempts, and tricks, even appearing completely naked when she first meets Holmes in order to thwart his effort to dissect her through sartorial clues. The episode also plays with Holmes' image as a man without sexual urges; Irene suggests that he does not "know where to look" at a naked woman, and the audience is told that Moriarty derisively calls Holmes "the virgin." Even Holmes' brother, Mycroft, gets in on the digs. When Sherlock delivers an irresistible straight line, "Sex doesn't alarm me," Mycroft cuttingly replies, "How would you know?" Inspired, perhaps, by the nude scene in the first Guy Ritchie film, *Sherlock* also treats viewers to glimpses of a naked Benedict Cumberbatch, although the full effect is more imagined than displayed. Like the Ritchie films, the second series also continues to explore the "bromance" elements of Holmes' relationship with Watson, provoking Watson to defend his heterosexuality against the idea that the two are, in fact, a couple. At every level, the episode shows its awareness of and engagement with the sexual aspects of the principal characters, consciously poking at viewers' ideas and persistent cultural perceptions. When Irene Adler says that "brainy's the new sexy," she aptly sums up the qualities that make Sherlock Holmes such a potent icon today.

The zeitgeist of current popular culture makes such Holmesian revision particularly timely. The 21st century has embraced a new masculine ideal that equates intellectual acuity with sexual desirability, with more television programs and films than ever before celebrating the sexy geek as icon, hero, and heartthrob. Even the ever logical Mr. Spock, already the object of adoration when the original *Star Trek* series aired in the 1960s, has come in for an amorous upgrade in the most recent *Star Trek* film, which depicts the Vulcan officer as embroiled in a serious romance with the lovely Lieutenant Uhura. Recent American television series have given us Dr. Gregory House (*House*), Chuck Bartowski (*Chuck*), Charlie Eppes (*Numb3rs*), and the adorable odd couple of Leonard and Sheldon on *The Big Bang Theory*. Across the pond, longtime cult hit *Doctor Who* has offered increasingly youthful and attractive stars in the title role, and romance has become a major aspect of the wandering Time Lord's experience. These characters, both old and new, suggest the increasing sense of compatibility between intellectual and amatory pursuits.

Ironically, this desire to embrace brilliant characters seems new to most of our cultural observers in the mainstream media, and yet it has been an important element in the revision and representation of Sherlock Holmes for over a century. Conan Doyle might have thought that his hero could be confined to cold calculations, but audiences have always sensed that there is something seductive about Sherlock Holmes, and the culture has persistently remade Holmes into the romantic figure of audience desire. Given our current cultural obsession with sexy, smart characters, it can hardly be surprising that

Holmes is enjoying renewed popularity, and it will be interesting to see how much the next iconic incarnation of the great detective embodies both superior intellect and sex appeal.

WORKS CITED

Bradshaw, Peter. "*The Private Life of Sherlock Holmes.*" Rev. of *The Private Life of Sherlock Holmes,* dir. Billy Wilder. *The Guardian.* 5 Dec. 2002. Web. 31 Dec. 2011.

Chabon, Michael. *The Final Solution: A Story of Detection (P.S.).* New York: Harper Perennial, 2005. Print.

Conan Doyle, Arthur. Letter to Joseph Bell. 16 June 1892. Print.

Conan Doyle, Arthur. *A Study in Scarlet. The Complete Sherlock Holmes.* Vol. 1. New York: Barnes & Noble Classics, 2003. 3–96. Print.

Davies, David Stuart. *Bending the Willow: Jeremy Brett as Sherlock Holmes.* Rev. ed. Ashcroft, BC: Calabash Press, 2002. Kindle ebook file.

Eyles, Allen. *Sherlock Holmes: A Centenary Celebration.* New York: Harper and Row, 1986. Print.

King, Laurie B. *The Beekeeper's Apprentice: Or, On the Segregation of the Queen.* New York: Picador, 2007. Print.

Martin, Dan. "Sherlock Makes Sunday Night TV Sexy." *The Guardian.* 23 July 2010. Web. 15 Mar. 2012.

Naslund, Sena Jeter. *Sherlock in Love.* New York: HarperCollins, 1993. Print.

Oglethorpe, Tim. "Sherlock's Got Sexy!" *MailOnline.* 23 July 2010. Web. 15 Mar. 2012.

Pointer, Michael. *The Sherlock Holmes File.* New York: Crown, 1976. Print.

The Private Life of Sherlock Holmes. Dir. Billy Wilder. Perf. Robert Stephens, Colin Blakely, Christopher Lee. United Artists, 1970. DVD.

Riley, Dick, and Pam McAllister. *The Bedside Companion to Sherlock Holmes: A Unique Guide to the World's Most Famous Detective.* New York: Barnes and Noble Books, 2005. Print.

Roberts, Lora. *The Affair of the Incognito Tenant: A Mystery with Sherlock Holmes.* McKinleyville, CA: Perseverance Press, 2004. Print.

Sabol, Autumn. *Elementary, My Dear.* Lincoln, NE: iUniverse, 2005. Print.

Sherlock. Created by Mark Gatiss and Steven Moffat. Perf. Benedict Cumberbatch, Martin Freeman, Una Stubbs. BBC. 2010–2012.

Sherlock Holmes. Dir. Guy Ritchie. Perf. Robert Downey, Jr., Jude Law, Rachel McAdams, Mark Strong. Warner Bros. 2009. DVD.

Sherlock Holmes: A Game of Shadows. Dir. Guy Ritchie. Perf. Robert Downey, Jr., Jude Law, Noomi Rapace, Rachel McAdams, Jared Harris, Stephen Fry. Warner Bros. 2011. DVD.

Sherlock Holmes in New York. Dir. Boris Sagal. Perf. Roger Moore, John Huston, Patrick Macnee, Charlotte Rampling. 20th Century–Fox Television, 1976. DVD.

Vernon, Polly. "Sartorial Style of Benedict Cumberbatch's Sherlock Holmes Points the Way for British Men." *The Guardian/The Observer* online. 7 Aug. 2010. Web. 14 Mar. 2012.

3

"Bromance is so passé"
Robert Downey, Jr.'s Queer Paratexts

KAYLEY THOMAS

"I think the word bromance is so passé. We are two men who
happen to be roommates who wrestle a lot and share a bed."
— *Robert Downey, Jr., qtd. in Carroll para. 9*

The dynamic between Sherlock Holmes and Dr. John Watson is, of
course, integral to any Sherlock Holmes adaptation. Both prior to and following the theatrical release of Guy Ritchie's *Sherlock Holmes* (2009) and its
sequel, *Sherlock Holmes: A Game of Shadows* (2011), critics and audiences have
debated the film's depiction of the famous partnership, with a particular
emphasis upon determining degrees of "bromance" or homosexuality in the
chemistry that Ritchie, Robert Downey, Jr. (Holmes), and Jude Law (Watson)
have concocted. Rumors of a gay Sherlock Holmes abounded before the first
film debuted, due in great part to Ritchie's, Law's, and Downey's suggestions
of homoerotic subtext at the very least, with more pointed emphases by
Downey of a more conspicuous homosexual relationship between Holmes and
Watson. The possibility of such an interpretation met with skepticism and
resistance by some, with debates arising over canonicity, marketability, and
the fundamental question: Would the actual film turn out to be more akin
to *I Love You, Man* or *Brokeback Mountain*? Would Ritchie's adaptation follow
in the long tradition of buddy narratives and employ elements of the recent
popular phenomenon of the bromance, or would it make the homosocial
homosexual, the subtextual textual? Downey's pre-film hype effectively created
a ready-made framework through which audiences were encouraged to view
the film. Rather than search within the films for instances of homoerotic subtext or seek to legitimate any existence thereof canonically or historically,
however, in this chapter I analyze the paratexts that promote such readings,

positing the influence of the actors and press in presenting and receiving the films as adaptations and as potentially queered texts. I consulted primarily popular media to aid in this analysis while employing Gérard Genette's theory of the paratext and Eve Kosofsky Sedgwick's theory of homosociality.

Pitching a More Equal Couple: (Re-)Interpreting and (Re-)Creating Holmes and Watson

Director Guy Ritchie situates his *Sherlock Holmes* films as participating in a distinctly adaptive process. Unlike Steven Moffat and Mark Gatiss's modern adaptation, *Sherlock*, however, Ritchie's films take place in Victorian England (and, in *A Game of Shadows*, France and Switzerland as well). Few audiences and critics would likely categorize these as period pieces, though; indeed, rather than serving as a mere transposition from one medium to another, the films engage in what Julie Sanders terms "*a process of creation*" in which "the act of adaptation always involves both (re-)interpretation and then (re-)creation" (8). Ritchie positions his adaptations as simultaneously part of a process of repetition, excavation, and revision:

> My original pitch to Warner [Brothers] was that I wanted something more along the lines of Butch and Sundance than the traditional, stodgy Holmes and Watson. I wanted a more equal couple. They're both very physical, which fits well with me. I had always read that Holmes is an action man.... As is Watson — he's a war hero [qtd. in Bentley para. 3–4].

Ritchie works in this statement to differentiate his interpretation from prior adaptations, indicating a desire at once for a Holmes and Watson emerging from his own vision of them and a pair that is authentic, loyally derived, and uniquely revived from Conan Doyle's stories. He responds to both his own experiences of the source text and adaptations of it, highlighting the intertextual nature of the adaptation process, in which every text is "a permutation of texts" (Kristeva 36). In establishing Holmes and Watson's masculinities and partnership as his objects of (re-)interpretation and (re-)creation, Ritchie in effect invites critics and audiences to determine precisely what interpretation of these men that his creation offers and if, as an adaptation, his text succeeds in the adaptive process of "repetition with variation" (Sanders 8) — a palatable fusion of fidelity and originality.

Sanders posits that audiences engage with adaptations "as palimpsests through our memory of other works" (8). Just as Ritchie approached *Sherlock Holmes* with the memory of previous adaptations as well as with the connection he had drawn between Butch and Sundance and Holmes and Watson, so do audiences bring other textual associations to their experiences of the movies.

In proposing both Holmes and Watson as men of action, Ritchie locates the films within the kind of action genre that one might understandably associate with the man behind *Snatch* and *Lock, Stock, and Two Smoking Barrels* with "a grand reputation for block camaraderie" and "knowing masculinity" (Kennedy para. 11). Ritchie's films occupy a highly masculine-oriented milieu, where male interests and male-male interactions take center stage. Likewise, in invoking *Butch Cassidy and the Sundance Kid*, Ritchie calls upon audience familiarity with another genre associated with masculinity and masculine bonds, the Western — and, in the case of Butch and Sundance, both the buddy film and what some have interpreted as "a thinly disguised homosexual love story" (Mellen 286), which, in the 21st century, is often referred to as a "bromance." In doing so, Ritchie proposes that amidst the action will not only be a focus upon a buddy dynamic but on Holmes and Watson as a *couple*.

Jude Law affirms, "Guy wanted to make this about the *relationship* between Watson and Holmes" (qtd. in Balls para. 6, emphasis added). Although such language certainly does not definitively position Ritchie's incarnation of Holmes and Watson as a homosexual couple, it does gesture toward a potential reading that has been powerfully adopted and, in a sense, adapted by Robert Downey, Jr. The actor's own (re-)interpretation and (re-)creation of Ritchie's conception, textually and paratextually — both in his performances in the films and, as this chapter is concerned with, his proclamations in the press — employ a queer framework through which to view Ritchie's adaptation. As a result, Downey envelopes the question of the fidelity and originality of Ritchie's interpretation and extends further the question of the adaptation's variation: whether he and Law portray a bromantic couple who, although more equal partners in Ritchie's adaptation, maintain a close but distinctly heterosexual friendship; whether the detective harbors a "homerotic attachment" (Jenkins para. 5) for his doctor in a series of films "seething with bi-sexual grudges and longings" (Atkinson para. 3); or if such polarizations are themselves passé, and rather "Watson and Holmes are an exploration of intimacy in all kinds of relationships" (Downey, "Kate Meets the Sherlock Stars!").

Interests of Men and Interest in Men: Bromance Is the New Homosocial

The term "bromance" has been frequently associated with Ritchie's *Sherlock Holmes*, with reviews entitled "Muscular 'Sherlock' a Victorian Bromance, with Fights" (Kennedy), articles identifying the films' "secret weapon" as the "bromantic chemistry between the two leads" (Crowther 82), and interviewers asking Downey, Jr. and Law to comment on "developing the Holmes/Watson bromance" (Downey, Jr., Robert, Jude Law, Noomi Rapace, and Guy Ritchie para. 4). The word gained popularity in the 2000s with films like *I Love You, Man* and *Superbad*, as well as such television series as *Scrubs* and *House, M.D.* (Drs. House and Wilson notably inspired in part by Holmes and Watson themselves), amongst others. A portmanteau of "bro" and "romance," a bromance designates a significant bond between men, described in *Time* as "the strong emotional attachment of one man for another" (Corliss para. 4), and more narrowly defined in *Merriam-Webster* as "a close *non-sexual* friendship between men" (emphasis added). Purportedly coined in the 1990s by *Big Brother* editor Dave Carnie to describe the camaraderie between skateboarders who spent much of their time together on tour (Corliss para. 4), bromance as a film genre can certainly trace its roots further back. Downey notes that the Holmes/Watson relationship reminds him of at turns *The Odd Couple*, *Lethal Weapon*, and *Butch and Sundance* (Downey, Jr., and Law, "Robert Downey, Jr., and Jude Law are Holmes and Watson" para. 16). These comparisons suitably evoke elements common to the bromance and prevalent in Ritchie's adaptations: back-and-forth banter, a love-hate dynamic, codependency, masculine physicality and action, male camaraderie and loyalty, and potential homoeroticism — what reviewers of the *Sherlock Holmes* films themselves identify as an "Oscar-and-Felix routine of quarrelsome affection" (Scott para. 8); "the best buddy cop movie since *Lethal Weapon 2*," whose "heart" is "the chemistry between best friends" (Demaret para. 7); and a "Redford/ Newman so lovingly, endearingly" reprised by Downey, Jr., and Law that their "love for one another" is "clear ... and convincing" (Thomas para. 4).

The concept of the bromance understandably resonates with *Sherlock Holmes* and can even be determined as drawing from the influence of Conan Doyle's own Holmes and Watson, the original odd couple alternately fighting for justice and Empire while together living outside the confines of ordinary existence — fighting for and, more so in Ritchie's adaptations, sometimes *with* each other. Cast as two men who relish one another's company and often prize their masculine bonds above those with women, the bromantic couple is epitomized in Downey's and Law's portrayals of Holmes and Watson: "two thrill-seekers who would rather be with each other than just about anywhere else" (Drake para. 1). Ritchie's adaptations expound on this in their focus on two men who, particularly in Watson's case, cannot live with each other and, as Holmes makes abundantly clear, cannot live without each other. Both Downey and Law position *Sherlock Holmes* as a story driven by a decisive conflict — and it is not the scheming Lord Blackwood, meddling Irene Adler, or devious Professor Moriarty at the center, according to Downey:

> We basically start [*Sherlock Holmes*] with Watson already having decided to get away from me.... It shows what Holmes is fighting for as much as anything else.

> It's no secret to anybody who's at all familiar with Holmes that he is incredibly devoted to justice — but this is second only to his need for Watson to not go and have a life away from him [Downey, Jr., Law, and Ritchie 79].

Holmes' attachment to Watson is positioned above Holmes' participation in a larger social system; while his devotion to a primarily patriarchal Victorian social order (i.e., the interests *of* men) is established, his desire for a bond with a particular man (i.e., an interest *in* men) dominates, as an examination of Eve Kosofsky Sedgwick's homosocialty will elaborate upon shortly. Law likewise positions the disruption of this "couple who have known each other eight or so years" as the "crisis" of the film (Downey, Jr., and Law, "Robert Downey, Jr., and Jude Law are Holmes and Watson" para. 20), acknowledging that "you could say this is a buddy film. Whether [Holmes and Watson] will or won't stay together and whether they will or won't drive each other around the bend before the end of the case is very much front and center in the story" (qtd. in Parks para. 5). Both actors establish for potential filmgoers the lens through which the desired audience should view the films.

Thus in declaring prior to the release of the first movie that "the word bromance is so passé" but then proceeding to tease that Holmes and Watson are "two men who happen to be roommates who wrestle a lot and share a bed" (Downey, Jr., qtd. in Carroll para. 9), Downey at once rejects and engages the concept of the bromance. His efforts function, in effect, as an adaptive act, correlating to Linda Hutcheon's observation of the "many different possible intentions behind the act of adaptation: the urge to consume and erase the memory of the adapted text or to call it into question is as likely as the desire to pay tribute by copying" (7). Downey's comment simultaneously invites the reader to consider the relationship between Holmes and Watson in association with the term "bromance," thus recalling other films and duos to which it has been attributed, and posits that either audiences should or should not perceive and read homoerotic subtext in this portrayal: Holmes and Watson can *happen* to be two men who engage in masculine, non-homosexual physicality (e.g., wrestling) and are perfectly comfortable sharing a bed, or they *happen* to be two men who share a bed in which they "wrestle," enveloping a physical component into "the strong emotional attachment of one man for another" while excluding the caveat that this must be "a close *non-sexual* friendship between men" (emphasis added). Downey works to displace the term but depends upon its meaning and associations in order to expand upon and surpass it, much as an adaptation does its source text.

Such a public remark serves as what Gérard Genette calls the *threshold* before the primary text (here, the film itself), which offers "the world at large the possibility of either stepping inside or turning back" (1). Not only can readers be drawn to or away from viewing the film because of Downey's declaration, but they can also determine whether to enter into his rejection of the bromance or turn back to its usefulness as a categorization of relationships between men, as many critics have. Despite Downey's disavowal of "bromance," the "passé" provision has often become lost in newsbytes that seize upon the popular portmanteau alone, resulting in articles touting or decrying the films' bromance without attention to Downey's own distinction (the interview itself was notably titled "Robert Downey, Jr., Jude Law Explore 'Bromance' On 'Sherlock Holmes' Set").

Bromance is closely aligned with another neologism: *homosocial*. Defined in the social sciences as "the seeking, enjoyment, and/or preference for the company of the same sex," homosocial bonds create a sphere of male sociality separate from the female sphere that develops and encourages a masculine system of value (Lipman-Blumen 16). Sedgwick notes that the term is "obviously formed by analogy with 'homosexual,' and just as obviously meant to be distinguished from 'homosexual'" (1). Her groundbreaking *Between Men: English Literature and Male Homosocial Desire*, with a strong focus upon 19th century literature, proves particularly appropriate in discussing the bond between Holmes and Watson. She posits the homosocial sphere of much of male bonding, particularly in contemporary society, as a heteronormative construct that depends simultaneously upon the use and exclusion of women and a fear of homosexuality (1–2).

Patriarchy as a system of "relations between men, which ... establish or create interdependence and solidarity among men that enable them to dominate women" (Hartmann 14) demands what Gayle Rubin terms a "compulsory homosexuality" in which "the suppression of the homosexual component of human sexuality, any corollary, the oppression of homosexuals, is ... a product of the same system whose rules and relations oppose women" (180). Sedgwick's feminist perspective informs her analysis of the bonds between men, often focusing upon the women between them that facilitate homosocial bonds at their own expense, but she also calls attention to the space between men in which lies a "carefully blurred, always-already-crossed line from being 'interested *in* men'" and pursuing the interests *of* men (89, emphasis added).

This line need not necessarily be crossed; Sedgwick's study does not seek to illuminate the inherent homosexuality in the literary characters that she analyzes. Rather she calls for more complex considerations of the relationships between men in which the often otherwise heteronormative, misogynistic, and homophobic realm of the homosocial might allow these close bonds to envelop the "potential unbrokenness of a continuum between homosocial and homosexual — a continuum whose visibility, for men, in our society, is radically disrupted" (1–2).

The broken homosocial continuum is perfectly embodied by the brand of bromance portrayed in popular films. Emotional bonds between men are allotted increasing visibility, yet many filmmakers and their characters display a continued wariness of straying into the homosexual end of the continuum. The potential for male intimacy to be interpreted as homosexual — or further, to develop into homosexual feeling or activity — may be acknowledged but is likely to be undercut by humor or policed by the inclusion of heterosexual love interests.

Superbad, for example, chronicles the efforts of two friends to lose their virginities to women before graduating high school; yet ultimately, as Corliss observes, "at the end of a night of wacky hijinks, the lads do wind up in a sleeping bag, exchanging intimacies with ... each other" (para. 2). Whether as rivals or compatriots, the pursuit of heterosexual pleasure as a plot device in such comedies has long relied upon the pleasure inherent in the bonding between men in the process. The modern bromance and its audiences recognize and revel in this. In *Superbad*, however, Seth's declaration that ultimately he just wants to "go to the rooftops and scream, 'I love my best friend, Evan'" is safely ensconced in the vulgar lads' humor throughout the film; the romantic image of the rooftop declaration thus adopts a genre convention to highlight the film's recognition of the homosocial element of its male intimacy but still land squarely on the side of "best friend." The male bond is valued above the initial heterosexual conquest premise, establishing the female objects of desire as necessary devices to develop that bond, but the homosocial bond remains resolutely heterosexual. On the other hand, when similar observations are made about the *Sherlock Holmes* films, their categorization as bromance more commonly conflates the heterosexual-homosocial with homoerotic subtext, complicating the assumption of male friendships as emotional *and* non-sexual.

In the first *Sherlock Holmes*, the two principle female characters are cast primarily as, in fact, standing between men and function, for many critics, to do little else. Scott identifies Irene Adler (Rachel McAdams) as "the beard" intended only to "dispel a few hints of homoerotic subtext" (para. 8) and likewise dubs Mary Morstan (Kelly Reilly) "a page of half-written dialogue" who "sends Holmes into a snit of jealousy," all of "which loses some of its interesting implications" when the film works to establish Adler as Holmes' love interest (para. 8). Scott's analysis envelopes a pointed homosexual element into the bromance. If the film does not fulfill the implications of its subtext, it is nonetheless marked as walking that always-already-crossed line of Sedgwick's, away from the concept of the bromance as a close non-sexual friendship between men. Atkinson further conflates bromance and romance in deeming Holmes and Watson's relationship

> an uncloseted bromance seething with bi-sexual grudges and longings ... we're supposed to smell the sexual tension ("Don't get excited," Holmes whispers when

fishing in Watson's pocket) and be as amused as the guys are by their predicament, stuck as they are between an eternal boyhood chasing villains and a respectable life of marriage and afternoon tea [para. 3].

An uncloseted bromance would seem to be the open acknowledgment of the emotional intimacy of a close male friendship — *Superbad*'s evocation of the rooftop declaration. Atkinson positions Holmes and Watson at once closeted and uncloseted, however: they seethe with unfulfilled longings, sexual frustration and codependency strangely masked, revealed, and tempered by bromantic banter about personal space issues and wearing each other's clothes. The film's action (and its posturing as an action movie) are for Atkinson "little more than loud diversions from the ironic and self-knowing tale beneath the tale, a story of two men in love ... and the ways in which they keep rescuing and then bickering with each other as they try to stay boys forever" (para. 4). Atkinson invokes here two seemingly different discourses: one of (un)closeted homosexual desire and one of compulsory heterosexuality. In casting Holmes and Watson's bromance in the homosocial continuum as a sort of Freudian, acceptable phase of male desire that must be outgrown, Atkinson highlights the films' simultaneous challenging of and submission to the heterosexual conventions of the bromance. Never one to follow conventions, Downey submits a challenge to a consideration of the films as bromances.

Queering the Paratext: The Way a (Sub)Text Makes a Movie of Itself

Appropriating Ritchie's initial vision for the films, Downey has on multiple occasions promoted the adaptations as potentially homoerotic. During the first film's production, his suggestion to the press that Holmes and Watson would wrestle and share a bed attracted critics' and audiences' attention. Just one comment in an MTV interview appeared in almost every early report on the film's development, inspiring headlines such as *Digital Spy*'s "Ritchie 'Casts Sherlock Holmes as Gay,'" *The New York Post*'s "'Gay' Sherlock Holmes Could Backfire for Guy Ritchie," and *The News of the World*'s "Queerstalker." Although Ritchie has never declared Holmes as gay — rather, he has elaborated that "while these guys are sort of in love with each other," they are "a heterosexual couple that at moments could seem gay" (qtd. in Ditzian para. 7) — Downey's inferences have dominated, serving as the defining paratext for the films.

Genette's theory of paratextuality posits seemingly external materials as an inextricable part of a text, with the prefix *para-* at once denoting that which is "separate from or going beyond" while also serving as "analogous or parallel to," according to the *OED*. Although Genette discusses the paratext in reference to literary works in particular, the concept can easily be applied to the filmic text. A literary paratext might include a book's cover, title page, preface, or even reviews about a book, whether quoted upon its jacket or encountered by a potential reader in a magazine. In the same way, a film paratext could be a movie trailer, DVD cover, title sequence, reviews from the press, or interviews with the writers, directors, and cast. Although we may not typically consider a trailer released months before the film's debut or a quote from an interview as a *part* of an actual movie, these do serve significantly to shape how we approach our viewing of the film for the first time as well as how we reflect upon it while viewing, after viewing, or upon revisiting it. Such paratexts can even create for us the text of a film we have not seen and perhaps, as a result of such paratexts, have chosen not to: Sherlock Holmes can become "that film about those two guys who wrestle a lot and share a bed" that one never sees but has categorized as such.

The paratext, for Genette, is "the means by which a text makes a book of itself and proposes itself as such to its readers, and more generally to the public" (261); in the same way paratexts are how a text makes a film of itself and proposes itself as such to its audiences. Thus Downey's comments serve as a paratext informing our viewing of the *Sherlock Holmes* films, infusing them with an *illocutionary force* (Genette 268). A paratext can "communicate pure *information*," such as the actors who star in the film and the release date, but it may also function to provide "authorial and/or editorial *intention* or *interpretation*," which, as Genette posits, is "the cardinal function of most prefaces" in books (268). Downey's interview did not necessarily communicate *accurate* information: Holmes and Watson never are actually shown sharing a bed, though, to be fair, neither are they shown sleeping separately, and *A Game of Shadows* delivers a rather notable wrestling scene, with a red-faced Watson's head clamped between Holmes' bare legs (the detective having donned wig, lipstick, and dress). Certainly Downey's press comments prefacing the films proffer a powerful interpretation to potential audiences and critics.

In the week prior to its release, Downey appeared on *The Late Show with David Letterman* to promote the first film. Letterman began the discussion of the film by acknowledging that "there was always the suggestion that there was a different level of relationship between Sherlock and Dr. Watson." The ambiguity of his comment was quickly assigned meaning by Downey, who quipped, "You mean that they were homos." At Letterman's speechlessness and nervous laughter, Downey prompted further, "That is what you were saying?" The conversation progressed as follows, with an interjection from Letterman's musical director, Paul Shaffer:

LETTERMAN: In a manner of speaking, yes ... that they were closer than just out solving crimes. It's sort of touched on in the film, but he has a fiancée, so we're not certain. Is that right?

DOWNEY: She could be a beard. Who knows?

SHAFFER: What are they, complete screamers? Is that what you're saying?

DOWNEY: Why don't we observe the clip and let the audience decide if he just happens to be a very butch homosexual. Which there are many. And I'm proud to know certain of them.

Downey's frank language and approach are not uncommon to him, but certainly his blunt commentary drew attention. Jeff Jensen recalls the "stir" Downey caused with his previous interview and identifies and critiques the actor's Letterman appearance as a "little clever schtick," determining that rather than "accomplish something more interesting and noble" such as "by spinning Holmes as gay ... trying to get people to confront their own attitudes and biases about homosexuality [and] the look and form of movie heroes," Downey "decided to get all provocative ... to push his latest very expensive franchise flick" (Jensen para. 4). Jensen's tone is deliberately mocking of such pretensions, and he proceeds to profess an openness to a queer interpretation of the duo and invites his readership to weigh in, but he draws attention to the notion that an actor's paratext is always suspect and seemingly harnesses not the illocutionary force of interpretation but of intent — it sells a text but does not meaningfully define it.

In examining the context of Downey's paratexts and their influence, the question becomes what role the actor plays as the author of a film text. Hutcheon considers whether actors can be considered as "conscious adaptors" (81). Some actors bring to their performances research they have conducted of the source texts for inspiration and background, but all actors in a sense adapt screenplays, "embody[ing] and giv[ing] material existence to the adaptation" in their decisions regarding glances, gestures, and tone of voice that can "interpret through incarnating characters in ways the initial creator never envisaged" (81–82). But scripts can also change through interactions between directors and actors, producing an end product that could be quite different from both the screenplay and the original adapted text. Hutcheon aptly summarizes William Goldman's vision of the final film product as "the studio's adaptation of the editor's adaptation of the director's adaptation of the actors' adaptation of the screenwriter's adaptation of a novel that might itself be an adaptation of narrative or generic conventions" (83). In addition to reading Conan Doyle in preparation, meeting with Sherlockian Leslie Klinger, and brainstorming ideas with Ritchie ("Robert Downey, Jr., & Jude Law are Holmes and Watson"), Downey's paratextual play presents him as a decidedly conscious and crafty adaptor, participating in the process through which a text makes a movie of itself— not only into a movie that people purchase tickets to but also a movie that people will as a result consider as an adaptation — and in this case, potentially a queer one.

Widening Your Gaze: Horizons of Possibility

In *Sherlock Holmes: A Game of Shadows*, reviewers have noted that Holmes and Watson's "bromance gathers steam, homoeroticism now less a subtext than extended routine in which Sherlock even dons full drag" (Nathan para. 5) and "the suggestion that the detective has a homoerotic attachment to his sidekick, floated in the first movie, is made even more explicit" (Jenkins para. 5). Although this suggests a potentially less disrupted conception of Holmes and Watson's positions along the homosocial continuum, semantic and conceptual conflicts inherent in deeming the film a "bromance" persist. Protesting the term, Downey elaborated in an interview prior to the sequel's theatrical release:

> To me bromance ... I hate to say that that cheapens it; I understand that it simplifies the description.... But really, you know, what's known as 'banter'—which is sometimes just waffle to get you from one action sequence to another — we really treated that like that's the poetry in the movie. So finishing each other's sentences, being at cross purposes but coming around to these circles of understanding and love is to me — Watson and Holmes are an exploration of intimacy in all kinds of relationships [Downey, Jr., and Law, "Kate Meets the Sherlock Stars!"].

Downey offers here a reading of the relationship between Holmes and Watson that resists simplification, opening it up to more evocative, emotional, and malleable language than the neologism seems to allow, despite its often conflated, conflicted employment. The interviewer, however, interpreted as a result: "So it works! It is a bromance! You'll love that word by the end!" Downey's counter, "I love that after *all* of that positive explanation you go, 'that's so great, okay, let me minimize what you just said and now we're ready to move on'" ("Kate Meets the Sherlock Stars"), albeit in good humor, positions his previous paratextual play as a persistent stance in the interpretive process — a particularly *queer* stance on bromance.

I adopt David Halperin's definition of queerness as an interpretive process, rather than an identity or category of sexuality. Although rooted in homosexual object-choice, Halperin positions queer identity as different from gay identity, in that it "need not be grounded in any positive truth or in any stable reality" (62). Rather, Halperin proposes that "'queer' does not name some natural kind or refer to some determinate object; it acquires its meaning from its oppositional relation to the norm.... It is an identity without an essence"

(62). Thus Downey's comments work to establish within the popularity and subsequent categorization of the bromance a queer space of potentiality, an essence to be filled and multiplied with meaning. To name something as queer, according to Halperin, posits

> a horizon of possibility ... for reordering the relations among sexual behaviors, erotic identities, constructions of gender, forms of knowledge, regimes of enunciation, logics of representation, modes of self-constitution, and practices of community — for restructuring, that is, the relations among power, truth, and desire [62].

Although Downey has positioned himself without a doubt as a conscious adaptor, this is not to say that he is a conscious theorist. Words are important, though, as he emphasizes, and his own words construct an interpretive framework that itself demands interpretation — "the audience can decide for themselves," as he told Letterman. What Downey has done as an adaptor has not been, or has not simply been, to offer a queer performance or a queer interpretation, but to draw attention to potentialities, to horizons of possibilities in language, adaptation, and analysis. Although Downey has not been able to exorcise the passé neologism, he has drawn attention to the rhetoric of the heterosexual bromance as a brokenness in the continuum between the homosocial and the homosexual. Although discussions of the Sherlock Holmes films continue to invoke the term, the common conflation in reviews of the bromance and the homoerotic points to a very queering of the word's understanding that might just "happen to be" part of a productive process of (re-)interpretation and (re-)creation.

WORKS CITED

Atkinson, Michael. "Review: Sherlock Holmes." *The Boston Phoenix*. 22 Dec. 2009. Web. 4 Jan. 2012.

Balls, David. "Ritchie 'Casts Sherlock Holmes as Gay.'" *Digital Spy*. 23 Feb. 2009. Web. 4 Jan. 2012.

Bentley, David. "Sherlock Holmes: Does It Survive Guy Ritchie's Action-Hero Reinvention?" The Geek Files. *Coventry Telegraph*. 4 Jan. 2010. Web. 4 Jan. 2012.

"bromance." *Merriam-Webster.com*. 2012. Web. 4 Jan. 2012.

Carroll, Larry. "Robert Downey, Jr., Jude Law Explore 'Bromance' On 'Sherlock Holmes' Set." *MTV*. 12 Feb. 2009. Web. 4 Jan. 2012.

Corliss, Richard. "*Superbad*: A Fine Bromance." *Time*. 17 Aug. 2007. Web. 4 Jan. 2012.

Crowther, Jane. "A Fine Bromance." *Total Film*. Dec. 2011: 80–85. Print.

Demaret, David A. "Review: Sherlock Holmes Is Best Buddy Cop Movie since Lethal Weapon 2." *29–95*. 25. Dec. 2009. Web. 4 Jan. 2012.

Ditzian, Eric. "Guy Ritchie Explains the Tender Bromance in 'Sherlock Holmes.'" *MTV*. 4 Aug. 2009. Web. 4 Jan. 2012.

Downey, Robert, Jr. Interview by David Letterman. *The Late Show with David Letterman*. CBS. 16 Dec. 2009. Television.

Downey, Robert, Jr., and Jude Law. "Kate Meets the Sherlock Stars!" Interview by Kate Garrway. *Daybreak.* ITV. 14 Dec. 2011. Web. 4 Jan. 2012.

_____. "Robert Downey, Jr., and Jude Law Are Holmes and Watson." Interview by Edward Douglas. *ComingSoon.Net.* 5 Mar. 2009. Web. 4 Jan. 2012.

Downey, Robert, Jr., Jude Law, and Guy Ritchie. "The Game's Afoot..." Interview by Damon Wise. *Empire.* 1 Jan. 2010: 78–82. Print.

Downey, Robert, Jr., Jude Law, Noomi Rapace, and Guy Ritchie. "*Sherlock Holmes: A Game of Shadows* Press Conference." Interview. *DIY.* 13 Dec. 2011. Web. 4 Jan. 2012.

Drake, Rossiter. "Prelude to a Kiss? Robert Downey, Jr., Jude Law Share an Intriguing Romance in 'Sherlock Holmes.'" *7x7SF.* 24 Dec. 2009. Web. 4 Jan. 2012.

"'Gay' Sherlock Holmes Could Backfire for Guy Ritchie." *New York Post.* 4 Aug. 2009. Web. 4 Jan. 2012.

Genette, Gérard. *Paratexts: Thresholds of Interpretation.* Trans. Jane E. Lewin. Cambridge, UK: Cambridge University Press, 1997. Print.

Halperin, David. *Saint Foucault: Toward a Gay Hagiography.* Oxford, UK: Oxford University Press, 1997. Print.

Hartmann, Heidi. "The Unhappy Marriage of Marxism and Feminism: Towards a More Progressive Union." *Women and Revolution: A Discussion of the Unhappy Marriage of Marxism and Feminism.* Ed. Lydia Sargent. Cambridge, UK: South End Press, 1981. Print.

Hutcheon, Linda. *A Theory of Adaptation.* New York: Routledge, 2006. Print.

Jenkins, Mark. "No Wit, 'Sherlock': 'Game of Shadows' Trades Brains for Brawn." *The Washington Post GoingOutGuide.*15 Dec. 2011. Web. 4 Jan. 2012.

Jensen, Jeff. "Robert Downey, Jr.'s Allegedly Gay 'Sherlock Holmes.' Seriously?!" PopWatch. *Entertainment Weekly.* 22 Dec. 2009. Web. 4 Jan. 2012.

Kennedy, Lisa. "Movie Review: Muscular 'Sherlock' a Victorian Bromance, with Fights." *DenverPost.com.* 25 Dec. 2009. Web. 4 Jan. 2012.

Kristeva, Julia. "The Bounded Text." *Desire in Language: A Semiotic Approach to Literature and Art.* Ed. Leon S. Roudiez. Trans. Thomas Gora, Alice Jardine, and Leon S. Roudiez. New York: Columbia University Press, 1980. 36–63. Print.

Lipman-Blumen, Jean. "Toward a Homosocial Theory of Sex Roles: An Explanation of the Sex Segregation of Social Institutions." *Signs* 1: 15–31. Print.

Mellen, Joan. *Big Bad Wolves: Masculinity in the American Film.* London: Elm Tree Books, 1978. Print.

Nathan, Ian. "Sherlock Holmes: A Game of Shadows." *Empire.* Web. 4 Jan. 2012.

"para-." *OED.* Oxford University Press, 2011. Web. 4 Jan. 2012.

Parks, Tim. "Downey Jr: 'Bromance Is a Passé Term.'" *Digital Spy.* 27 Aug. 2009. Web. 4 Jan. 2012.

Rubin, Gayle. "The Traffic in Women: Notes toward a Political Economy of Sex." *Toward an Anthology of Women.* Ed. Rayna Reiter. New York: Monthly Review Press, 1975. Print. 157–210.

Sanders, Julie. *Adaptation and Appropriation.* New York: Routledge, 2006. Print.

Scott, A.O. "The Brawling Supersleuth of 221B Baker Street Socks It to 'Em." *The New York Times.* 24 Dec. 2009. Web. 4 Jan. 2012.

Sedgwick, Eve Kosofsky. *Between Men: English Literature and Male Homosocial Desire.* New York: Columbia University Press, 1985. Print.

"Sherlock Holmes." *Box Office Mojo.* IMDb.com. Web. 4 Jan. 2012.

Sherlock Holmes. Dir. Guy Ritchie. Warner Brothers, 2010. DVD.

Sherlock Holmes: A Game of Shadows. Dir. Guy Ritchie. Warner Brothers, 2011. Film.

Superbad. Dir. Greg Mottola. Columbia Pictures, 2001. DVD.

Thomas, William. "Sherlock Holmes." *Empire.* 2010. Web. 4 Jan. 2012.

4

The Watson Effect
Civilizing the Sociopath
APRIL TOADVINE

When asked about one of his father's most famous characters, Adrian Conan Doyle commented that his father, Sir Arthur, often claimed that anyone who thought John Watson was an idiot was missing the point of the character. "Who was Watson?" he asked, and continued, "I do not mean the bumbling ass that is Hollywood's conception. I mean the *real* Watson of whom my father said to me in so many words on more than one occasion — 'those who consider Watson to be a fool are simply admitting that they haven't read the stories attentively.' ... Certainly Watson was no fool" (cited in Accardo 102, emphasis in the original).

Questions about John Watson, and what to make of him, have continued since the character's introduction. In the 2009 Guy Ritchie movie, *Sherlock Holmes*, Holmes, played by Robert Downey, Jr., and Watson, played by Jude Law, walk down a busy street in search of clues in the disappearance of Lord Blackwood and are stopped by a woman who reads Watson's palm. The woman claims to see two men, brothers, which both Watson and the audience are supposed to understand as a description of his relationship with Holmes. This relationship is at the heart of the original stories and essential to the recent adaptations, which focus as much on the relationship as they do on any crime solving.

In Arthur Conan Doyle's stories, Watson was a competent war veteran with a medical practice. Although he was never a detective, he was certainly important because he represented the prevailing late–Victorian morality of the society in which he and Holmes lived. Classic movie and television depictions of Holmes and Watson have focused on Holmes as the intellectual superior of a slower-witted, almost buffoonish Watson, as indelibly portrayed in a series of movies in the 1940s by Nigel Bruce. In more recent portrayals, however, Watson has changed; both the 2009 film and the recent BBC series

Sherlock portray John as similar to Sherlock, so similar in fact, that he and Sherlock share personality traits. Therefore, when the title character[1] of BBC's *Sherlock* claims to be a "high-functioning sociopath" (in "A Study in Pink"), John's character is equally called into question. In this chapter, I contend that the character of John Watson, both in the 2009 movie and in the BBC series, is depicted as a sociopath on par with the character of Sherlock Holmes. Given the character's role as moral representative, his transformation is important because it calls into question the character of Holmes himself and, by extension, the culture that created him. In order to examine the way that the character of Watson reflects shifts in cultural understanding of morality and the construction of sociopaths, I compare the original literary depiction of the character with recent depictions of Watson's increasing antisocial impulses.

The Victorian Sociopath

One of the hallmarks of the mid–Victorian period is the importance placed on morality, especially as it was demonstrated through relationships in and around the family. Because of the influence of domestic ideology, which idealized the home and the role of women as a civilizing influence on their husbands and the business world, the expectations for moral behavior for both men and women revolved around duty to family, duty to those less fortunate, and respectability, usually demonstrated by scrupulous personal integrity and cleanliness. Buttressed by a strong work ethic and the influence of the Church, these values allowed the middle class to take cultural superiority from those in the upper classes who had long held cultural and economic power over the country. As Richard Altick points out in *Victorian People and Ideas*, "[t]he moral code of Protestantism ... put high value upon such qualities as frugality, self-denial, dedication to one's appointed occupation" (169). By the end of the century, a thriving materialist culture made the dedication to individual work even more important as it became the marker of social status for middle-class men who were defined in particular by their professional identities. The fears of degeneration in men stemming from the combination of Britain's wars in the Crimea and South Africa, not to mention the difficulties of maintaining the Empire in far-flung, dangerous places, led to worries that young men were physically inferior to their predecessors, to those they were to rule, and worse, to their enemies. Although fears of men being effeminate as a result of too much mental labor were certainly not new, the growing number of men who no longer lived by manual labor meant that more men were at risk for this particular problem. At the same time, a growing emphasis on athleticism in men, especially for young middle-class men, meant that men were expected to be physical, athletic, and certainly courageous in the face of physical danger. Intellect, while never an unwanted quality, was not emphasized to the same extent. James Eli Adams notes that the rise of muscular Christianity meant that men were expected to be vigorous, with "animal spirits" (108) that made them energetic, vital, and physically strong. These expectations were difficult to display for non-military professional men, particularly those whose daily lives did not involve manual labor. Men in non-manual professions were expected to display the kind of emotional and physical self-discipline that showed them capable of exerting and, more importantly, controlling themselves on par with those whose labor required this exertion daily (17).

Those who were unwilling or unable to control themselves, or who did not fit social views of traditional morality, were often diagnosed as mentally ill. During the 19th century this was particularly true of those who seemed antisocial. Christopher Lane's work on antisocial behaviors in the Victorian period shows a shift during the 19th century in which, by the end of the century, antipathy towards others moves from being a sign of idealistic belief in the good in humanity to a sign of illness (Lane 13). During the mid–Victorian period, some forms of mental illness were diagnosed as moral deficiency, and much of the treatment involved moral instruction in one form or another. In particular, the mental illness afflicting sociopaths was termed "moral insanity" by those practitioners in the 19th century who were attempting to specify those whose lack of empathy and disinterest in relationships with others distinguished them from those whose illness involved delusions or mental incapacity. After 1835, Victorian doctors assumed that individuals suffering from what was known as "non compos mentis" did so as a result of many different causes, among them excess emotional response, brain disease, and over study (Pedlar 2).

Writing in 1835, James Prichard describes moral insanity as "a morbid perversion of the feelings, affections, and natural impulses, without any remarkable disorder or affect of the intellect of knowing and reasoning facilities" (cited in Pedlar 4). Unlike lunatics, for example, those afflicted with moral insanity were not considered intellectually inferior to others, which made their cases even more difficult for the medical establishment to understand. The morally insane were recognizable because their feelings were noticeably different than others. Prichard refers to lack of affection and natural impulses as a means to say that the morally insane were unable to emotionally connect to others in ways that the medical establishment of the time considered natural.

In 1897, as Conan Doyle was writing, Henry Maudsley argued that some criminal offenders had no "moral sense" as a result of genetic degeneration of the criminal classes. Although he was certainly influenced by class considerations, by describing individuals without the ability to maintain interpersonal relationships, he was describing antisocial behavior in the offenders he saw. His definition of moral sense involved exactly that set of interpersonal skills (e.g., relationships, empathy) that are difficult for people whose behavior is antisocial. Maudsley based his claims on a belief in a genetic component to the problem, a belief that seems to have continued to the present (Millon et al. 146).

The definitions of antisocial personality disorder have shifted from the Victorian concern with moral health to the contemporary interest in preventing the sociopath from committing acts of violence towards others, from "moral insanity" to "antisocial personality disorder." Although there is the lack of empathy and the inability to form meaningful relationships, the sociopath is not currently seen as morally insane as much as developmentally damaged by an early inability to form relationships that could teach empathy. While there is still some belief in heredity as a possible factor in the development of the disorder, it is equally likely to occur from physical brain damage and environmental considerations. Contemporary definitions of sociopathy involve looking at the various ways this lack of empathy manifests itself in the way the sociopath deals with society. Some sociopaths are aggressive; some are able to build relationships with a very few people, whereas others have relationships with no one at all. Some feel that social norms do not apply to them, that there is another code of behavior for them than for others. In addition, there is the possibility that the sociopath might enjoy harming or frightening others (Lykken 26). The lack of specificity in the way this lack of empathy is expressed is one of the reasons why the sociopath is so difficult to recognize. Current treatment for individuals with antisocial personality disorder involves behavioral modification and medication, if the individual can actually be convinced to get help.

In their book, *Politics of Madness*, Joseph Melling and Bill Forsythe point out that the majority of those who are considered antisocial are young men, usually of lower socio-economic status (xii). The potential for stereotyping young men into this category as a result of their class status could be seen as a holdover from the Victorian expectations of mental illness in the poor. Because neither Holmes nor Watson is a member of the lower economic classes, they do not seem to fit the stereotype that associates mental illness with the poor. Additionally, because of their class status, Holmes' behavior, which easily can be considered erratic and a sign of instability, is considered a sign of his intellect rather than inadequacy. Watson is solidly middle class and is defined by the qualities that would have been representative of a Victorian man.

Watson, the Middle-Class Man

The first way that Watson is delineated as middle class is in the way his character is identified. His first name, while mentioned, is rarely used; instead, he is usually referred to by his professional title: Doctor. As a marker to identify his middle-class status, his professional title signals his education and a level of social ability that is at odds with the traditional Hollywood representation of Watson as a buffoon. Rather, his professional association underscores his capability. Conan Doyle's version of Watson is a military veteran who is able to eventually build a medical practice. The character displays a strong belief in progress and science. Although not a detective himself, he has the ability to appreciate Sherlock Holmes and to see what he does as scientific and rational. Others, Lestrade, for example, might make use of Sherlock Holmes but do not see him as anything other than an amateur with an interest in crime. By contrast, John Watson has the middle-class Victorian interest in science and progress, which allows him to see that Sherlock Holmes possesses above-average ability. At the same time, Conan Doyle's Watson is a man who often is the one Holmes asks to accompany him when there is likely to be a fight. It is clear that he is good in a difficult situation because of his military experience. With his physical capabilities and his average, though not genius intellect, John Watson meets the definition of the hearty, average middle-class man described earlier.

His very averageness makes him the representative of societal norm, unlike Sherlock Holmes. After all, while Conan Doyle's Watson is capable and professional, his Holmes is something more. Holmes is undoubtedly exceptional to such an extent that he does not fit into the normal categories of professional. While he claims that he is the world's first "consulting detective" because he has invented the position, he has, in fact, set himself up as a crime specialist — as distinct from a regular detective in the way a medical specialist would be distinct from a general practitioner of medicine. That Conan Doyle's Watson is not a specialist but is instead a general practitioner is in no way a denigration of him. Instead, it underscores the character as average, and therefore representative.

In describing Watson, Stephen Knight refers to his narrative tone as that of a "mildly self-satisfied bourgeois who feels he has a mastery of things," which Knight believes helps align readers with the more intellectual, elite Holmes, who is able to understand and unravel the mysteries surrounding the cases they solve (cited in Jann 24). Although Watson certainly has the bourgeois voice, I argue that this allows readers to see themselves as Watson, middle-class voice and all. Readers are expected to side with Watson in his repeated marveling in his friend's abilities, particularly because the narrator rarely allows readers all of the information until Holmes explains the solution. Conan Doyle's Watson, therefore, is no less intelligent than average readers who, try as they might to follow the clues, cannot solve the mystery and must wait for Sherlock Holmes to explain.

Watson's Victorian Morality

As a professional man, Conan Doyle's Watson is a skilled physician; as an average man his reactions to Holmes often stem from a familiarly Victorian code of behavior that privileged work ethic, respectability, and modesty. His earliest complaints of Sherlock Holmes stem from the haphazard way that objects are stored in the apartment. When Watson sees the great detective sitting inactive on the couch, his reaction is disapproval, particularly when he realizes that the lassitude is chemically induced. At the beginning of "A Sign of Four," Watson describes himself as "exasperated" with Holmes' manner of injecting himself and finally decides to confront him. As with so many middle-class men, Conan Doyle's Watson judges his companion by a work ethic, until he realizes that, like other professionals, Holmes works with his mind. Watson then uses Holmes' concern for his mind to convince him to stop by asking him, "why should you, for a mere passing pleasure, risk the loss of those great powers with which you have been endowed" (89)? In fact, the very lack of neatness at 221B would indicate, for some, a lack of respectability, given the importance placed on clean and orderly homes as a marker for middle-class families. Watson is thus a voice of social norm at 221B.

Unlike John Watson, Sherlock Holmes is not interested in family or any social connection so important to other Victorian men. The doctor describes him as someone who "never spoke of the softer passions, save with a gibe and a sneer" and mentions that he "loathe[s] every form of society with his whole Bohemian soul" (Conan Doyle 161). Unlike the doctor, who does find duty to family important, Sherlock Holmes does not, an attitude which is a significant departure from the ostensible importance Victorians placed on an idealized view of the family.

Conan Doyle's Watson demonstrates this importance through his relationship with Mary Morstan, the woman who eventually becomes his wife. His feelings about the relationship are seen through the lens of late–Victorian modesty in the face of two quintessential Victorian issues: money and appearances. Both of these nearly cost John Watson his wife, because his fear of the social implications of being seen as financially profiting by their relationship was enough to convince him not to approach her. In the story "The Sign of Four," Conan Doyle's Watson forces himself to sound happy about a fortune that will place the woman he loves out of his reach. He describes the moment when he realizes that her treasure, and therefore her fortune, is gone by saying "a great shadow seemed to pass from my soul. I did not know how this Agra treasure had weighed me down until now that it was finally removed. It was selfish, no doubt, disloyal, wrong, but I could realize nothing save that the golden barrier was gone from between us" (142–3). Not only does he feel strongly that he should not be seen as a financial speculator who would take advantage of a young woman's new wealth, he feels guilty for wishing she is not going to be rich. This combination of difficult emotions shows John Watson in the midst of a moral quandary based on an ingrained moral code regulating his behavior toward women. His belief in respectable behavior and personal integrity causes him to say nothing to Mary if he could possibly be seen to be taking advantage of her.

More than just socially norming, Conan Doyle's Watson is also the moral authority at 221B. Not only does he wish to avoid taking advantage of Mary, he also attempts to correct Holmes' behavior when he thinks it wrong. For example, as the two are discussing the account of a previous case at the beginning of "The Adventure of the Copper Beeches," Sherlock Holmes' comments offend the doctor because they seem to be too self-serving. Their conversations about Doctor Watson's writing usually center on Sherlock Holmes' belief that the doctor has missed the essential details of the case in favor of color and human interest. The doctor feels that the detective is perhaps asking for more praise in the press and says, "I was repelled by the egotism which I had more than once observed to be a strong factor in my friend's singular character" (317). His belief in the moral value of modesty, already apparent in his dealings with Mary, comes to the forefront when dealing with his friend's lack of it.

Watson in Adaptation

The Watson of the recent Guy Ritchie films is portrayed as similarly average compared to other men (except, of course, Holmes). His clothing is well constructed but nondescript, and he faces financial concerns that ring true to the audience. He represents concerns most middle-class men can understand when he tries to smooth the meeting of his friend and his soon-to-be fiancée. In the first film, *Sherlock Holmes,* Watson is involved in the case of Lord Blackwood not just because Holmes is, but because he is a medical professional and defines himself that way. Although there are plenty of available doctors in London who could be called upon to examine Lord Blackwood and pronounce him dead, Watson has the job. Even the injury that keeps him sidelined for a portion of the movie shows him to be noticeably average; he is obviously not superhuman in his recuperative ability.

Similarly, whereas *Sherlock's* John is as professionally skilled as his literary predecessor, he is nondescript—so much so that compared to Sherlock, he is blend-into-the-woodwork average. Although he is a doctor, he has some trouble finding a job, making his professional identity problematic, unlike previous versions of the character. When he does find a job, he seems somewhat underemployed because, rather than working at a hospital or as part of a practice, he is working at what appears to be a small clinic. Given 21st century concerns of a difficult economy and returning from a war zone, John represents economic and emotional instability familiar to many in the audience. His need to find work, to re-establish his identity after leaving his previous employment, is the experience of many who have lost their jobs and are searching for work. In no way does John display any special abilities that allow him to avoid or at least weather these pitfalls any differently than others would in the same situation. John's mediocrity allows him to be representative in the same way as Conan Doyle's Watson represented his time. Martin Freeman's quiet delivery makes John seem almost monotone when compared to the varying degrees of emotion exhibited by Benedict Cumberbatch's Sherlock. The juxtaposition of this monotone with John's moments of frustration, which is the only time he seems to become louder and more animated, allows the audience to see his attempt to keep his emotions in check. John's calmness could either be seen as self-discipline or the loss of emotional range as a result of trauma. In the early part of the series, John's emotions seem either on or off, depending on the situation; only as the series continues and he is stimulated by the excitement of crime solving does John show more emotional range. It is clear how difficult he finds restraint when he is unable to stop punching Sherlock in "A Scandal in Belgravia"; his visibly shaken reaction at the beginning of "The Reichenbach Fall" also shows a previously unseen depth of feeling.

John's relative quiet belies his importance as a reflection of social norm in *Sherlock*. In both the television and recent film adaptations, the character of Watson both reflects norms as well as significantly straying from them. In the Ritchie films, the portrayal of Watson gives a nod to social norms and Victorian morality while at the same time calling into question Watson's commitment to those norms. Initially, in *Sherlock Holmes,* the two characters are in conflict about Watson's intent to move out of their rooms into his own home with his soon-to-be-wife. Watson repeatedly expresses his disapproval of Holmes' actions, particularly in his attempts to lure him back into the case. Explaining that he is no longer interested in the case, Watson tells Holmes that he is looking for a normal life, full of normal events like having tea with his prospective in-laws. In fact, one of the plot sequences in the film revolves around his search for the right ring to propose to Mary.

In *Sherlock Holmes: A Game of Shadows,* the character of Watson begins on a note of normalcy as he marries Mary and anticipates their honeymoon together. The bachelor party scene is illustrative of Watson's desire for common social rituals, because he looks around the bar after arriving with Holmes and asks where his other friends are, friends who were ignored and uninvited by Holmes. In essence, he is attempting to continue building social relationships. Holmes, by contrast, loses Irene Adler and is living in the midst of images representing Moriarty's latest conspiracy. Watson's wry observation upon seeing the rooms where Holmes is still pursuing his theories is as much a comment on Holmes' living arrangements as on his case, accompanied as it is by a swift look at an untidy room.

In the same way that Conan Doyle's Watson represents the social norm, Jude Law's Watson is equally disapproving of Holmes' actions when they seem to challenge convention. For example, in the first film, Watson must run the gauntlet into Holmes' rooms when Mrs. Hudson is too afraid to enter because Holmes is shooting at the wall. After Holmes' desperate attempt to follow Irene Adler after she leaves the house, Watson comments that the only woman Holmes could love would of course be a criminal. Watson's anger at Lord Blackwood after the near-death of one of his victims is the justifiable moral outrage that one might expect. More personally, he defends his fiancée, Mary, from Holmes' assumption that she might be a gold-digger, a reaction that parallels Conan Doyle's Watson and his concerns about a similar label. Watson is just as concerned that Mary not be labeled in such a way, and for similar reasons. Whether on a case or in his personal life, Watson displays moral outrage at appropriate times.

Throughout the first two seasons, *Sherlock*'s John is characterized in much the same way as Conan Doyle's Watson, a combination of physical strength, courage, loyalty, and professional skill. He contrasts the more intellectual and socially inept Sherlock in that he is able to recognize and use social cues in a way that Sherlock does not. More importantly, though, he complains that Sherlock enjoys crime and crime scenes more than he should — the assumption being that Sherlock's enjoyment is immoral because it seems to be at the expense of the victims. John's reaction indicates that he has a stronger moral compass than his companion; he is genuinely affected by the thought of individuals in danger and by Sherlock's seeming lack of empathy.

Like the film version, *Sherlock*'s John displays repeated moral outrage. In "A Study in Pink," when the cabbie responsible for killing four people is suddenly shot, Sherlock deduces a "strong moral principle" in the unknown shooter; the camera suddenly shifts to John as Sherlock realizes who saved his life. John's frequent outbursts at Sherlock usually come when he believes Sherlock does not exhibit moral behavior — a failure to care sufficiently about the victims. In, for example, "The Great Game," John reminds Sherlock that lives are at stake, and he berates the detective for playing a "game" with Moriarty instead of considering the victims. Despite his frustration with Sherlock, who is certainly not the easiest roommate to have, John defends Sherlock, even when he barely knows him. John refuses to back down from his first confrontation with a mysterious man who tries to bribe him to spy on Sherlock, though he eventually learns that this man is Sherlock's brother, Mycroft. This scene shows John's unusual, immediate loyalty to Sherlock.

In *Sherlock,* John is frequently forced to smooth over social situations. For example, despite Sherlock's often rude treatment of others, especially the police, John makes small hand gestures to acknowledge the authority of the police when Sherlock examines evidence. In "A Study in Pink," John tries to explain to Sherlock that "real people have relationships," but Sherlock obviously does not value them to the same degree. Sherlock manipulates Molly, the lab technician who does not hide her attraction, in order to get special treatment. John repeatedly acts as a go-between for Sherlock and his brother, whose similar abilities make for a difficult relationship. It is John's sense of duty that causes him to remind Sherlock that Mycroft, and by extension the British government, need him on occasion, even when Sherlock does not wish to comply. When contrasted with John's own strained sibling relationship, however, it seems that neither John nor Sherlock is particularly able to maintain a familial relationship easily.

Both Law's and Freeman's depiction of John Watson shows the character as a moral and social counterweight to Sherlock Holmes, but what is even more interesting is the way that the more recent versions of Watson also undercut his relationship to social norms and contemporary ideas of morality. While the literary character is closely linked to Victorian ideas of family and duty, neither the Ritchie films nor BBC version maintains the same connection.

Moral Ambiguity: Watson's Malfunctioning Moral Compass

In the Ritchie films, Watson's duty to his fiancée and his friend aside, the character often can barely restrain himself from violence. He threatens Lord Blackwood, punches Holmes for insulting his fiancée, and chooses to become involved in several brawls alongside Holmes (*Sherlock Holmes*). He displays similar proclivities in *A Game of Shadows,* although some violence (e.g., shooting a pistol, getting involved in a brawl) is mainly in self-defense. He seems unafraid to use violence, especially if Holmes is in danger.

Not only is Jude Law's portrayal of Watson very physical, but his characterization also undercuts notions of Watson as a representative of social norms, particularly moral ones. In *Sherlock Holmes,* Watson repeatedly claims that he wants a more stable life, and he does continue seeing patients despite Holmes' loud disturbances in their shared work space. Watson's search for a wedding ring for Mary shows him attempting to carry on with his life despite the interruptions of Holmes' case. Although he frequently disapproves of Holmes, his disapproval is done with a wink. For example, during a carriage ride, Watson argues with Holmes about a waistcoat the detective appropriated from his friend's wardrobe. Watson eventually is able to retrieve his waistcoat, only to toss it out of the carriage window in a fit of pique. His shared grin with Holmes shows that he knows he has just done something unacceptable but does not care. The only time that Watson is truly offended by his friend's manners occurs when Holmes insults Mary during dinner; Watson reprimands Holmes and then leaves the restaurant.

More important, however, is how Watson as a reflector of social norms reflects a lack of morality. At one point in *Sherlock Holmes,* the detective must remind Watson to check that the man he has just rendered unconscious is still breathing. It is clear that Watson is not very attached to his Hippocratic Oath. He has no compunction about attacking or injuring others or, conversely, not helping those who would hurt Holmes. In *A Game of Shadows,* this portrayal continues when Watson uses a very large weapon to bring down a building in order to save Holmes. Watson's morality is strongly situational.

Sherlock's John similarly is attracted to a violent lifestyle and is portrayed as an adrenaline junkie. He has difficulty readjusting to civilian life after fighting in Afghanistan. His apparent PTSD has forced him to undergo therapy and has also left him with trembling hands and a limp that disappear when he begins chasing criminals with Sherlock. When Sherlock asks John if he wants to come on a case ("A Study in Pink"), his exclamation of "Oh, God yes!" indicates both relief and excitement that he does not attempt to contain. When John tells Sherlock that the police think Sherlock will at some point become a criminal because he enjoys the thrill of new cases so much, Sherlock tells him, "I said dangerous, and here you are," a reminder that although Sherlock is interested in the chase, John needs it just as much. Despite his many positive traits, John does not provide the same moral compass for the detective as Watson does in Conan Doyle's stories.

Because John is not adjusting as well as Conan Doyle's Watson, whose injuries were mostly physical, he brings an element of emotional damage to the character as a result of his experiences in Afghanistan. For example, after John shoots the cabbie to save Sherlock, he repeatedly asserts that he is fine. He and Sherlock trade quips about the cabbie (e.g., "he wasn't a very nice man," "and a bloody awful cabbie"), and both begin to laugh. While John recognizes that it is not right to be laughing at the situation, it does not stop him; his reaction could be attributed to the adrenaline rush of relief that he is alive, but it is obvious that both men find the situation funny, again, a reflection of situational morality.

In fact, the more recent portrayals have shown a relationship between Sherlock Holmes and John Watson that is more than a Johnson/Boswell relationship in which the great detective is extolled by the adoring, bumbling doctor. The Ritchie films and BBC series show the Holmes-Watson relationship as tense not because the two are so different that they cannot get along, but because they are too much alike.

In *Sherlock Holmes*, the detective instigates the meeting with the fortune teller who warns Watson not to get married and refers to the men as brothers. In essence, Holmes is making a plea based on shared personality traits in order to keep Watson from leaving. These shared traits come into play in *Sherlock Holmes: A Game of Shadows* in several sequences, the most important of which puts Watson in the position of detective while Holmes is dealing with Professor Moriarty. As Holmes says, "You know my methods," and he trusts his friend to follow them to help solve the case. Although Moriarty openly scoffs at Holmes' suggestion that Watson is a worthy accomplice, the doctor indeed shows not only that he knows Holmes' methods, but that he can use them well. In "The Reichenbach Fall" episode of *Sherlock*, John refers to this as "the face" that Sherlock makes when he assumes that John is following his line of reasoning — an assumption that John is quick to deride. However, it is John who actually puts the pieces together for the audience to explain how Moriarty is able to have enough information about Sherlock to set a plan in motion to destroy him. John may not intend to be a detective, but he ends up in that position.

Recent adaptations have shown Watson to be more capable, more professional than earlier film predecessors; at the same time, his character displays moral confusion consistent with 21st century life. He may display moral outrage at the plight of victims, but his morality becomes situational and inconsistent as the character is placed in more difficult situations.

Watson the Sociopath

In addition to the adaptations' increased emphasis on John Watson's moral ambiguity and his similarity to Sherlock Holmes in his enjoyment of the chase, Watson's characterization calls into question his own ability to maintain social connection to, or more importantly, empathy for others. In *A Game of Shadows*, Watson's behavior is more than a little strange for a newlywed; when his new wife is unceremoniously thrown off the train taking them to their honeymoon, Watson engages in an initial struggle with Holmes but, once assured that Mary is safe with Mycroft, does not ask another question about her. While the movie clearly emphasizes the connection between Holmes and Watson, the newly married man's behavior also suggests that he lacks concern for his wife, despite his claims to the contrary. This lack of concern for his wife, as well as others he harms in the pursuit of Moriarty, shows him exhibiting symptoms consistent with antisocial personality disorder.

The connection between antisocial behavior and Watson is even stronger in the BBC series. When Sherlock declares himself a sociopath, audiences are encouraged to see John as the voice of reason rather than for who he is, a trained killer transplanted to London and uncomfortable in his new environment. As Mycroft tells him in "A Study in Pink," "You're not haunted by the war, Dr. Watson. You miss it." It is clear that John responds positively to danger because his hand stops trembling whenever he faces a threat. Instead of the traditional PTSD pattern in which stimuli that bring up war memories results in increased stress, John becomes calmer when presented with danger because he suddenly feels engaged. John's lack of remorse after killing the cabbie, for example, is a sociopathic response to the situation, and his and Sherlock's reactions to this death show that both of them fit the label of sociopath.

Nor is the killing of the cabbie the only example of John's sociopathy. When he calmly tells Sarah at the clinic that the mundane work of the clinic will be good, he is clearly lying or at the very least indulging in wishful thinking. He knows very well that he has been bored until meeting Sherlock. One signal of a sociopathic personality is the constant need for excitement or stimulus, and John fits that description. In this respect he is no different than Sherlock, who, in addition to demanding data, frequently complains of boredom and the need for something to do.

John may have problems fitting into social norms after his military service, but Sherlock usually upholds the social order. Even his treatment of Irene Adler in "A Scandal in Belgravia" in consistent with a belief that she has been punished enough for her crime; what is more interesting is that it is Sherlock who makes the decision and acts on it in lieu of more traditional authority figures who are incapable of quick, decisive action in the situation.

As the person who shows that society is capable of policing itself, of catching offenders, Sherlock is the symbol of order. He never challenges the police force's existence, despite his unmistakable superiority. Conan Doyle's Holmes treats the police as useful for the mundane jobs of catching everyday criminals; despite their limited skills, they are perfectly capable of catching people whose criminal skills are equally limited. Holmes' status as a specialist means that he can focus on the cases the police cannot solve, which must be rare, because he is the only consulting detective in existence. Similarly, television's Sherlock prefers interesting cases that are worth his time, and he refuses to investigate the mundane problems clients bring to him, as we see in both "A Scandal in Belgravia" and "The Hound of the Baskervilles."

In the Ritchie films, Holmes' challenges to social order are limited to flouting social convention by offending Mary or irritating his landlady. In the first movie, he shows little reverence for aristocracy but works closely to develop a plan with Lestrade that allows him to escape custody in order to pursue Lord Blackwood. In fact, Holmes becomes an emissary of the police, acting in their stead to stop the threat to the social order. In *A Game of Shadows* Holmes becomes involved with members of world governments as the film raises the stakes for Holmes' success. The attempt to forestall a world war is, by definition, upholding social order.

On television, Sherlock's relationship with the police force is tenuous at best; Lestrade uses him for information but also resorts to blackmailing him by searching his apartment for drugs to get his help ("A Study in Pink"). As a result, Sherlock seems less an extension of the police force than his predecessors. Nevertheless, because Sherlock does work to stop criminal behavior, he represents a societal force that attempts to preserve order, even though his relationship with the police is uneasy. Despite the suggestion in first-season episodes that at some point in the future Sherlock will want to commit crimes rather than solve them (which seems to be the case in "The Reichenbach Fall"), the audience never really seriously questions Sherlock's commitment to solving crimes. In fact, because Sherlock is antisocial, he has become the expert in understanding and countering antisocial behaviors in order to stop crime. In each of his cases, the police force's ability to contain crime is limited, but not in a way that challenges society's ability to regulate and maintain the antisocial impulses that create crime. The audience is reassured that Sherlock can go beyond the limits of the police to preserve society from the threat of truly antisocial personalities.

Because, in recent adaptations, John Watson is portrayed as similar to Sherlock Holmes in response to danger and crime, he must also represent social order. In this respect he is similar to Conan Doyle's Watson, who not only fails to question Holmes about the need to catch criminals but actively assists him in stopping dangerous men from preying on others. In effect, he also preserves society from the potential threat of crime. In *Sherlock Holmes*, Watson represents the official medical establishment at an execution, a very symbolic moment of the state's imposition of order on the body of a person found guilty of crime. By assisting the police in confirming Lord Blackwood's death after his hanging, Watson grants tacit approval for the state's actions. Not only does Watson represent a force of order in the sense that he is able to treat or cure physical ills, but he is a cure for social ills as well.

The adaptations' emphasis on John Watson's military training, especially his ability to be a sniper as well as a medical doctor (as shown in *A Game of Shadows* and "A Study in Pink"), allows him to represent a similar combination of medical and social healing. At the same time, this combination is problematic, a fact that becomes clear in "A Scandal in Belgravia." Although he asks John to pummel him during a case, John's enthusiasm for attacking Sherlock troubles the detective, who reminds his friend that he is a doctor. John, however, growls that he is also a trained killer who "has bad days"—all the while holding Sherlock in a headlock. The fact that John Watson is both a doctor and a capable killer is indicative of modern society's split personality and increasing acceptance of moral ambiguity.

The Damaged Detective

One reason why individuals with antisocial personality disorder are often depicted as abnormal and a threat to society is that society uses those depictions to mark the boundaries of acceptable behavior, which the detective then must enforce (Carrabine 112). Without these boundaries, society would have little reason for the police or the detective. Just as the detective is the avatar of social order, the antisocial personality has become the exemplar of disorder. When the detective, however, is equally antisocial, the boundaries between social and antisocial behavior blur. In Conan Doyle's original texts, John Watson has acted as a stand-in for readers, asking questions that they need Holmes to answer. As a result, readers feel slightly superior to Watson, because, however wrongly, they get the sense that Watson is less capable than they.

In *Sherlock*, however, John asks questions but does so in such a way that viewers never think that he is inferior. The moral position Conan Doyle's Watson occupies in the original stories allows him the ability to judge Holmes and classify him as eccentric but not morally insane, despite his dislike of people. The film versions continue the focus on Holmes' eccentricities by portraying Watson as the judging, socially and morally stable member of the pair, but even the film Watson seems to be showing signs of sociopathy. Without a solidly moral John Watson to provide judgment, a characterization missing in *Sherlock,* the detective emerges as sociopathic, and the society that he polices as a detective is equally so.

If, instead of representing sociopaths as poor, lower-class unfortunates who are inadequate to the tasks of daily life, those with antisocial personalities (e.g., John Watson, Sherlock Holmes) are presented as everyday professionals, these adaptations gloss over the problem by showing that, despite their eccentricities, individuals with antisocial personalities are normal and capable of coping with the stress of daily life. If it has become acceptable, even in a time of war, to display a complete lack of remorse for the killing of another and, more importantly, to cover up that killing, then the society represented in particular by John Watson is one with a split personality, outwardly decrying the violence of crime while creating the conditions for its continuance.

Precisely because John Watson is such an average member of the middle class, it is so important to account for his recent representation as a sociopath. This depiction raises questions not only about the status of the sociopath in 21st century society, but also the status of that society itself. As represented by the John Watson portrayed in the recent adaptations, sociopaths are professional, well-educated, and capable members of society; in fact, they represent the norm for the early 21st century middle class, just as the original Watson represented middle-class norms in Victorian England.

WORKS CITED

Accardo, Pasquale. *Diagnosis and Detection: The Medical Iconography of Sherlock Holmes.* Cranbury, NJ: Associated University Presses, 1987. Print.

Adams, James Eli. *Dandies and Dessert Saints: Styles of Victorian Masculinity.* Ithaca, NY: Cornell University Press, 2005. Print.

Altick, Richard. *Victorian People and Ideas.* New York: Norton, 1973. Print.

"The Blind Banker." *Sherlock.* Writ. Mark Gatiss, Stephen Moffat. Dir. Euros Lyn. BBC. 31 Oct. 2010. Television.

Carrabine, Eamonn. *Crime, Culture, and the Media.* Malden, MA: Polity, 2008. Print.

Conan Doyle, Sir Arthur. *The Complete Sherlock Holmes.* New York: Barnes and Noble, 1992. Print.

"The Great Game." *Sherlock.* PBS. Dir. Paul McGuigan. Television.

Jann, Rosemary. *The Adventures of Sherlock Holmes: Detecting Social Order.* New York: Twayne, 1995. Print.

Lane, Christopher. *Hatred and Civility: The Antisocial Life in Victorian Britain.* New York: Columbia University Press, 2004. Print.

Lykken, David. *The Antisocial Personalities.* Hillsdale, NJ: Lawrence Earlbaum, 1995. Print.

Melling, Joseph, and Bill Forsythe. *The Politics of Madness: The State, Insanity and Society in England, 1845–1914.* New York: Routledge, 2006. Print.

Millon, Theodore, et al., eds. *Psychopathy: Antisocial, Criminal, Violent Behavior.* New York: Guilford Press, 1998. Print.

Pedlar, Valerie. *The 'Most Dreadful Visitation': Male Madness in Victorian Fiction.* Liverpool: Liverpool University Press, 2005. Print.

"The Reichenbach Fall." *Sherlock.* Dir. Toby Haynes. Perf. Bennedict Cumberbatch, Martin Freeman. Dailymotion.com. Online Video. 28 Jan. 2012.

"A Scandal in Belgravia." *Sherlock.* Dir. Paul Guigan. Perf. Benedict Cumberbatch, Martin Freeman. *Daily Motion.com.* Online video. 14 Jan. 2012.

Sherlock Holmes. Dir. Guy Ritchie. Perf. Robert Downey, Jr., Jude Law. Warner Brothers, 2009. DVD.

Sherlock Holmes: A Game of Shadows. Dir. Guy Ritchie. Warner Brothers, 2011. Film.

"A Study in Pink." *Sherlock.* PBS. WFYI, Indianapolis. 24 Oct. 2010. Television.

NOTE

1. For the purposes of this chapter, I refer to the characters in the 2009 Guy Ritchie movie as Holmes and Watson, and the characters in the BBC's *Sherlock* as Sherlock and John. For the original stories, I use Sherlock Holmes and John Watson, or refer to them as Conan Doyle's.

5

"Don't Make People into Heroes, John"
(Re/De)Constructing the Detective as Hero

FRANCESCA M. MARINARO *and* KAYLEY THOMAS

In 1840, essayist Thomas Carlyle wrote in *On Heroes, Hero-Worship and the Heroic in History* that "the history of what man has accomplished in this world is at bottom the history of the great men who have worked here. They were the leaders of men, these great ones ... all things that we see standing accomplished in the world are ... the practical realization and embodiment of thoughts that dwelt in the great men sent into the world" (1). The Carlylian hero epitomized the strength, ambition, and moral fortitude that the Victorians sought in their leaders during the golden age of empire. Perhaps one of the most popular and complex heroic figures in 19th century fiction is Sir Arthur Conan Doyle's Sherlock Holmes, whose greatness as characterized by Dr. John Watson speaks to Victorian notions of leadership embodied in the Carlylian hero. Upon first meeting Holmes, Watson reflects, "Surely no man would work so hard or attain such precise information unless he has some *very good* reason for doing so" (Conan Doyle, "A Study in Scarlet" 12, emphasis added). This description encapsulates Carlyle's vision of the hero — the man who uses his skills and talents to serve and to better mankind.

For over a century, readers have taken their cue from Watson in constructing Holmes as a heroic figure; most recently, Robert Downey, Jr., who plays the detective in Guy Ritchie's 2009 and 2011 film adaptations, echoes this characterization in describing Holmes as the "first superhero" (qtd. in Levy para. 1). Yet Sherlock Holmes, often self-absorbed and selfishly motivated, appears to be a character with the potential, if not the desire, to respond to the call to heroism. Steven Moffat and Mark Gatiss' modern day television adaptation, *Sherlock* (2010–present), offers us a somewhat more problematic characterization—"a dynamic superhero" who is "driven by a desire to prove himself cleverer than the perpetrator and the police — everyone, in fact," as Piers Wenger, Head of Drama at BBC Wales, terms him (qtd. in "BBC to Make a Modern-Day Sherlock Holmes"). These contradictory readings of Holmes challenge us to question the legitimacy of constructing Holmes as a heroic figure. Ritchie's adaptations and the BBC series re-evaluate the construction of Holmes-as-hero by highlighting an understated aspect of Conan Doyle's stories — Watson's oft-assumed characterization of Holmes as heroic. Though Conan Doyle's Watson avidly admires and even hero-worships Holmes, viewing the pair's relationship in these contemporary adaptations reveals that what Watson identifies in Holmes is heroic potential rather than actual heroism. Because it is Watson as Conan Doyle's narrator through whom readers have constructed a heroic Holmes, the legitimation of this construction is achieved by Watson's own heroism, complementing and cultivating Holmes as a hero.

Hero-Worshiping Holmes

For Watson, heroism is directly associated with service to mankind. Having endangered his life in the service of the Empire as a military doctor, he responds to a precise definition of Victorian notions of heroic, civic duty. Holmes characterizes him in *The Hound of the Baskervilles* as "born to be a man of action" (128). Ritchie's Holmes praises Watson (Jude Law) as "strong" and "brave," and BBC's Sherlock (Benedict Cumberbatch) identifies John (Martin Freeman) as a man "with a history of military service" and "strong moral principle" ("A Study in Pink").

In Watson's construction of heroism, the "very good reason" for which Holmes would cultivate his talents must relate directly to the service of others, for upon first meeting Holmes absorbed in chemical research to identify blood stains, Watson inquires whether he intends to enter the medical profession (Conan Doyle, "A Study in Scarlet" 12). To a military doctor fresh from Afghanistan, the medical profession is inextricably linked to imperial duty, and thus Watson ascribes to Holmes what he deems a noble ambition to safeguard the health and welfare of the Empire. As we shall argue, situating Watson's characterization of Holmes within a Carlylian framework demands devoting attention to the usage of such terms as "great" and "good" as they are applied to Holmes.

Holmes and Watson respectively represent the two essential elements that create the hero: greatness and goodness. To identify greatness and goodness as individual character traits is to seek to understand the born versus the cultivated aspects of heroism. In Carlyle's heroic configuration, he identifies what he envisions in man as the raw material that can be molded — or cultivated — into the hero: "a strong untutored intellect; eyesight, [and] heart" (69). In Holmes' greatness — in his natural abilities — Watson identifies heroic potential — the "untutored," or untrained hero — for although Holmes has amassed a considerable body of knowledge, that knowledge remains largely uncultivated. He uses his detective work as a vehicle through which to exercise his skills, but self-serving as that work is, it cannot satisfy the "very good reason" that characterizes heroism.

The Ritchie and BBC incarnations of the great detective convey to their good doctors a preference for the work itself above all else, with Holmes declaring in Ritchie's first film, "My mind rebels at stagnation — give me work," and the BBC's Sherlock echoing, "All that matters to me is the work. Without that, my brain rots" ("The Great Game"). In episode one of the BBC series, Sherlock displays a callous indifference to the suffering of others, seemingly unable to understand how a victim might focus upon the memory of a daughter long dead in her own dying moments. "That was ages ago! Why would she still be upset?" he shouts in frustration. Upon observing the disbelieving faces of John and the Scotland Yard detectives, he adds, somewhat sheepishly: "Not good?" to which John confirms, "Bit not good, yeah" ("A Study in Pink"). Sherlock cannot properly connect to what is "good" here. Whereas Ritchie's Holmes is able to declare in *Sherlock Holmes: A Game of Shadows* that he sees "everything — that is my curse," Moffatt and Gatiss' John highlights the potential problem with such a statement, observing in his blog, "Sherlock sees right through everyone and everything.... What's incredible, though, is how spectacularly ignorant he is about some things" ("The Great Game"). Sherlock Holmes possesses Carlyle's "eyesight" but lacks the emotional perception of Dr. Watson — the heart. To that end, the Ritchie and BBC adaptations seek to clarify the ways that goodness (as embodied by Watson) informs greatness (as embodied by Holmes).

If Conan Doyle's Watson, despite his perplexity about Holmes, seems to hero-worship him, Ritchie and Moffat and Gatiss present a Holmes that departs from this characterization. Ritchie's Watson actively questions both his assessment of Holmes' character and his involvement with him, declaring "I've been reviewing my notes of our exploits over the last seven months. Would you like to know my conclusion? I'm psychologically disturbed" (*Sherlock Holmes*). Holmes' response that "You never complained about my methods before" recalls Watson's seemingly unconditional adoration of Holmes familiar to readers. Yet Watson's frustration with Holmes' treatment of him reveals a moment of doubt as he struggles to reconcile the image of "the great Sherlock Holmes" with this self-absorbed, inconsiderate creature. To question his own view of Holmes is ultimately to question the audience's, because our understanding of Holmes' character is largely dependent upon Watson's.

This scene presents a clear disconnect between Holmes and Carlyle's heroic configuration: Watson has never criticized, nor is he now complaining about Holmes' methods; rather the objections he raises about Holmes — his lack of consideration, his secrecy, and his attempts to "sabotage [Watson's] relationship with Mary" — relate not to Holmes' mind, but to his emotion, with the "heart" that makes the truly great man good. It is the conflict between these two contradictory images of Holmes that the films seek to resolve. Watson's attempts to detach himself from Holmes and Baker Street through his settlement into married life and private practice is a domestic construct suggesting retirement from public, heroic duty, yet he continually returns to Holmes' side. Before Watson can fully retire from heroic duty, his final act of heroism is to cultivate Holmes' heroic potential.

BBC's *Sherlock* similarly experiments with this notion of John as the audience's point of access to Sherlock in order to consider the extent to which our construction of Holmes-as-hero relies upon Conan Doyle's construction of Watson as hero-worshiper. The unaired pilot episode of "A Study in Pink" includes an additional scene following Sherlock's examination of the murdered woman in pink. In the pilot, as Sherlock rushes from the crime scene to locate her missing suitcase, John glances up while searching for a cab. He sees Sherlock's silhouette on the roof in a strikingly superhero-like pose, coat billowing around him like a cape. With Sherlock standing in an elevated position to John's admiring gaze, this scene situates John and Sherlock in the respective positions of hero-worshiper and hero-worshiped, acknowledging and challenging the notion of a heroic Holmes. While the angle from which John glimpses Sherlock reflects his admiration of him and recalls to the audience that our view of Sherlock is filtered through John, the comically exaggerated superhero stance exposes this heroic view of him as perhaps unrealistic. Removing this scene from the televised episode suggests an endeavor by Moffat and Gatiss to offer a more ambiguous interpretation of Sherlock, requiring greater consideration on the part of the audience before we can identify him as a heroic figure.

If Season One offers us a caveat against casting our heroes in this one-dimensional mold, Season Two challenges us through similar imagery to revisit the possibility of Sherlock's heroic potential. Upon their arrival in Dartmoor in "The Hounds of Baskerville," Sherlock climbs atop a rock to gain a better perspective of his surroundings while John studies a map of the village. Echoing the unaired pilot, he stands in an elevated position to John with one marked difference: without John's gaze fixed admiringly on him, the scene lacks the same exaggerated heroic configuration. Sherlock's coat still billows dramatically in the wind, his collar turned up in what John later identifies as a dramatic affectation, one which he and the audience observe Sherlock enact repeatedly throughout the episode. While his suggestively heroic stance on the roof is unintentional, this gesture is deliberately enacted: in the unaired pilot, Sherlock is unconscious of John's gaze, but now the detective anticipates an audience. More pointedly, where previously John held witness in awe, in this instance he is preoccupied with his own tasks and alternates throughout Season Two between ignoring and critiquing Sherlock's more eccentric behavior.

Having become a familiar figure in the public eye, Sherlock actively responds to the image of the brooding hero of popular imagination. Yet if he seems to adopt a characterization that the show has previously resisted, Sherlock does so in a manner that suggests performativity rather than genuine heroic embodiment — an appropriation of the heroic image without the desire to respond to its call. Observing this gesture later in the episode, John's notably more critical gaze redirects Sherlock's behavior: "Can we not do this this time? ... You being all mysterious with your cheekbones and turning your coat collar up so you look cool" ("The Hounds of Baskerville"). It is John who reminds Sherlock to "stick to the facts" when the case begins to emotionally overwhelm the detective; John who criticizes Sherlock's near-maniacal laughter upon solving the case when his client is still visibly shaken; John who, focusing on solving the case rather than on Sherlock's self-elevating antics, ultimately re-grounds Sherlock in "the work," bringing purpose to his performativity. In the finale of Season Two, Sherlock reprises this pose once more, further complicating the division between performativity and true heroism, as we will address later in this chapter.

Watson's Heroic Quest

In marked contrast, the broadcast version of "A Study in Pink" adds a scene not present in the unaired pilot which works to cast John in a heroic light. Both versions open with John, the entrance character through which we begin our journey — the everyman, the audience surrogate who invites us into his adventures with the great Sherlock Holmes. Moffatt and Gatiss' John is hardly an everyman, however; he is characterized rather as a hero of Joseph Campbell's type, "the redeeming hero, the carrier of the shining blade, whose blow, whose touch ... will liberate the land" (11). Campbell's prototypical hero of myth and folklore "ventures forth from the world of the common day" (23) into "darkness, the unknown, and danger" (64), where powerful "forces are there encountered and a decisive victory is won" (23). This quest can be figured as a man gone to war, but where John has certainly acquitted himself bravely in battle, he returns wounded and despairing from a war unwon. Even for the hero whose quest is completed, Campbell notes that one of his difficulties is to re-enter the "banalities and noisy obscenities of life" (189).

Although both the unaired and televised versions of Episode One proffer a despondent John bound by the confines of a small, sparse hotel room, the aired episode pointedly presents us first with John waking from a dream of war. Before proceeding like the unaired pilot to focus painfully upon John in the present, limping to his desk only to stare dully at a blank computer screen, the camera dissolves his image as he sits up in bed upon waking, and he fades back into focus on the other side of the room, ghost-like. Here Moffat and Gatiss establish John as a man between worlds, a wounded hero dreaming of war, unfit for the humdrum existence of civilian life. Thus when the scene changes to John's appointment with his therapist, during which she suggests that blogging "everything that happens to you" will help him adjust, his response that "nothing happens to me" is grounded in the visual rhetoric of transition and instability. John is a man of action with no adventures to chronicle, a soldier lost without the war, as Mycroft (Mark Gatiss) proposes later in the episode: "You're not haunted by the war, Dr. Watson — you miss it."

John Watson is cast then as a hero in need of a quest, and as a result, he gravitates toward Sherlock Holmes. In Campbell's configuration of the heroic quest, the "call to adventure" can begin with "the merest chance" which "reveals an unsuspected world," and the hero is thus "drawn into a relationship with forces that are not rightly understood" (42). In "A Study in Pink," a random encounter with old college chum Mike Stamford tumbles John headfirst into life with Sherlock, the "mad ... but strangely likeable" consulting detective who is decidedly "not safe" but, as John reflects in his blog, promises a life in which John is sure that he at least is "not going to be bored" (Lidster para. 2).

John's call to adventure comes when Sherlock insists to Lestrade that he needs an assistant and invites John along, the "very *good*" army doctor who, despite having seen "more than enough" danger, cannot resist the summons to encounter more ("A Study in Pink," emphasis added). Campbell allows that a hero can resist the call to adventure, but the result is usually that he is "walled in boredom, hard work, or 'culture,'" exchanging "the power of significant affirmative action" for a life that "feels meaningless" (49). We have already seen John presented with this stark reality, so when Sherlock proposes that John could "stay home and watch telly" or accompany him to a crime scene, John heeds the call.

The crime scene and his meeting after with Mycroft function as Campbell's stage of crossing the threshold between a menial life and a new quest in a world unknown, with both Sergeant Sally Donovan (Vinette Robinson) and Mycroft standing in as "threshold guardians" (64). Sally warns John to stay away from Sherlock's psychopathy, and Mycroft emphasizes the danger that embarking with Sherlock entails, offering John the chance to turn back. Campbell posits that "the usual person is more than content ... to remain within the indicated bounds" (64). But John is not the usual person, as Mycroft suggests: "Most people blunder around this city, and all they see are streets and shops and cars. When you walk with Sherlock Holmes, you see the battlefield." Sherlock is established for John as a heroic quest in the same manner as the battlefield he was forced to quit.

These adaptations present Dr. Watson as a man out of place and out of time, though in both accounts he has seemingly completed his hero's journey: in Moffat and Gatiss' origin story, he returns from war; in Ritchie's *in medias res*, he has adventured with Holmes but ultimately fallen in love, the common progenitor of a hero's happy ending.

Whereas the BBC's John embarks upon a new quest, Ritchie's Watson endeavors to leave his. In both Ritchie films, Watson cannot seem to escape Holmes' needy clutches, however, and it is at times unclear if he truly wants to. Although he manages to wed Mary Morstan (Kelly Reilly) in the second film, Watson is drawn back into Holmes' adventures. The night before the wedding, Holmes responds to Watson's dreams of domesticity in a manner that highlights his desire for Watson to remain by his side: "So you'll settle down and have a family, and I'll die alone?" Yet at both points in the film in which Holmes faces death, he is pointedly not alone. Holmes' near demise on the train back from Germany elicits an impassioned response from Watson, whose tearful, desperate efforts at reviving him expose his unwillingness to let Holmes go. Likewise, when Holmes goes over the falls at Reichenbach with Moriarty, Watson holds witness, able afterward to chronicle his seemingly dead friend as "the best and wisest man I have ever known." Rather than being freed of Holmes, Watson must be torn away from his writing by Mary, who cannot quite succeed in redirecting his attention to her. Presumably when Watson learns of Holmes' survival he will, as in Conan Doyle's stories, follow Holmes once more, neither able to settle down nor leave Holmes alone.

Ultimately Holmes' greatness cannot persist without the accompaniment of the goodness Watson embodies, Moffat and Gatiss portraying a Sherlock whose potential heroism cannot be reached without it and Ritchie presenting a Holmes whose existence is dependent upon it. Thus John Watson is tasked with the making and the maintaining of the great man.

Holmes as Anti-Hero

The great man is worthy of heroic identification not by his greatness alone; his heroism springs from the desire to utilize his greatness for the benefit of mankind rather than for self-aggrandizement. Thus what Conan Doyle identifies through the characters of Watson and Holmes and what these adaptations further illustrate is the distinction between greatness and goodness.

The BBC series directly defines this distinction toward the conclusion of "A Study in Pink," with Detective Inspector Lestrade (Rupert Graves) informing John that "Sherlock Holmes is a great man, and I think one day, if we are very, very lucky, he might be a good one." Lestrade does not preclude Sherlock from heroism in indicating the absence of "good" in the detective's character, but he does powerfully remind in his evocation of the words "great" and "good" that there is more to Carlyle's Great Man than great talent or achievement: there must be goodness as well.

Whether Sherlock can attain this status is posed as questionable: At the close of "A Study in Pink," Mycroft remarks, "Interesting, that soldier fellow. He could be the making of my brother, or make him worse than ever." Thus Moffat and Gatiss ask us to consider whether Sherlock is capable of becoming a hero and what kind of impact John will have upon his development, placing John as the key component in determining Sherlock's heroic status. The BBC's construction of the hero is one in which greatness and goodness are two ingredients which together create the truly estimable and heroic man.

Even Robert Downey, Jr.'s characterization of the consulting detective as the first superhero seems somewhat more congruous with the heroic configuration than BBC's Sherlock: "He doesn't do it to show everyone how smart he is or that he has figured everything out when they haven't. He is actually a crusader" (qtd. in Levy para. 1).

If Downey, Jr.'s Holmes is, however flawed, ultimately heroic, Cumberbatch's "high-functioning sociopath" demands the intense scrutiny of his audience even as he seems to defy a definitive characterization ("A Study in Pink"). In "The Great Game," Sherlock cautions John (and by association the audience) against viewing him in a heroic light: "don't make people into heroes, John. Heroes don't exist, and if they did, I wouldn't be one of them." Sherlock's remark proves perceptive within the context of the evolving heroic model over the past century and our continued desire to ascribe the heroic identity to Holmes. There is no denying that the desire for heroes remains as prevalent in the 21st century as it did in Victorian England; as with the Victorian motivation of love of Empire, the call to end political injustice and the threat of terrorism to Western democracy demands the strength and bravery of heroes. Indeed, Moffat and Gatiss make it clear that *Sherlock* is a series that — among other things — calls us to re-examine our definition of the hero against the backdrop of war.

Holmes' detective work is often tied to nationalist/political interests, particularly when they concern his brother Mycroft — a man who claims in the BBC series to occupy a "minor position in the British government" but to whom Holmes refers as "*the* British government" ("A Study in Pink"). Ritchie's films and *Sherlock* utilize this nationalist connection to Holmes' work to challenge the legitimacy of his heroism. In the Ritchie films, it takes the form of Holmes managing to avert a political and national disaster by thwarting Lord Blackwood's (Mark Strong) plot to overthrow Parliament and Professor James Moriarty's (Jared Harris) threat to spark international warfare. In *Sherlock*'s "The Great Game," it takes the form of Sherlock's involvement — via Mycroft — in investigating the Bruce-Partington program. The two adaptations underscore Holmes' heroic ambivalence by highlighting his relationship to and, more specifically, his detachment from the public institutions of social order — the government and the police force. Holmes' work contributes to the maintenance of law and order, but not because he views that work as socially or morally upright — solving crimes best exercises his powers of deduction.

Thus when Mycroft attempts to enlist Sherlock's aid in the Bruce-Partington case, a case of "national importance," as both Mycroft and John stress, Sherlock's initial refusal poses a pointed rejection of any interest in the greater good. Rather he disavows the sense of the good associated with John, pitting John's humanism against his rationalism. Mycroft hopes that "perhaps [John] can get through to him" after Sherlock first turns down the case, highlighting a deduction on his part that John does, in fact, have an influence upon Sherlock and is capable, if anyone is, of channeling Sherlock's energies into a socially productive cause. Sherlock declares John's concern over the case's national importance as "quaint," however, mocking John's alliance with "Queen and country." More importantly, though, John shows himself to be invested not just at the national level but at the local level, which becomes evident when Sherlock dismisses the Bruce-Partington case in favor of the challenge presented by Moriarty:

SHERLOCK: The only mystery is this — why is my brother so determined to bore me when somebody else is being so delightfully interesting?
JOHN: Try and remember there's a woman who might be dying.
SHERLOCK: What for? This hospital's full of people dying, Doctor. Why don't you go and cry by their bedside and see what *good* it does them? (emphasis added)

Although Sherlock pinpoints John's compassion as an illogical, unserviceable factor in the actual solution of a problem, he manages to draw attention to his own emotional motivations in the process. His, however, focus upon self-gratification rather than the interests of others in the desire for his mind to be stimulated by Moriarty's machinations. Holmes' antisocial behavior, his self-absorption, and his general lack of emotion suggest a kind of anti-heroism, if the anti-hero is defined in terms of a refusal to subscribe to the socially appropriate path of dedicating one's life and talents to the service of community or country.

It is important here to emphasize the distinction between the anti-hero and the villain: the anti-hero is characterized by emotional detachment — from family, community, nationalism or patriotism — the institutions and ideologies on which social order is founded, because to attach oneself to such notions commits the anti-hero to subscribing to social mores rather than acting based upon his own personal code of conduct. We can better understand Holmes' anti-heroism if we situate it in terms of an important distinction between the heroic character and a heroic act; as Lynnette Porter pinpoints in her discussion of anti-heroism, a "heroic act" does not inherently constitute heroism (12). To capture or kill a villain — as Holmes so often does — is undeniably a heroic act, but if the motivations behind that act are not clearly aligned with the greater good, we cannot define it as absolute heroism.

Yet if we cannot identify Downey, Jr.'s Holmes as definitively heroic, neither can we term him a villain, as seen when we compare him to Blackwood and Moriarty. The villain is arguably motivated, though to a more dangerous degree, by the same desires that motivate the hero: power, wealth, and recognition. The hero, however, pursues those desires for the greater good, whereas Blackwood (*Sherlock Holmes*) and Moriarty (*A Game of Shadows*) seek power by appropriating political and nationalist ideology for personal gain: Blackwood mobilizes his followers through the desire to "fulfill England's destiny," reclaiming control of the U.S. and erasing a blot from British history; Moriarty endeavors to spark international warfare by orchestrating a series of bombings and assassinations and targeting world dignitaries in order to grow rich on the sale of war materials. The anti-hero similarly constructs a universe in which he is the focal point, yet he desires none of the power that the villain seeks for himself or that the hero attains for his people, for with power and authority come responsibility. Thus, despite a remark from Lord Coward (Hans Matheson)— one of Blackwood's followers — that Holmes would have been "a valuable ally," Holmes neither responds to this invitation to direct his talents toward villainy nor definitively aligns himself with the social institutions (namely, the police force) that seek to defeat Blackwood.

This moment serves pivotally in Holmes' heroic cultivation, laying the groundwork for legitimating that characterization in *A Game of Shadows*. True, Holmes' investigation of the series of crimes orchestrated by Moriarty is personal rather than political; he is initially concerned less with averting war than with defeating Moriarty in an intellectual contest. Yet if the first film shows him actively distancing himself from association with the greater good — shielding his face in press photos of the Blackwood case and deliberately ignoring Lestrade's orders — in the second he at least acknowledges that solving the case would "prevent the collapse of Western civilization." Furthermore, because it is Watson to whom we (and Holmes) look to cultivate

Holmes' heroic characteristics, it is fitting that Holmes commits his most heroic act through Watson. When Moriarty targets Watson and Mary to draw Holmes deeper into his web of crime, Holmes goes to great lengths to protect the newlyweds in a gesture that locates his work within the interests of Queen and country, however tangentially. As the pair is ambushed on the train traveling to their honeymoon, it is Mary whom Holmes removes from danger and delivers directly into the arms of the British government by enlisting Mycroft (Stephen Fry) to rescue her. Holmes' protection of Mary supports Watson's dream of marriage and family — the two social institutions that directly service the Empire with children and future citizens. Even if Holmes' heroic act is personally rather than politically motivated, the protection of Watson and Mary for Watson's sake reveals the moral fiber that makes the great man good. Holmes' return to Watson at the film's end, following his supposed death, and the question mark he inserts at the end of Watson's narrative, if not an active declaration of his desire to submit to heroic cultivation, challenge Watson to complete his heroic quest and the audience to determine if Holmes can ever be worthy of hero-worship.

Alternatively, Moffat and Gatiss' characterization of Sherlock seems at times to dangerously dissolve the already blurred boundaries between villainy and anti-heroism. Like Porter's villain, Sherlock has "few if any socially acceptable qualities" and has "much to overcome before viewers accept [him] as 'good'" (145). If Ritchie acknowledges the dangerous potential of Holmes, he nevertheless presents a potentially heroic character somewhat easier to accept than Moffat and Gatiss' Sherlock; when Holmes declares to Moriarty in *A Game of Shadows*, "My horror at your crimes is matched only by my admiration at the skill it took to achieve them," clearly the horror resonates more strongly. Even as he acknowledges an inevitable meeting of the minds in this great game, he asks pointedly of Moriarty, "[Watson] is out of the equation. I trust you will take that into consideration." When Moriarty targets Watson to get to Holmes, Watson is drawn back into the equation, and Holmes, through Watson's heroic influence, is thus positioned in direct opposition to Moriarty.

If Ritchie offers us a glimpse of Holmes' heroic potential, Moffat and Gatiss remind us that his character might just as easily have gone to the opposite extreme. Here is a Sherlock indecently transparent about his motivations for solving crimes: "There's no point sitting at home when there's finally something fun going on! ... Who cares about decent? The game, Mrs. Hudson, is on!" he exclaims about the serial suicides in "A Study in Pink" — an expression of delight over death and destruction hardly socially appropriate. This dissolving of the boundary between villain and anti-hero is epitomized in Sherlock's relationship to Moriarty (Andrew Scott), which is constructed more as a game between two brilliant minds than a battle between hero and villain. Sherlock's ultimate goal is to meet Moriarty, not to save the lives at stake. Yet when explaining the motivations of a serial killer to John in "A Study in Pink," Sherlock observes, "That's the frailty of genius, John. It needs an audience." On the one hand, this comment denotes the intense desire for attention that ultimately leads to the criminal's downfall—an emotional interference to which Sherlock would never allow himself to succumb. On the other, the remark seems singularly personal to Sherlock; the frailty of his own genius could ultimately lead to his downfall if he is in fact hovering on the edge of devious criminality. His emotional attachment to Watson ennobles Holmes throughout Ritchie's films; in the BBC series, Sherlock is poised upon a precipice of not only criminality but another potentiality—of an empathy with a man of heart and action that might strengthen his fragility. Thus John has the potential to save Sherlock from himself—John can cultivate Sherlock's "untutored intellect" for a socially productive, "good" cause.

Cultivating a Heroic Holmes

This potential for social and emotional development emerges markedly in "The Great Game," where Sherlock's interest in Moriarty over the consulting criminal's victims is countered by John's concern for their welfare. When an elderly woman dies in part because of Sherlock's preoccupation with Moriarty, Sherlock remarks that, despite the failure to save her life, "technically I did solve the case." Faced with such conspicuous evidence of Sherlock's emotional detachment and socially contrary priorities, John cannot leave the detective unchallenged:

> JOHN: There are lives at stake, Sherlock, actual human lives! Just so I know: do you care about that at all?
> SHERLOCK: Will caring about them help save them?
> JOHN: No.
> SHERLOCK: Then I will continue not to make that mistake.
> [...]
> SHERLOCK: I've disappointed you.
> JOHN: That's good. That's a good deduction, yeah.

Sherlock's rejection of emotion in favor of logic suggests that the heart only complicates or detracts from the great mind. Conversely, while John does not reject the intellectual truth of Sherlock's position, he believes that caring for the victims remains important. What John notably indicates as a *good* deduction, however, gestures towards the significance of Sherlock's own recognition of John's emotions, in which he observes that he has disappointed John in his disavowal of the heroic. Sherlock's prior claim that heroes do not exist and his refusal to be characterized as one if they did position him as cognizant of what makes a hero and that John may, in fact, be attempting to construct him as one. John's presence and reactions to Sherlock's behavior enable Sherlock to register emotional context, potentially equipping him to learn through John's efforts to integrate his heart-head dichotomy.

Although Sherlock's interactions with Moriarty in "The Great Game" separate him from the more recognizable heroism of Holmes in *A Game of Shadows*, his emotional response to John at the episode's end anticipates the heroic potential depicted in Ritchie's first film. In *Sherlock Holmes*, a confrontation with Blackwood leaves Watson injured, drawing Holmes to his bedside. In an effort to assuage his guilt, Mary assures Holmes, "This is not your responsibility; it was his choice. He'd say that it was worth the wounds," echoing Watson's observation in Conan Doyle's "The Three Garridebs" of a Holmes who fears that Watson has been mortally wounded:

> It was worth a wound — it was worth many wounds — to know the depth of loyalty and love which lay behind that cold mask [:] ... a great heart as well as ... a great brain. All my years of humble but single-minded service culminated in that moment of revelation [624–625].

The unfeigned admiration of Conan Doyle's Watson is here reciprocated, and the recollection of this moment in Ritchie's film positions the detective as a great man worthy of the good doctor's service.

To that end, in the final showdown in "The Great Game," Moriarty's men train their sniper rifles upon Sherlock's head and John's heart, aligning the two men in their respective roles of greatness and goodness: Sherlock, whose great mind has been led here by its attraction to Moriarty's, and John, the brave hostage willing to sacrifice his life in order that Sherlock might escape. When Moriarty threatens to "stop [John's] heart," he contextualizes his later declaration that rather than kill Sherlock, he will "burn the heart out of" him. Sherlock's insistence that he does not possess one only causes Moriarty to respond, "we both know that's not quite true." Thus John is established as at once the heart to Sherlock's head and perhaps the key to the emergence of Sherlock's own heart. When Moriarty first leaves them, an uncharacteristically frantic Sherlock rips away the bomb strapped to John's chest, barely able to articulate "that thing you did ... that was, um, *good*" (emphasis added). Sherlock can here recognize and appreciate John's display of loyalty and devotion; his concern for John's well-being presents a marked contrast to his previous disregard of Moriarty's other hostages, revealing the heart that Moriarty insists that Sherlock does, in fact, have. Where initially Sherlock and John seem to be established as head and heart, potentially forming through their partnership an effective whole, this scene suggests that just as Watson has learned enough of Holmes' deductive methods to solve the case in *A Game of Shadows*, so might the BBC series' Sherlock learn and adopt John's methods — the goodness and heart behind the man of action. Indeed, after Sherlock's emotional display, Moriarty returns, as do the snipers' beams — notably trained now upon Sherlock's heart.

This heart emerges perhaps most strongly in the last episode of Season Two, "The Reichenbach Fall." Having been hailed by the public as "the Reichenbach Hero," Sherlock now faces the threat of being exposed to the press as a fraud through Moriarty's machinations. In a scene nearly identical to the heroic pose in the unaired pilot, the finale finds Sherlock standing on the roof of St. Bart's, yet again in an elevated position as John gazes up at him. Whereas Sherlock was unaware of John's worshipful gaze before, here Sherlock pleads with him to "keep your eyes fixed on me" ("The Reichenbach Fall"). This scene notably departs from Conan Doyle's "The Final Problem" and *A Game of Shadows,* where in the former Watson must deduce from the cliff itself Holmes' end and in the latter he only catches one last glimpse of Holmes as he plummets. In both instances these men see enough to believe in, mourn, and tell the tale of the detective's heroic demise. *Sherlock*'s John, however, is forced to watch as Sherlock falls so that he will not only believe Sherlock to be dead but also that he might legitimate Moriarty's story in bearing witness to Sherlock's "suicide." Sherlock trusts John to accept the injunction to "tell anyone who'll listen to you" and perpetuate the myth of Sherlock's fraudulence because John, as the "good" man and faithful blogger, has a responsibility to testify to the truth, and it is his testimony that the public is most likely to still accept as truth ("The Reichenbach Fall"). John is unable to believe Sherlock's own insistence upon Moriarty's lies, but he believes in Sherlock, and that is the story he, like the Watson of Ritchie's films, ultimately imparts to the audience. As our access point to Sherlock, John serves particularly in the end of Season Two as the only remaining link to our belief in a heroic Sherlock — and rather than confirm the fall of the Reichenbach hero, John eulogizes a Sherlock who rises in "The Reichenbach Fall" to his heroic potential.

Sherlock's final problem comes down not only to putting a stop to Moriarty but to prevent Moriarty from putting a stop to, once more, John Watson's heart. Moriarty's threats to burn the heart out of Sherlock have come to encompass by this point both the reputation as a great detective that he has gained for himself worldwide and the good people he has let into his life — John, Mrs. Hudson, and Lestrade. "The Reichenbach Fall," in the end, presents the fall of a great man and the rise of a good man. Sherlock sacrifices all that makes him great — his intellect, his superiority, his carefully constructed persona — to do what is good, and it is for this that John is determined to remember and honor both of those aspects of the heroic in him. Standing before Sherlock's gravestone, John declares: "You told me once that you weren't a hero ... but you were the best man, the most human ... human being that I have ever known, and no one will ever convince me that you told me a lie" ("The Reichenbach Fall"). In recalling his conversation with Sherlock about heroism from "The Great Game," John, in fact, addresses two lies he arguably believes that Sherlock *has* told him: he is not a hero, and he is a fake. At the same time, John's reference is elliptical; he does not confirm Sherlock as a hero outright. Instead, he establishes him as, rather than "the best and the wisest" as in "The Final Problem" and *Game of Shadows*, the best — the greatest, he could as easily say — and the most human, thus imparting to Sherlock emotional and social capacity — heart. His plea with Sherlock, "don't be dead," is as much a plea with the heroic image of Sherlock as with the man himself, demanding that the audience, along with John, cling to our belief in heroes and Sherlock's worthiness of that characterization.

Both Ritchie's films and the BBC television series ultimately establish Sherlock Holmes as not strictly a hero but a man whose heroic potential must be shaped by Dr. Watson. Holmes can only achieve true greatness if his genius is tempered by goodness. Holmes' insertion of a question mark at "The End" of Watson's chronicles in *A Game of Shadows* suggests, like the shadowy figure of Sherlock observing John at his gravestone in "The Reichenbach Fall," that the good doctor's quest with the great detective is not yet over. The ongoing BBC series has positioned Sherlock as someone with both heroic and anti-heroic potential, and although John has been tasked by Mycroft with the making of Sherlock, there always remains the possibility that Sherlock might proceed as "worse than ever," particularly as his self-enforced exile removes him from the more immediate influence of "the side of the angels" — and despite the seeming culmination of his heroism in "The Reichenbach Fall," Sherlock still declares that although he may be on the side of good, he is himself no angel. Key to Sherlock Holmes' continued development, then, is John Watson's rejection of the old mode of hero worship, his ability to challenge Holmes and, in securing his affections, providing the cerebral, emotionally distant detective with the key to accessing true greatness — empathy for another human being, for something more than the self.

WORKS CITED

"BBC to Make a Modern-Day Sherlock Holmes." *The Telegraph.* Telegraph Media Group Limited. 19 Dec. 2008. Web. 31 Dec. 2011.

Campbell, Joseph. *The Hero with a Thousand Faces.* 3rd ed. Novato, CA: New World Library, 2008. Print.

Carlyle, Thomas. *On Heroes, Hero-Worship and the Heroic in History.* Ed. Carl Niemeyer. Lincoln: University of Nebraska Press, 1966. Print.

Conan Doyle, Sir Arthur. "The Adventure of the Three Garridebs." *Sherlock Holmes: The Complete Novels and Stories Volume II.* 1986. New York: Bantam Classics, 2003. 610–626. Print.

_____. *The Hound of the Baskervilles. Sherlock Holmes: The Complete Novels and Stories Volume II.* 1986. New York: Bantam Classics, 2003. 1–159. Print.

_____. "A Study in Scarlet." *Sherlock Holmes: The Complete Novels and Stories Volume I.* 1986. New York: Bantam Classics, 2003. 1–120. Print.

"The Great Game." *Sherlock: Season One.* Writ. Mark Gatiss. BBC Worldwide, 2010. DVD.

"The Hounds of Baskerville." *Sherlock: Complete Series Two.* Writ. Stephen Thompson. Hartswood Films, 2012. DVD.

Lidster, Joseph. "My New Flatmate." *The Personal Blog of Dr. John H. Watson.* BBC. Web. 31 Dec. 2011.

Levy, Emanuel. "Sherlock Holmes: Interview with Star Robert Downey, Jr." *Emanuel Levy Cinema 24/7.* n.p. Web. 31 Dec. 2011.

Porter, Lynnette. *Tarnished Heroes, Charming Villains, and Modern Monsters: Science Fiction in Shades of Gray on 21st Century Television.* Jefferson, NC: McFarland, 2010.

"The Reichenbach Fall." *Sherlock: Complete Series Two.* Writ. Mark Gatiss. Hartswood Films, 2012. DVD.

Sherlock Holmes. Dir. Guy Ritchie. Warner Brothers, 2010. DVD.

Sherlock Holmes: A Game of Shadows. Dir. Guy Ritchie. Warner Brothers, 2011. Film.

"A Study in Pink." *Sherlock: Season One.* Writ. Steven Moffat. BBC Worldwide, 2010. DVD.

"A Study in Pink (Pilot)." *Sherlock: Season One.* Writ. Steven Moffat and Mark Gatiss. BBC Worldwide, 2010. DVD.

6

Making the Transition
The Modern Adaptation and Recreation
of the Scientist Detective Hero

ANA E. LA PAZ

Sherlock Holmes may not have been the first private detective, but he was the first to inspire such interest, admiration, and imitation. He and Dr. Watson are considered heroes by many because of the inspirational qualities that can be found in the characters and their stories. Readers love the Holmes stories and the two central characters. Audiences idolize them, live through them, believe in them, and recreate them. They need such heroes who can solve any problem or resolve any mystery, no matter how difficult or impossible it seems. According to Scott T. Allison and George R. Goethals, authors of *Heroes: What They Do and Why We Need Them,* "[t]here is an underlying human need for heroes to show us the best side of human nature.... Heroes model exemplary behavior and challenge us to rise to their level. Heroes inspire us to aim higher" (188). People want and need to believe in the highest and best attributes of humanity. Throughout their book, Allison and Goethals repeat the idea that heroes embody, or, through the circumstances they are dealt, come to embody those traits which are the best parts of humanity. During the Victorian era, when the Holmes stories were written, and today, as they are still being read and recreated, intellect and ability, in combination with some kindness, are the very highest attributes that humans strive to achieve. Therefore, audiences look to detectives like Sherlock Holmes and Dr. Watson, the best models of those attributes, for hope and guidance.

Allison states that, in a survey conducted for the book he co-authored, participants indicated that fictional heroes were more real than non-fictional heroes. In light of this finding, it is easy to see why fans idolize Holmes and Watson and why television showrunners create detectives to step into their shoes, so to speak. We want them to be real, especially in law enforcement, because the ideals they represent provide us with something to look up to and that makes us feel safe. Sherlock Holmes, with the help of Dr. Watson, is a great hero, and the fact that he and his style of detection are quintessential to society's need for the detective hero can be seen in many recent television dramas, especially in the U.S. television series *Bones*.

The Holmesian Hero

When Sir Arthur Conan Doyle published the Holmes stories, he little imagined the great effect they would have on readers. Surprisingly, when, in 1887, Sherlock Holmes made his debut in *Beeton's Christmas Annual*, he did not receive much acclaim. In fact, the Holmes mysteries did not become widely popular until after their publication in *Strand Magazine* in 1891. However, since then, Holmes' fame has become international, and the reading or viewing public clearly exhibits a basic human need for the detached and knowledgeable hero detective. Holmes is so influential because he leads the way in fictional forensic detection.

Ellen Burton Harrington, in a *CSI*-focused article, states that "[f]orensic science shows hammer home the notion that human beings leave traces of themselves wherever they go, inviting us to believe that the criminals will inevitably be caught by the idealized scientists who wield innovative procedures" (378). The notions that people always leave evidence and that all criminals are "catchable" is definitely one upheld in the Holmes mysteries. It is also one which makes Holmes, and all detectives like him, heroic. According to Allison and Goethals, a hero must have the following "great eight traits" (62), which go along with "a number of closely related traits in each cluster" (62):

Smart: intelligent, wise
Strong: leader, dominating, courageous, gallant
Selfless: moral, honest, humble, altruistic
Caring: compassionate, empathetic, kind
Charismatic: eloquent, dedicated, passionate
Resilient: determined, persevering, accomplished
Reliable: loyal, true
Inspiring: admirable, amazing, great [62]

The forensic Holmesian scientist has all of these traits. Intellect is shown in many ways, but mostly in the ability to observe and interpret data at a crime scene. Holmes does this by searching the scene thoroughly, either by use of his five senses alone or with the aid of a magnifying glass. Once he finds the data, he relies on his vast knowledge of forensic science to interpret that data, once in a while also employing his chemistry lab to aid him. The new, recreated Holmesian detective conducts investigations with a team, each of whom specializes in one area of forensic science. This team gathers and interprets the data they collect through the use of computers and knowledge of their field. Such modern displays of intellect reassure audiences that the people in law enforcement have the resources and knowledge needed to apprehend criminals.

But intellect must be paired with strength in order to be effective. Strength is depicted when the detective or scientist leads the way in the investigation, figuring out the clues and showing everyone else the way to the criminal. Scientist detectives must have strength and intellect because, without the strength to spend grueling hours interpreting data and then also assisting in tracking down and catching the criminal, their intelligence would not be seen as inspiring and selfless. Selflessness can be seen whenever detective scientists place the good of others before themselves. They exhibit resiliency in their indefatigable pursuit of truth and justice. They make the right decision in the face of a serious moral dilemma and protect others even when they risk their own well-being.

Holmes and Watson, and other Holmesian characters, exhibit caring when they sympathize and/or empathize with the victim(s) of a crime, showing that they feel for the hardships of others. Whenever scientist detectives solve the crime, they show charisma in their dedication to catching the criminal and their presentation of the solution to the mystery. This presentation is usually quite dramatic, and the speaker(s) are eloquent and attention-grabbing. The charismatic presentation is also almost always given toward the end of the story so that its dramatic quality is heightened.

Reliability is yet another trait of Holmesian characters. Detectives and scientists can count on each other for assistance and timely responses, but the victims and the families of victims can also count on them for a speedy resolution to the problem. Even criminals can rely on law enforcers to eventually and inevitably catch them.

All of these characteristics make the detective scientist inspirational, people to be looked up to for the example they set and the guidance they can offer. All of these characteristics are present in the Holmes stories and, because of their connection to Holmes, are present in *Bones* episodes as well. Holmesian heroics are essential to the detective scientist model and have thus been carried through in modern translations and representations of the tales.

Holmes in Translation

Not only have the Holmes stories been translated in many languages, they have also been analyzed and used as a jumping off point for other works of fiction. Within the last twenty years, there has been a surge in the popularity of television detective shows, each with a different approach. U.S. television shows like *Law & Order* and *CSI* headed the movement which has produced many additions to the detective fiction genre, such as *Psych* and *Criminal Minds*. Each show is written to be unique. However, as these shows' detectives have gained popularity, many have been compared to that original great detective, Sherlock Holmes. Harrington notes that "[d]rawing from Sherlock Holmes stories, which prioritize the collection of trace evidence as well as deduction, *CSI* and its fellow shows present a reliable detective formula" (366). Like Holmes, the characters in these shows are presented with difficult murder or kidnapping cases which must be solved. Also like Holmes, the characters manage to pull through, often at the last minute, and reveal who the killer is or where the missing person is being hidden.

Bones, a Fox network television series which premiered in 2005, is a very effective and highly successful modern adaptation of Conan Doyle's characters. It furthers our need for the hero detective by borrowing and restructuring Conan Doyle's character's skill sets and personality traits, thereby creating a Sherlock Holmes story for the new millennium.

Bones *Basics*

Dr. Temperance Brennan, a highly intelligent forensic anthropologist, works with Special Agent Seeley Booth to solve murder cases for the FBI. Dr. Brennan works with a team of specialists: Dr. Jack Hodgins, an entomologist and mineralogist; Angela Montenegro, a classically trained artist; Dr. Daniel Goodman, an archaeologist; and Zack Addy, Dr. Brennan's graduate student. This team, including Special Agent Booth, works together to fight crimes in much the same way that Holmes and Watson do. Because of cast and character changes in later seasons, the focus of this study lies only on the first season, but the show's premise has remained the same in subsequent seasons. The *Bones* team specializes in crimes which are thought to be impossible to solve. Their range of specialties uniquely assists them in this pursuit. Conan Doyle's original crime-fighting scientist detective and doctor together specialize in many fields, including but not limited to forensic pathology, tattoos, psychology, and forensic medicine. Holmes also has extremely keen perception. Because of the scientific and technological advances that have been made since Holmes' time, no one character at the beginning of the 21st century can be accepted as a specialist in all of the areas in which Holmes, working in the late 1800s, specializes. Holmes himself states, in "The Five Orange Pips," that it is necessary that the reasoner [the scientist detective] should be able to utilize all the facts which have come to his knowledge; and this in itself implies, as you will readily see, a possession of all knowledge, which ... is a rare accomplishment. It is not so impossible, however, that a man should possess all knowledge which is likely to be useful to him in his work, and this I have endeavoured in my case to do [207].

Holmes does know everything that he needs to know in order to solve the cases he is presented with, and if he does not have the information memorized, he has it on hand and can find it readily. However, the amount of knowledge which scientist detectives need has grown exponentially since Conan Doyle wrote of the adventures of Sherlock Holmes. Today it is more practical and practicable for one person to specialize in one field. Therefore, in *Bones,* the attributes which make Holmes and Watson great detectives are spread amongst Dr. Brennan, her team, and Special Agent Booth. Using their intellect and the technology available to them, which is quite considerable, the characters in *Bones* represent detecting and crime-fighting skills in their most advanced stages, much as Holmes and Watson do in the late 1800s. Their character traits and skill sets, which closely mimic those of Holmes and Watson, assist them in solving these crimes. Although they utilize sophisticated machinery in their pursuit of justice, their intelligence, like Holmes', is shown in their ability to interpret the results that their technology produces.

The Man of Science

Sir Arthur Conan Doyle, speaking of Holmes, said "I thought of my old teacher Joe Bell.... If he were a detective he would surely reduce this fascinating unorganized business to something nearer to an exact science. I would try if I could get this effect" (qtd. in *The Complete Sherlock Holmes* x). He certainly succeeded. Holmes is "a calculating machine" (Conan Doyle, "The Sign of Four" 82), and Watson often comments on his skills, stating at one time that Holmes has "brought detection as near an exact science as it ever will be brought in this world" (Conan Doyle, "A Study in Scarlet" 21). He excels in chemistry, as well as other scientific pursuits, writes treatises on subjects such as the identification of different kinds of tobacco ash, discusses the use of fingerprinting during a time when it was being introduced in police work, and performs scientific experiments in his rooms. He uses technology, but his powers of observation, wide knowledge base, predilection for creating new investigative tools — such as using plaster of Paris to imprint footmarks — and ability to see evidence without allowing his emotions to skew his judgment are what make Holmes a great detective as well as a heroic and reassuring figure. In many recent detective television productions, audiences can see a representation of this man of science. In the original *CSI* series, there was CSI Grissom, the knowledgeable, poker-faced leader of the CSI crew. Other detective series usually have at least one character who is highly intelligent and less emotional than the others.

In *Bones*, Dr. Temperance Brennan fills that role. Like Holmes, she is the incarnation of "that ... rational, intelligent, and wise man or woman who can explain all mysteries and solve all problems" (Nick Rennison qtd. in Hockensmith 27). Brennan works at the Jeffersonian Institute. Her main occupation in the beginning of the series is the identification, and sometimes the excavation, of people who have been dead for so long that only their bones are left. She works most closely with Zack Addy, her graduate student and a near mirror image of herself in academic interest, emotional suppression, and interpersonal interaction skills. Due to her specialty, Agent Booth gives her the nickname "Bones."

Because she is the best forensic anthropologist in the country, the FBI requests her assistance with cases in which the murder victim has somehow, either naturally or unnaturally, been stripped of flesh. Brennan not only identifies the victim but can give time and cause of death, along with an identification of the murder weapon. Like Holmes, Brennan is "trained ... in the art of observation and analysis" (Hogan and Schwartz 157), which is what makes her the best in her field. Like the legendary detective, Brennan notices the small bits and pieces of the puzzle which help pull the larger fragments together. Small pieces of bone, snippets of string, tiny gouges and fractures — none of these escape Brennan's notice. In the third episode, "The Man on Death Row," Booth and Brennan are discussing a hand found inside a bear, and Brennan immediately notices "kerf marks. Marks made from a cutting tool," which she observes could not have come from the necropsy on the bear because "it's not a straight edge. [There are] residual cross section striations." She notices these details from a photograph of the hand. This level of observation closely resembles Holmes' close observational skills.

Holmes once comments on Watson's appearance, saying "I know that you have been getting yourself very wet lately, and that you have a most clumsy and careless servant girl" (Conan Doyle, "A Study in Scarlet" 12). Watson, of course, admits to the truth in these observations but claims that he cannot see how Holmes knows these things. "It is simplicity itself," Holmes claims, "my eyes tell me that on the inside of your left shoe, just where the firelight strikes it, the leather is scored by six almost parallel cuts. Obviously, they have been caused by someone who has very carelessly scraped round the edges of the sole in order to remove crusted mud from it. Hence, you see, my double deduction" (Conan Doyle, "A Study in Scarlet" 13). Brennan has the Holmesian characteristics of observation and deduction. She is greatly intelligent like Holmes, and she is also like him in personality, especially in her reclusive tendencies.

For both characters, a hermetic lifestyle seems to stem from a high IQ. Holmes finds the world boring and refuses to participate in it, save for when it offers him stimulation in the form of a mystery. He feels little for others; as Watson observes, "[a]ll emotions ... were abhorrent to his cold, precise but admirably balanced mind" (Conan Doyle, "A Study in Scarlet" 11). Brennan also finds emotions to be a muddying influence on her intellect. However, whereas Holmes can still reasonably function around others, Brennan puts people off with her lack of tact and feeling. In her first interaction with a victim's parents, she exhibits her lack of interpersonal skills. When the parents ask whether she is sure of whom the victim is, Brennan begins rattling off scientific information: "[w]e established 22 matching points of comparison" (Pilot) and is only stopped from continuing by a glare from Booth. Later, in a conversation with Angela, Brennan admits her social inadequacies, stating, "[m]y most meaningful relationships are with dead people!" (Pilot). However, those relationships with dead people give her an edge in her field, one she shares with Dr. Watson.

Although Holmes knows something of forensic medical science, he sometimes relies on Watson's medical abilities in order to solve a case. Brennan's medical knowledge brings that Watsonian knowledge into *Bones*, making her a perfectly informed forensic anthropologist. When she evaluates wounds, she carries over the role which Watson plays in the Holmes stories. Readers do not often see Watson filling the role of forensic medical professional. However, in "The Boscombe Valley Mystery," Watson has a chance to exhibit his abilities. An elderly man has been murdered by blunt force trauma, and, in an effort to clear the accused, Watson examines the medical evidence in hopes that "the nature of the injuries [would] reveal something to [his] medical instincts" (Conan Doyle, "The Sign of Four" 82). They do. The accused was arguing, face to face, with the deceased. Watson finds that "the posterior third of the left parietal bone and the left half of the occipital bone had been shattered," and when he uses his own head as a model to ascertain exactly where that type of injury would land, he concludes, "[c]learly such a blow must have been struck from behind" (Conan Doyle, "The Sign of Four" 82).

This evaluation is much like the ones that Brennan does for every case. Like Watson, she analyzes the wound and comes up with a reasonable evaluation of how it might have been caused. While examining the remains of the victim who was eaten by a bear, Brennan notices bite marks and remarks that they cannot be from the bear, which had "premolars that are small and pegged like," nor could they be from a wild pig, which would have a double cusp pattern with six incisors. She states "[t]hese marks show a double cusp pattern ... [and] were made by four incisors, like a chimp, but these teeth form a continuous arch." From this information she very calmly concludes, "[w]e don't just have a killer on our hands, we have a cannibal" ("The Man in the Bear"). In the end, Brennan could not be as efficient if it were not for technology. She often uses x-rays, MRIs, highly powered microscopic lenses, and computer imaging in order to examine evidence. Whereas Homes and Watson could only observe the information visible to the naked eye or through a low-powered microscope, Brennan often uses scans and digital 3-D renderings to more closely examine human remains. However, without the knowledge needed to read and interpret this data, the evidence would be meaningless. Brennan's technology ultimately only highlights her vast intelligence, which she frequently references. In the pilot episode, Booth teases her by saying that "[w]hen cops get stuck, we bring in people like you. You know? Squints. You know, you squint at things," to which Brennan replies, "[o]h, you mean people with very high IQs and basic reasoning skills." Although Brennan is highly knowledgeable, she would not be able to solve the mysteries alone. She is unable to interact efficiently with others, and she lacks certain skills which are necessary to the solving of crimes.

Tact and Other Small Matters

Tact, as well, as the remaining Holmesian skills, are provided by the rest of the team, starting with Dr. Goodman and Dr. Hodgins. These men are highly intelligent; however, they are able to interact with others in a socially acceptable way. Dr. Goodman is the resident archaeologist at the Jeffersonian. Like Brennan, he possesses the skill of close observation. He looks at the artifacts, noticing, like Holmes, small scrape marks on a tool or wear marks on clothing. However, Goodman possesses an additional Holmesian skill which Brennan does not: supposition. He can imagine what the information he observes might mean. While examining a corpse, Goodman waxes prosaic about the dead man's interests, habits, and work, imitating Holmes' frequently used trick of exposing a person's habits and career through close observations of gloves, hands, shoes, and cuffs. In the tenth episode, "The Woman at the Airport," the Jeffersonian is asked to authenticate a skeleton possibly from the Iron Age. Dr. Brennan is away on a case, so Dr. Goodman leads the study of the corpse. He examines the bones and artifacts and deduces that the 6' 1" dead man was "a big man for his time. Feared by his foes, respected by his neighbors." He bases these claims on the facts that "[h]is bones bear the marks of battle. His weapons are of good quality, well used." Also, he notices that the friends and family—the neighbors—of the dead Iron Age man showed their love and respect in the way they buried him. This type of deduction, in which Brennan would not take part because these social details cannot be proven, is exactly the type of deduction Holmes illustrates in instances such as deciphering a typist by the wear and ink on gloves or fingers. However, Goodman is an administrator first and, therefore, only an occasional part of the team. His administration duties keep him much more in contact with the world outside of the Jeffersonian. He is personable and polite, much like Watson. This connection to people enables him to infer a victim's life story from clothes and body. This kind of cognitive-imaginative leap is important to a case at times. However, it is foreign to strict scientists like Brennan and Dr. Hodgins, who is frustrated by Goodman's speculations.

Dr. Hodgins plays a large role in the series and is very emotional. In fact, at the beginning of the series, viewers are given to understand that Hodgins is undergoing anger-management therapy due to his overt displays of emotion. His emotional nature, especially once its explosive nature is under wraps, is quite endearing and allows him to form close bonds with his co-workers and to feel sympathy and even empathy for the victims. However, Hodgins is highly intelligent and very scientifically minded, so this empathy is often expressed in an enthusiasm for finding the truth through empirical data, much like Holmes displays. Whereas Brennan, Zack Addy, and Goodman work with people, Hodgins works with soil and insects. Although the study of insects was pursued by some scientists in France and Germany in Holmes' time, major advances and worldwide recognition of etymology did not occur until the 1960s (Benecke). However, Holmes is much concerned with soil. Watson describes him as being able to identify types of soil within a fifty-mile radius of London. In "The Five Orange Pips," Holmes, talking to a client, casually says, "[y]ou have come up from the south-west I see…. That clay and chalk mixture which I see upon your toe caps is quite distinctive" (Conan Doyle, 201). He often uses this skill in order to ascertain a suspect's guilt, reasoning that if the suspect wears the soil of the crime scene on his clothing, he is most assuredly guilty. Holmes' tactic of pointing out this evidence to suspects often elicits a confession which may not have otherwise been obtained.

Like Holmes, Hodgins is able to identify different types of soil. In "The Man on Death Row," the team finds a piece of evidence which appears to be a small bone shard, but Hodgins, after looking at it under a microscope, states that it is "not a bone. It's inorganic. Mineral, possibly quartz." Later, he is able to give the location of the crime scene based on the specific type of gravel. Hodgins is able to identify a wide range of materials accurately, which means that he is also able to be much more specific than Holmes. Whereas Holmes only has his keen eyesight, reasoning skills, and sometimes the assistance of his magnifying glass, Hodgins has such implements as high-powered

microscopes, computer imaging, a computer database, and the mass spectrometer. With this technological assistance, Hodgins is not only able to be more
specific in soil analysis but to analyze samples which are merely specks to the
naked eye, a feat which Holmes would have been glad to be able to accomplish.
However, the ability to recognize and analyze soil is an intelligence that Hodgins spent years cultivating. The technology does assist in his work; however,
in the end, it serves as a magnifier of the knowledge he already possesses.
Hodgins is also like Holmes and Brennan in that he can mostly distance himself emotionally from a crime. Although he does at times get a bit shaken by
the things he sees, he is not as emotionally involved as Angela Montenegro.
The only non-scientist on the Jeffersonian team, artist Angela finds each case
to be a personal trial. Like Watson, she emotionally identifies with the victim,
feeling the horrible reality of each crime as clearly as if it had happened to a
close friend. Within the plotline of the television series, she serves as the foil
to Brennan. Unlike Holmes, who plays violin and displays a creative side,
Brennan is not subject to duality; she is purely the empirical scientist. Holmes'
artistic leanings are described by thus: "[m]y friend was an enthusiastic musician, being himself not only a very capable performer but a composer of no
ordinary merit" (Conan Doyle). However, Holmes also produces some sketches
which Watson implies are quite good.

Angela provides this artistic influence on crime solving. Although she is
not a musician, she was raised by one but follows her passion to become an
artist. She creates mostly abstract art but can produce accurate renderings of
victims. However, most of her work is done digitally. Angela can also create
computer programs and invents a machine dubbed the Angelator that mixes
her technological and artistic skills. It is capable of rendering 3-D images and
playing 3-D action sequences based on the information Angela inputs. She
takes the parameters given to her by the other members of the team and builds
the image or scenario, eliminating Holmes' need to imagine the circumstances
of the crime. In the pilot episode, Angela uses the bone markers that Brennan
provides from the skull in order to identify the victim; after she enters the
markers and the dimensions of the skull into the program, the team can see
the image of the murder victim in a three-dimensional rendering. The Angelator can show the victim and a fact-based rendering of the crime so that they
may be analyzed in realistic three-dimensional images. Although Holmes has
to be content with his sketch artist and deductive abilities, Angela can input
the measurements of the victim or the parameters of the crime, and the computer will render exact and lifelike images.

The precise work of Angela and others at the Jeffersonian allows Agent
Booth to be equally precise. What Booth lacks in scientific or artistic ability,
he makes up in his ability to intimate facts about the victims, intuitively read

people, and analyze their words and actions. In "The Woman at the Airport," Booth describes his part in the team in this way: "I usually ... [get] a feel for the person [victim]: what they wanted, how they felt, what was going on in their lives." Like Watson, he connects emotionally to people, which makes him able to relate to them and get them to open up to him. When he talks to suspects, he makes them feel at ease, which in turn makes them tell him things which they would never have told stiff and unyielding Brennan. Like Holmes, Booth is able to closely observe suspects' actions and make inferences as to their motives and future actions. When a soldier is found dead in Arlington, lying on top of his unit commander's grave, Booth infers that the soldier may have had survivor's guilt, which could have induced him to commit suicide. Although the soldier is later proven to have been murdered, Booth's inference is pulled from personal experience, is quite reasonable, and could easily have accounted for the soldier's death ("The Soldier on the Grave"). He can put himself in another person's place and evaluate a situation from someone else's perspective. Similarly, Holmes, in "The Empty House," reasons that the person who tries to kill him after his narrow escape at Reichenbach Falls is a compatriot of Professor Moriarty and, therefore, would not give up seeking revenge for Moriarty's death. Holmes states

> Moriarty had not been alone. A confederate ... had kept guard while the Professor had attacked me. From a distance, unseen by me, he had been a witness to his friend's death and of my escape. He had waited, and then, making his way round to the top of the cliff, he had endeavoured to succeed where his comrade had failed [Conan Doyle, "The Empty House" 457].

After Holmes' return to London, two years after the incident at the Falls, he confides in Watson that, just as he suspected, that confederate, "the bosom friend of Moriarty, ... the most cunning and dangerous criminal in London ... is after me tonight" (Conan Doyle, "The Empty House" 460). Holmes knows not only that Moriarty's friends will hunt him, but that they are so loyal to Moriarty that they will never let up in their chase. This type of deductive reasoning from personality traits and sets of circumstances is exactly what Seeley Booth brings to the detection team in *Bones*.

Heroic in Any Time

Each character, in his or her own way, fills a role originally incorporated into the characters of Holmes and Watson. People feel a need for someone who has or can find all of the answers. Sherlock Holmes was the first character to truly fill this role, and in some form or another, he has been doing so for more than a century. Holmes also is at the cutting edge of science and technology for his time. He and Watson thus also fulfill our need for the scientific detective hero. Watson is the perfect foil to Holmes, and the two are a crime-fighting team who provide the audience with the comforting idea that no problem is too difficult to resolve if one has the right help. The characters in *Bones* repeat this theme, showing the audience that even murders committed long ago or by the cleverest of fiends can be solved with the right team and cutting-edge technology. The characterization of the empirical, analytical, detail-oriented, but conversely artistic scientist and the personable and competent doctor are well represented in these modern heroes. Brennan, her team, and Booth bring Holmes and Watson to life in the 21st century. They, and their television descendants, encourage our faith that real people can similarly solve crimes and keep us safe.

WORKS CITED

Allison, Scott T., and George R. Geothals. *Heroes: What They Do & Why We Need Them.* Oxford: Oxford University Press, 2011. Print.

Benecke, Mark. "A Brief History of Forensic Entomology." *Forensic Science International.* 120.1–2 (2001): 2–14. Web. 10 Dec. 2011.

Conan Doyle, Sir Arthur. "The Empty House." *The Complete Sherlock Holmes.* Christopher and Barbra Roden, eds. New York: Barnes & Noble, 2009. 453–465. Print.

_____. "The Five Orange Pips." *The Complete Sherlock Holmes.* Christopher and Barbra Roden, eds. New York: Barnes & Noble, 2009. 200–210. Print.

_____. "The Sign of the Four." *The Complete Sherlock Holmes.* Christopher and Barbra Roden, eds. New York: Barnes & Noble, 2009. 75–141. Print.

_____. "A Study in Scarlet." *The Complete Sherlock Holmes.* Christopher and Barbra Roden, eds. New York: Barnes & Noble, 2009. 3–71. Print.

Harrington, Ellen Burton. "Nation, Identity, and the Fascination with Forensic Science in *Sherlock Holmes* and *CSI.*" *International Journal of Cultural Studies* 10.3 (2007): 365–382. *MLA International Bibliography.* Web. 1 Feb. 2011.

Hockensmith, Steve. "The Eternal Detective: The Undying Appeal of Sherlock Holmes." *Mystery Scene* 93 (2006): 26–33. *MLA International Bibliography.* Web. 1 Feb. 2011.

Hogan, John C., and Mortimer D. Schwartz. "The Manly Art of Observation and Deduction." *The Journal of Criminal Law, Criminology, and Police Science* 55.1 (1964): 157–164. *JSTOR.* Web. 1 Feb. 2011.

"The Man in the Bear." *Bones.* Fox. 1 Nov. 2005. Television.

"The Man on Death Row." *Bones.* Fox. 22 Nov. 2005. Television.

"Pilot." *Bones.* Fox. 13 Sept. 2005. Television.

"The Soldier on the Grave." *Bones.* Fox. 10 May 2006. Television.

"The Woman at the Airport." *Bones.* Fox. 25 Jan. 2006. Television.

7

A Singular Case of Identity
Holmesian Shapeshifting

RHONDA HARRIS TAYLOR

After being introduced to the world by Sir Arthur Conan Doyle over a hundred and twenty-five years ago, the World's Greatest Detective, Sherlock Holmes, is still very much alive. As mystery writer Steve Hockensmith, creator of the Holmes on the Range book series, has noted, "Holmes isn't just the most popular character ever to emerge from the mystery genre: He *is* a genre — virtually an industry — unto himself" (27). Hockensmith joins a plethora of scholars, media commentators, and fans, present and past, who have analyzed and marveled at Holmes' enduring popularity (e.g., Dalrymple; Meyer; Moorman; Morley; Strebeigh). Sherlockian (and member of the Baker Street Irregulars) De Waal explained the popularity and recurrences of the fictional world's first consulting detective by placing Holmes (and Watson) within the familiar confines of 221B Baker Street and declaring "That magical 221b Baker Street and all the Canonical characters who inhabit our minds and hearts are a world in themselves" (De Waal). The appeal of the nostalgia of that archaic setting and its accoutrement has not paled for 21st century, technologically-savvy fans, as can be seen in the graphics chosen for the websites of Sherlockian Scion Societies, which are easily accessed through the web portal, Sherlockian Who's Who.

Recent Holmes offerings from the British also have retained the trappings of the original stories. As noted on its book jacket, English author Anthony Horowitz's 2011 contribution to the Holmes saga is distinguished by the fact that, "[f]or the first time in its one-hundred-and-twenty-five-year history, the Arthur Conan Doyle Estate has authorized a new Sherlock Holmes novel." Not surprisingly for a book authorized by the Doyle Estate and authored by an individual who has long been fascinated by "the rich atmosphere of 19th century London" (Neary), *The House of Silk* is true to the flavor of the original setting of time and place and personages. The two most recent Sherlock Holmes movies, directed by Britain's Guy Ritchie (*Sherlock Holmes*; *Sherlock Holmes: A Game of Shadows*), present Holmes as a big-screen action hero, but the time period, the costumes, and settings are familiarly 19th century. Even the BBC's series of a contemporary, young, technologically adept Holmes still retains such familiar trappings as the original characters, 221B Baker Street, and Holmes' cape-like, flowing overcoat (*Sherlock*), which has generated its own fanbase (e.g., Kingsnorth and Petridis). Although British audiences may feel more culturally proprietary about Holmes, American audiences have been Holmes' fans since he was brought to them via *Lippincott's Magazine*'s 1890 publication of *The Sign of the Four*.

What can be characterized as broadly popular versions of Holmes for the 21st century U.S.? One place to seek those is in the realm of the not-quite pastiche. On Adrian Nebbett's website for Sherlockian pastiches, he provides a category that he terms Periphera, which are "novels and stories that are almost but not quite Sherlockian enough to appear in the main section." This collection contains publications that "may be Sherlockian in title alone, or their Sherlockian content may be limited to a line or two, or an illustration, with no real impingement on the plot." He has a separate category for Pretenders & Puns, collocating works with "Sherlockian-style characters appearing in pastiches and parodies, and those that impersonate and dress up as canonical characters. Word-plays, mis-heard, mis-pronounced and disguised names of canonical characters and cases." This category includes endeavors ranging from Hockensmith's Holmes on the Range novel series (in which a 19th century cowboy is inspired by the Holmes stories to start solving mysteries) to Robert L. Fish's humorous Schlock Homes (who resides at 221B Bagel Street) short stories to Gladys Mitchell's *Watson's Choice* (in which Mrs. Bradley, amateur detective and psychiatrist, investigates a murder at a party with a Sherlock Holmes theme). Nebbett's indecision about where to place items that are recognizable, even if tangentially, as Holmesian and yet are not quite pastiches or parodies is understandable. His Periphera and Pretenders & Puns categories would benefit from the addition of a third category, which could be a container for the two series (one television and one book) that will be considered here as Holmesian shapeshifting (and that phrase could be a label for that third category!).

Detecting a 21st Century American Holmes

For the first decade of the 21st century Holmes has thrived in unexpected incarnations who can appeal to a wider audience than the traditional fanbase seeking an in-universe visit. These modern iterations avoid the familiar, now trivialized, trappings of the magnifying glass and deerstalker representation of Holmes. How ubiquitous these images have become is evidenced by the graphics that appear when "detective" is searched on Microsoft's free clip art website (Microsoft). The majority of the almost three screens of results are deerstalker hats, magnifying lenses, and/or recognizable Holmes profiles that are men, women, children, and an animal. These signifiers have taken on a life of their own, separate from the *real* Sherlock Holmes. Knight says that even Holmes' very name is "a synonym for a detective" (67), while suggesting that his survival may be simply "as a standard totem of detection in passing references or jokes" (104).

However, separating the omnipresent signifiers such as deerstalkers and magnifying lenses from the fundamental characteristics of the Holmes/Watson duo does not negate the characters as recognizable, regardless of the guises they have, for two reasons. The first is the concept of surrogacy, and the second is the post–September 11, 2001 paradigm shift for the United States.

Surrogacy, Avatars, and Shapeshifting

Tim Berners-Lee brought the web into being in 1990, and within a year commercial applications appeared. Since the last decade of the 20th century, and growing incrementally, individuals shop online, bank online, date online, and publicly present themselves and their ideas and creations through websites, blogs, social networking sites like MySpace and Facebook, and YouTube videos. Thus the possibility of having multiple public self-identities has become comfortable for many people. A December 2007 report from the Pew Internet and American Life Project on its study of *Digital Footprints* noted that 47 percent of Internet users searched for information about themselves online, up from 22 percent five years previously (Madden et al.). Also, 60 percent of Internet users were not worried about how much online information about them was available.

It is a short journey from shaping the presentation of one's identity through the mediation of social networking to surrogacy, which can be simply defined as the substitution of one person for another ("Surrogate"). The epitome of surrogacy in mediated Internet space is the virtual world of Second Life ("Second Life"), launched in 2003 and populated by the avatars created by and representing its individual citizens in whatever 3-D world(s) they choose to inhabit. Usually, such surrogates bear no physical resemblance to the real people who design them, but invariably they capture one or more essential personal characteristics important to the individuals that they represent.

Surrogacy is increasingly a familiar idea for many 21st century Americans in their personal lives, and it has also found a broad audience appeal in fiction presentations. One form of surrogacy is the avatar, which can be defined as "a variant phrase or version of a continuing basic entity" ("Avatar"). An avatar is still an accurate representation of some fundamental of the original, albeit the physical appearance has changed. The contemporary concept of avatar almost invariably carries with it the connotation of technological intervention. This vision of the avatar is very familiar to 21st century moviegoers. While the genre of science fiction has delivered these representations, the numbers of viewers of these popular and acclaimed films surpass those of the traditional science fiction fanbase.

Steven Spielberg's 2001 *A.I. (Artificial Intelligence)* (nominated for 3 Oscars, among numerous other awards) is the story of an innovative robot that serves for a time as a surrogate for a couple's terminally ill child. In the case of this surrogate, the artificial child appears as a physical replication of the robot creator's deceased son: an android ("Android"). Per the definition of the term, this surrogate *resembles* a human being: the child is capable of feeling love but lacks the ability to be fully human. Avatars gained even greater exposure with James Cameron's 2009 blockbuster 3-D movie, *Avatar* (nominated for 9 Oscars and received 3, among other awards). The hero in *Avatar* retains his own identity/personality even as he is linked into a lab-created, genetically alien/human body. A-list actor Hugh Jackman stars in the 2011 film, *Real Steel* (nominated for a visual effects Oscar), set in a not-so-distant future where robots are the contenders in the boxing ring. The bond between a boy and a special robot teaches lessons in fatherhood to his former-boxer parent. In turn, the father is coerced into teaching the robot how to box as he once did—the robot becomes a surrogate for his former talents.

In contrast to the avatar's creation through the use of technology, a shape-shifter morphs biologically. In biology, shapeshifting is metamorphosis, when an organism changes its form or structure as part of a natural process of growth. In myth and folklore, a shapeshifter changes from the appearance of a true self into the guise of another. For example, shapeshifting Native Americans are portrayed in the wildly popular *Twilight Saga* movies, begun in 2008. The movies are based on the equally popular book series of the same titles by Stephenie Meyer, which first appeared in 2005 as young adult offerings that soon found many adult fans. These shapeshifters are humans who can be transformed suddenly and dramatically into giant wolves but with their human identities intact. Similarly, today's ordinary humans who utilize avatars online are shapeshifters with sophisticated powers offered by the mediation of technology—they can assume multiple guises, including their own original ones. More importantly, they assume those roles simultaneously rather than sequentially, as is the case with the fictional shapeshifting *Twilight* wolves. The concepts of avatars and shapeshifters offer insights about how Holmes surrogates can thrive in the ever-more technological and competitive environment that the current century offers to consumers of popular culture.

Surrogates and the Detective Conundrum

Two shapeshifters who re-flesh Holmes for new audiences are Detective Robert Goren and FBI Agent Aloysius Pendergast. Goren is the main protagonist in the long-running television series, *Law & Order: Criminal Intent*, which began in 2001 and ended in mid–2011. Pendergast is the central character of a book series from the team of Douglas Preston and Lincoln Child. He first appeared as a minor character in *The Relic* and *Reliquary* in the late 1990s and then became the main character in *The Cabinet of Curiosities* (2002) and subsequent titles. Flourishing in the first decade of the 21st century, they are Holmes' American surrogates. However, because Holmes is a consulting detective who accepts employment as a free agent, and Goren and Pendergast are law enforcement officers, terming them surrogates for Holmes overtly violates the traditional distinctions of the categories of the mystery story. For instance, Cawelti placed Holmes in the classical detective story formula, distinguished from "the hard-boiled detective story, the spy story, the police procedural tale, the gangster saga, and the Enforcer's caper" (80). Malmgren used broader, separate categories, classifying mystery, detective, and crime fiction (8–9). But, in his 1981 work, Porter deliberately adopted the inclusive phrase "detective novel" rather than more traditional distinctions, arguing that

> The attempt to devise strict categories and locate the by now vast corpus of published works within those categories is valuable only insofar as it draws attention to the range of possibilities in the genre and is a nuisance where it multiplies superficial differences. If we do hesitate between available terms in assigning a given work to a specific category such as mystery story, crime story, problem story, detective adventure story, police novel, thriller, or spy thriller, it is because in so many cases there is significant overlapping [4].

I focus my analysis within Porter's broad schema and emphasize the attributes that are shared fundamentals for Conan Doyle's Holmes and for Goren and Pendergast. The characteristics required for Goren and Pendergast to be true surrogates include those of context: the intentionality of their creators, the recognition of Goren and Pendergast as Holmesian by critics and fans and the embracing of them by Holmes fans, and their appropriateness for a contemporary time period that is very similar to the social tensions of late 19th century Britain. Also necessary are attributes found in a mirroring of the settings for Holmes' work, his person and personality, and his relationships.

9/11 emphasized to the American people that extreme danger lies in the unaffiliated loner and that future security lies in more structured and encompassing law enforcement (as exemplified by the establishment of the umbrella agency of Homeland Security) and more regulation (as exemplified by the USA Patriot Act). If that is the environment that will be more secure, then the Holmes surrogates would naturally be affiliated with law enforcement, where they are regulated by job requirements and have the information, technological, and personnel resources of large agencies. They would not be the "loose cannons" of private consulting detectives.

The intentionality of their creators is an important factor for determining the relationship of Goren and Pendergast to Holmes. In this sense they are avatars, deliberately created to resemble the original. The creator of the *Law & Order* franchise, Dick Wolf, has repeatedly said of the *Criminal Intent* series that Goren is Sherlock Holmes and Alexandra Eames is Watson (Wolf). The Pendergast series features multiple homages to the Conan Doyle stories. Pendergast's surname is remarkably similar to Prendergast, the last name of the leader of the mutiny of the *Gloria Scott* (Conan Doyle, "The 'Gloria Scott'") and also the last name of a falsely accused major whom Holmes clears (Conan Doyle, "The Five Orange Pips"). Continuing along these lines, there is an amusing exchange in *Cold Vengeance* in which an individual being questioned by Pendergast addresses him first as Pendergrast and then as Prendergast (286). Viola (a variation of Violet) is the name of a romantic interest of Pendergast's. Violet is the first name of three different characters who were the subjects of Holmes' cases (Conan Doyle, "The Adventure of the Illustrious Client," "The Adventure of the Solitary Cyclist," "The Adventure of the Bruce-Partington Plans"), besides being the name of the only woman in whom Watson ever hoped that Holmes would have a "further interest" (Conan Doyle, "The Adventure of the Copper Beeches"). Pendergast's villainous brother is named Diogenes, which is also the name of the club of Holmes' brother Mycroft. Diogenes' fatal fall from a cliff in Italy (Preston and Child, *The Book of the Dead*) brings to mind Holmes' confrontation with Moriarty at Reichenbach Falls in Switzerland (Conan Doyle, "The Final Problem").

Reviewers also recognize these relationships among Holmes, Goren, and Pendergast. At the end of *Criminal Intent*'s run, an online reviewer noted that the show had been "*Law & Order's* modern twist on Sherlock Holmes" (Young). The Internet Movie Database's review of the series referred to "the offbeat, Sherlock Holmes–like Detective Robert Goren" (Barjenbruch). A *Publishers Weekly* review dubbed Pendergast "a ruthless descendant of Holmes" and noted that New York police officer Vincent D'Agosta is "Watson to Pendergast's Sherlock" ("PW Forecasts" 36). The same publication commented about *The Dance of Death* that Pendergast and his brother Diogenes are "Sherlock Holmes locked in a death struggle with his smarter brother, Mycroft" ("Reviews" 59). The interviewer of authors Preston and Child for a *Writer* article noted that Pendergast's "character and unique style would fit just as easily into a Sherlock Holmes novel as a contemporary action piece" (Ayers).

Both Pendergast and Goren also have been embraced as Sherlockian by their many fans. For example, in 2006, a blogger provided a lengthy essay on "Aloysius Pendergast, the Modern Sherlock Holmes" (Roberts). A December 2011 posting to a website for *Law & Order: Criminal Intent* fan reviews raged against the diminishing roles of Goren and Eames, declaring "Detective Goren is our equivalent of Sherlock Holmes" (Sabreanimal4180). An Amazon.com customer posting for the first season DVD of the series asserted that Goren is "a modern-day Sherlock Holmes–type detective" (Whitenack).

As with Holmes, both Goren and Pendergast have been broadly and enduringly popular. *Criminal Intent* was a ratings leader in its original Sunday time slot throughout its first three years, and it remained in production for ten years (ending in June 2011), although it was moved in 2007 from its original NBC venue to the USA Network (owned by NBC). Reruns continue to be shown. All Pendergast books to date (2011) have appeared in the top 150 best-selling books list compiled by *USA Today* ("Best-selling"). *The Book of the Dead, Cabinet of Curiosities, Cold Vengeance, Dance of Death, Fever Dream, Still Life with Crows, The Relic,* and *The Wheel of Darkness* have also appeared on *The New York Times Bestseller* lists ("Best Sellers").

Just as Holmes has appeared on the radio, in movies, plays, graphic novels, computer games, etc., Goren and Pendergast are also cross-media translations and have moved beyond their initial formats. Their canons, as with that of Holmes, are extended by Apocrypha. The USA Network website for the *Criminal Intent* series offers fans interactive games, trivia challenges, mobile fan club, Facebook fan page, and weekly poll (USA, "Law"). Fans can, and do, create and add to an official website their own mash-ups of clips from the series (USA, "Law ... [Mash-ups]"). Vivendi Universal has produced a video-game based on the *Criminal Intent* series.

Similar to the *Criminal Intent* universe, the Pendergast world has expanded. On the Internet, fans can read an interview with Special Agent Pendergast, with authors Preston and Child posing the questions (Preston and Child, "Authors"). There is a website for Corrie Swanson, who is Pendergast's exceptional young protégé (*Corrie*) and who is reminiscent of the Baker Street Irregulars. Unofficially, these two series have online fan communities, many which post fan fiction. As with Holmes, Goren and Pendergast have lengthy entries about them on Wikipedia.

Surrogacy and a Post-9/11 World

A 19th/early 20th century Holmes and the late 20th/early 21st century Goren and Pendergast are products and reflections of their readers'/viewers' social and cultural environments, but those environments are similar.

Queen Victoria's reign from 1837 to 1901 bounds the fictional world of Sherlock Holmes. That era was characterized by increasing industrialization, urbanization with huge slums, rapid population growth (including immigration), and a new middle class with its own concerns. By the end of the 19th century, Britain was a rich colonial empire occupying Asia and Africa, but rebellion was beginning. Also, particularly important, in comparison to contemporary America, this era was a "time when the knowledge explosion of the nineteenth century threatened to swamp the generally educated man in a tide of specialization" (Jann 53). Many commentators (e.g., Knight 67; Jann 126) have iterated that much of Holmes' appeal was because of the realities faced by his readers; they needed him for reassurance in a turbulent world. Conan Doyle's stories were "'addressed to the privileged majority, it plays on their fears of social disturbance and makes use of Sherlock Holmes and what he stands for to reassure them'" (Pierre Nordon in Symons 22; Knight 67).

Contrast the Victorian world of Holmes with the first decade of the 21st century in the United States. The consequences of the September 11, 2001 attacks on the World Trade Center and the Pentagon began the decade and instigated a series of social changes:

> ID cards required everywhere. Airline passengers waiting patiently in line to take off their shoes, belts, jewelry — and to have their bags searched and perhaps their bodies as well. Fans searched as they enter football stadiums. People on the watch for suspicious characters — including those who might take photos of bridges and tunnels. People fearing to retrieve lost bags in case they are booby trapped. Increased government surveillance of individual Americans, including their telephone calls overseas [Zakheim 3].

Zakheim's summary of the consequences of the 9/11 attacks also emphasizes the astronomical national debt burden accumulated from two wars, economic losses from the attack, and increased domestic security changes. He notes the social programs and other government obligations on which the debt has an impact. The country's current presidential campaigns have highlighted other challenges that existed before 9/11 and have exacerbated: rapidly accelerating changes in information technology in every arena, including personal interactions; the shift from a production economy to a service economy, including outsourcing of jobs beyond the U.S.; the role of immigration; concern about the current status and future of the country's middle class; globalization, which emphasizes the gulf between rich and poor nations and the use of world resources; and the jockeying for national identity and leadership in a world where other powers are emerging to boldly compete. Audiences living in this environment should be receptive to the reassurance of a Holmes figure, but not to one who appears as the too-familiar icon that is used as a graphic to advertise everything from insurance to bars to trailer parks. Today's Holmes needs to possess the same attributes as the original, but he must shapeshift (which implies a responsive evolution) to be accepted in this modern context. Those attributes fall into three categories: the settings, persons and the personalities, and relationships, including *The* Woman.

The Settings

Holmes' place is urban (London); he only retreats to the rural when he retires from active practice. As explained in "The Adventure of the Cardboard Box," Holmes "loved to lie in the very centre of five millions of people, ... responsive to every little rumour or suspicion of unsolved crime" (Conan Doyle, 888). This potential identity of the city as urban jungle/frontier allows Holmes to master it but never to be "a routine, assimilated denizen of the city" (McLaughlin 45). As a hero of the urban jungle, Holmes' "work involves the intellectual purity of detection without his becoming involved in the bloodthirsty task of punishment" (McLaughlin 44). In the center of the urban jungle, however, is Baker Street, where reason prevails. Metress notes that the Holmes stories "begin in Baker Street" (and it should be mentioned, upstairs), move "out into London" (that urban jungle), and "in the end, they return to Baker Street" (186). The progression "establishes the power of Holmes' reason" (186) as he first solves a "minor problem or mystery" (187) and then exposes the chaos of the mystery in the outside before returning to the space where "reason confidently discovers or recovers order" (187). Thus, London is a duality of both urban jungle (the hunting ground) and a constructed city that represents reason, culture, achievement, and order. Holmes himself was adamant about preferring the city to the evil of the rural world, because, as he said, "the lowest and vilest alleys in London do not present a more dreadful record of sin than does the smiling and beautiful countryside" (Conan Doyle, "The Adventure of the Copper Beeches" 323). Where better to locate stories that are "celebrating the power of reason" (Metress 185) than the city?

Thus, where better to locate Holmes' modern day surrogates than the city? Both Goren and Pendergast reside and work in metropolitan areas, the former in New York City and the latter in New York City and New Orleans. Goren, as a New York City police officer, spends his days on the upper floors of a building which he leaves to investigate the crimes of the city, to make a foray into the disorder. By the end of the plotlines, he is usually back in the office interrogating a suspect, from whom he wrangles a confession through intellectual prowess. In a similar vein, Pendergast has a very large four-story family mansion in New York City, which is a decidedly unusual structure. However, it is a location which serves as a haven. This is where his ward, Constance Greene, a victim of his great-grand uncle, dwells under his protection and has an almost normal life. The basements of the mansion are the mysterious areas, with "other tunnels, older and more secret, that burrowed beneath the mansion into dark and unknown depths" (Preston and Child, *Dance of Death* 319)—normalcy resides above. Pendergast also maintains a very elegant residence above the city in the Dakota, overlooking Central Park. It contains a teahouse and garden and facilitates a "meditative spirit" (Preston and Child, *Cemetery Dance* 34). However, Pendergast might well agree with Holmes' assessment of rural areas, because one of his most macabre cases, *Still Life with Crows* (Preston and Child), is set in rural Kansas.

The Persons and the Personalities

The physical description of Holmes is as so: "In height he was rather over six feet, and so excessively lean that he seemed to be considerably taller. His eyes were sharp and piercing, save during those intervals of torpor to which I have alluded; and his thin, hawk-like nose gave his whole expression an air of alertness and decision" (Conan Doyle, "A Study in Scarlet" 20). He is also described as having "pale cheeks" (Conan Doyle, "The Adventure of the Six Napoleons" 594) and "thin hands" (Conan Doyle, "The Adventure of the Priory School" 554). Pendergast is very similar to Holmes in appearance. He is "thin—his skin almost transparent, his blue-gray eyes so light they looked luminous" (Preston and Child, *Still Life with Crows* 21), and he has a "long, pale face, white-blond hair, marble features" (Preston and Child, *The Wheel of Darkness* 4). Also, "his touch [is] as light and airy as a leaf's" (Preston and Child, *The Wheel of Darkness* 10). Although a television series does not provide a written description of its characters, viewers do see that Goren, like Holmes, is very tall, and the backstory for the series has him playing basketball in school. As with Holmes and Pendergast, one of Goren's more noticeable physical characteristics is his hands, which the camera emphasizes as he makes a point, commands the attention of suspects, or gathers clues. For Holmes, Pendergast, and Goren, physical appearances that may be more closely associated with the aesthete or even the ascetic do not negate demonstrated prowess in marksmanship, physical strength, or hand-to-hand combat. Holmes cannot be just an intellectual—he must be, as Knight suggests, a "hero in action," appealing to the "world-view of a basically uncerebral audience" (72). His two surrogates are of the same mold. Pendergast was in Special Forces (Preston and Child, "Authors"), and Goren was in the U.S. Army.

Besides their physical characteristics, these three characters are linked by the attributes of their personalities, intellect and other skills, and knowledge. It is important to emphasize that Holmes is both "one of us" (on our side) and yet apart from us, and that dichotomy, which is actually integrated in his personality, is reflected in what seem to be contradictory self-presentations. According to Symons, Holmes' attractiveness is that he "was a kind of saviour of society, somebody who did illegal things for the right reasons, who was really one of us" (22). For several reasons, it is necessary that Holmes be "the aloof, super-intellectual and slightly inhuman detective" (Symons 22). The intellectual prowess is needed to master science, because, as Knight says, "the importance of science — more exactly, of the aura of science — in Holmes' methods ... mobilises for the audience's fictional protection the contemporary idea that dispassionate science was steadily comprehending and so controlling the world" (79). Rauber even goes to the extent of asserting that "the detective is a popularized version of the scientist" (485). It would seem that the detective capable of effectively mastering Jann's "knowledge explosion of the nineteenth century" (53) would have to be of superior intellect. Also, his super-intellect in the Holmes stories mean that they "never suggest the reader can match the hero's intellectual power; he is accessible but not imitatable" (Knight 92). Holmes' "aloof, sometimes arrogant personal qualities" (Knight 79), coupled with his power over science, enhance the profile of "a superior being, a super-man whose world differs from ... and often baffled people like Watson" (79). Even his drug habit, which could be viewed as weakness, adds to the sense of his being superior, because it was "at that time, seen as an excitingly dangerous means of elevating and isolating the consciousness, closely bound up with the romantic artistic persona" (Knight 79). Of equal importance to his superiority, Holmes "treated all problems individualistically" (Knight 80), and he is "enlivened when he engages with human problems" (80). Thus, his "aloofness, self-assertion, irritation with everyday mediocrity was not merely forgivable — they were necessary parts of a credible comforting hero" (80).

Pendergast exhibits the same extraordinary intellectual and personal attributes as Holmes. In the "interview" (Preston and Child, "Authors") with him, Pendergast reveals that he graduated from Harvard (*summa cum laude* in anthropology) and from Oxford (with dual doctoral degrees and firsts in philosophy and classics). When Pendergast becomes a mentor for a bright teenager who is a misfit in her small community, she thinks that it is strange "someone as remote, as aloof, as unlike her as Pendergast was" (Preston and Child, *Still Life with Crows* 558) should care. He tells her that he will send her to boarding school, and when she worries that she will not "fit in," he tells her that as far as fitting in, "*I* never did" (558). When she hugs him, Pendergast is embarrassed, saying that he is "unused to physical displays of affection" (559).

Holmes is a walking encyclopedia of knowledge, and Jann says that the 19th century's knowledge explosion and specialization meant that "Holmes' mastery of so diverse an array of information would have been particularly reassuring" (53). Similarly, the 21st century world presents a landscape of unfathomable quantities of digitized information generation. Eric Schmidt, former CEO of Google, has been repeatedly quoted as saying in 2010 that as much information was being created every two days as had been created from "the dawn of civilization through 2003" (e.g., Kirkpatrick). As with Holmes, Goren and Pendergast seem to be knowledgeable about everything, and both speak multiple languages fluently. In an information explosion environment, Pendergast and Goren's facile recall of pertinent information (controlling the information at an individual level) should be just as reassuring as Holmes' ability to do the same.

Besides the knowledge of his own brain, Holmes also needs flexible methods of investigation, so that he can "be a convincing respondent to the variety and difficulty of the problems he tackles; the varying form creates an aura of spontaneity, of resource vigour that strengthens ... [his] authority" (Knight 76). He must be information literate, "able to access the relevant information from a vast array of knowledge and to select the exact constellation of facts to solve a particular mystery" (Jann 53). Holmes demonstrates that mastery in the range of information resources that he accesses, from his own files to daily newspapers to the Baker Street Irregulars and reformed criminal Shinwell Johnson. Similarly, Pendergast also uses many information resources, including a diverse pool of individuals: Corrie Swanson, a small-town teenage misfit; Wren, a book restorer; and the invalided Mime, a computer whiz. Goren is also a model of the "man who knows everything," but he frequently does library research on aspects of his cases, and he states that his library card is his "most important investigation tool" ("Dead"). He, too, has interesting human sources of information. For instance, in the very first episode, he uses a tattooed informant to identify a prison tattoo on a body ("One").

The many facets of Holmes' superiority are absolutely critical for successfully accomplishing the task of the detective, which is to answer the important question of "how will justice be done?" (Porter 125). It is requisite that "the action itself always focuses on the acts of the hero who is summoned ... to pursue and punish the villain and ... to rescue the victim and restore the status quo ante as well" (Porter 125). Sometimes those acts mean skirting the law. As Holmes says, "I am not in an official position, and there is no reason, so long as the ends of justice are served, why I should disclose all that I know" (Conan Doyle, "The Adventure of the Priory School" 558). His autonomy means that he is free to administer justice in ways that might not fit legal codes. This occurs, for example, in his choosing not to report the actions of guilty parties in "The Adventure of the Blue Carbuncle," "The Adventure of Charles Augustus Milverton," "The Adventure of the Priory School," and "The Adventure of the Sussex Vampire" (Conan Doyle), as well as in other cases. Because he is not part of the police or of a prosecutorial entity, he can avoid the "bloodthirsty task of punishment" (McLaughlin 44) and decide for himself how to bring justice. Even though Pendergast is an FBI agent and Goren is part of the New York police, they, too, manage to circumnavigate legalities in the quest for justice. For example, in *Still Life with Crows*, Pendergast appears in a small town that has had multiple murders and presents himself to the local sheriff as an FBI agent who is on vacation. He assures law enforcement that "I will not interfere with your investigation. I will operate independently. I will consult with you regularly and share information with you when appropriate" (25). It is worth noting that Pendergast is assuming the right to decide what constitutes appropriate information for the police. In *Cold Vengeance*, Pendergast is on a leave of absence while he investigates his wife's murder. However, he uses his potential authority as law enforcement and his family's generous charity to intimate informants. He also engages in breaking and entering, vandalism, and attacking and shooting people — all in a good cause, of course. Goren, a police officer, also takes a stance at odds with standard operating procedure. In the episode "Magnificat," Goren, thwarted in attempts to have a father prosecuted for his role in the murder of his children, assists the grandmother with securing legal aid in a custody battle for a surviving child. In "Want," Goren argues vehemently with his law enforcement colleagues for a life sentence rather than the death penalty for a serial killer. He ensures that outcome by convincing the man to confess. In "Untethered," Goren seeks answers to a murder by going undercover, against orders, in an institution for individuals who are mentally ill. This embracing of quasi-legal approaches to crime solving and justice suggest that Pendergast and Goren are very appealing Holmes surrogates for a country that is still wrestling with legal and ethical boundaries, post 9/11, of security versus individual rights. Those thorny issues have included preemptive military strikes, warrantless detentions and surveillance, free speech, and definitions of torture. In this paradigm, the extraordinary individual who is both bounded and authorized by a legal structure but is secure in making difficult judicial decisions outside of those limits would be considered heroic.

The Relationships, Including The Woman

On the personal relationship level, "Holmes lives outside conventional relationships in a society in which romantic love and family ties are so often shown to be a source of vulnerability and disorder" (Jann 75). Family ties for Holmes seem to be non-existent other than his brother, Mycroft, who is as genius and eccentric as Holmes. Watson does not even know Holmes has a brother until he appears in a case (Conan Doyle, "The Greek Interpreter" 435). There is also Holmes' cryptic remark ("Art in the blood is liable to take the strangest forms") about his talent for deduction and its connection with his lineage from a French artist's sister (Conan Doyle, "The Greek Interpreter"). For Pendergast and Goren, having "disordered" family ties that leave one "vulnerable" is a definite understatement. Pendergast's family tree is stranger than Holmes' genealogy; it includes a strong tendency for insanity as well as family members who are murderers or serial killers. Goren does not fare much better. His mother is institutionalized for schizophrenia, and his homeless brother is a drug addict with a gambling problem, who is killed by Goren's nemesis. His nephew has bipolar disorder. Goren's biological father is a serial killer.

Eschewing romantic entanglements means that a character such as the adventuress Irene Adler, who is *The Woman* in Holmes' memory and whose memento Holmes carries, is not a romantic interest (Conan Doyle, "A Scandal in Bohemia"). Also, by the end of the case she is married and fled with her husband to who-knows-where, so she is out of the picture. After all, "women who signify sexuality [as did Adler] have no place in mystery and detective fiction" (Jann 113). One reason for the absence of the feminine is Wilson's suggestion that "the sexually repressed hysterical male is more powerful, more conservative and more masculine than his married Watson-like counterpart" (38). Pendergast is also of the Holmes mold. He attributes his discomfort with physical displays of affection to his early family life (Preston and Child, *Still Life with Crows* 559). However, Pendergast was once married but is now widowed (his wife Helen supposedly dies tragically on an African safari but might have been murdered). He also has a romantic connection with Dr. Viola Maskelene, an archaeologist, but it is apparently long distance.

Other than his attention to his institutionalized mother, Goren seems to have no life, romantic or otherwise, outside of work. There is a reference to a former girlfriend ("Enemy Within"), but the one woman who does appear repeatedly in his life is his nemesis, murderer Nicole Wallace. His everyday social interactions can be grating, and even his own police partner, Eames, is put off by him as a colleague, especially in the early days of their relationship. Even Goren admits, "I am an acquired taste" ("In the Wee Small Hours").

However, it is worth observing that one way to accomplish "easing women into mystery and detective fiction ... is to dress them in the costume of the pal" (Roth 127). After all, Irene Adler dressed as a young man in order to best Holmes (Conan Doyle, "A Scandal in Bohemia"). Goren's police partner, Eames, whom he usually addresses by her surname, is slightly built and frequently wears trousers. Rarely is she seen in what would be considered particularly feminine attire. Even a pregnancy for Eames (to accommodate the pregnancy of the actress) lends her a distance from the traditional female role of mother. This pregnancy is explained as a surrogacy role for a sister, and the child is considered a nephew. Also, the relationship between Eames and Goren is friendship and not romance.

Apparently one way not to ease a woman into a detective story is to have her marry the Watson character. Watson's wife/wives were very accommodating of his returning to Baker Street to assist Holmes with various cases. D'Agosto, Pendergast's Watson-like friend, actually separates from his domestic partner in order to assist Pendergast (Preston and Child, *Dance of Death*). Goren's Watson, Eames, is a widow, so there is not a demanding spouse in the background. The romantic connections of the Watson characters serve to highlight the contrast with the Holmes characters' aloofness from ordinary human entanglements, but they also emphasize that the detective is the primary loyalty for the Watson characters.

Holmes, and readers, need that loyal pal/partner figure as part of his world. For Holmes, Watson the partner "is the hero-worshipper of boys' fiction and in *this* respect acts as a surrogate for the reader" (Roth 106). Readers know him to be supportive of Holmes, though often baffled and irritated by him. The same can be said of D'Agosto's relationship with Pendergast and Eames' relationship with Goren. The fact that Eames is a woman is a different spin on the traditional Watson figure. However, Eames is a member of a police family and appears "tomboyish" in appearance and general bearing. She is usually the "bad cop" for the good cop/bad cop interactions with suspects. Also, gender-switch possibilities have a long history in Sherlockiana, ranging from mystery writer Rex Stout's 1941 Baker Street Irregulars speech about "Watson Was a Woman?" to the 2004 university press monograph about *Ms. Holmes of Baker Street* (Bradley and Sarjeant).

In addition to a partner, Holmes needs an archenemy, and because the battle between them must be believable, the villain must match Holmes' superiority. Holmes has Moriarty, the "Napoleon of Crime" and "the organizer of half that is evil and of nearly all that is undetected" in London (Conan Doyle, "The Final Problem" 471). Holmes defeats Moriarty by throwing him into Reichenbach Falls, which does evoke the image of Lucifer being cast out of heaven. This is a battle of cosmic proportions: "There, deep down in that dreadful cauldron of swirling water and seething foam, will lie for all time the most dangerous criminal and the foremost champion of the law of their generation" (Conan Doyle, "The Final Problem" 480). Pendergast's archnemesis is his own brother, Diogenes, an insane murderer. Pendergast races to the ultimate confrontation, knowing that "one of them would walk back down the mountain; the other would be thrown into the Sciara" (Preston, *The Book of the Dead* 432). Diogenes does meet a death very similar to Moriarty's demise, except that it is not Pendergast who thrusts him off a cliff. It is Constance Greene, Pendergast's "sheltered, fragile, confused" ward, who plays out the final scene of "enemies, joined in mortal struggle, heedless of the wind, or the roar of the volcano, or the extreme peril of the cliff edge" (Preston, *The Book of the Dead* 435). Goodness, as an extension of Pendergast, has triumphed over evil. The recurring archvillain in Goren's life is a woman (not surprising because Alexandra Eames is Watson), Nicole Wallace, who has murdered multiple times, for gain and for revenge. She is a woman who has used her sexuality to seek power and wealth. She fulfills "the actions of female characters [who] almost always conform to the stereotypes that Holmes accepts: "Women ... are naturally secretive ... pertinacious, and cunning ... or have a greater capacity for anger when wronged" (Jann 107). Wallace is eventually killed by another murderer (Goren's former mentor, a psychological profiler), who reports that her last words were to tell Goren that "he's the only man I've ever loved" ("Frame"). Because one of Goren's most effective skills is using his understanding of a suspect's psychology to elicit a confession, this presumed deathbed admission is, in one sense, Wallace's fall from a cliff, albeit a psychological one. As Jann observes, "Women are allowed their female intuition ... but this is the kind of skill always conceded to primitive, untutored intellects; it is no real match for logic and reasoning" (107). At the end of her life, Wallace, who is both Moriarty and Adler, has succumbed to her emotions. This finale also spares Goren (Holmes) the ignominy of killing a woman (Moriarty). After all, this is the character about whom Watson confirmed, "he had a remarkable gentleness and courtesy in his dealings with women," and while he "disliked and distrusted" women, Holmes was "always a chivalrous opponent" (Conan Doyle, "The Adventure of the Dying Detective" 932).

Roth has said that the villain is invisible because "he or she is a split figure with two faces, and the only one showing is a face of social respectability" (148). Thus, "as a creature of multiple identities, the criminal resembles mythical and rhetorical shapeshifters" (149). Therefore, Holmes' 21st century surrogates are shapeshifters involved in deadly battles with other shapeshifters in a quest to bring justice and restore order.

Knight says that "Holmes was a hero shaped for a particular time and place, but like many other heroes he has survived out of context as a figure of heroism" (104). Holmes' survival has been bolstered by his shapeshifting into fresh guises to accommodate new nuances of time and place while retaining his own identity. More than a decade into the 21st century, Holmes is returning to America in his original identity: CBS has cast a series titled *Elementary*. In it, Holmes is seeking addiction rehabilitation in New York City, and his partner is Joan Watson, a surgeon who has lost her medical license. Cyber chatter has speculated about the potential success of the series, given the plot, the characterizations, and the casting of actors. However, the far more interesting question is, 11 years after the September 11 attacks and a year after the death of the individual who claimed to be the mastermind behind them, is an American audience ready to again believe that a freelance consulting detective, separate from law enforcement, is a bastion against the fears of a restless age? That is the conundrum in the ultimate Sherlockian "case of identity."

WORKS CITED

A.I. Artificial Intelligence. Dir. Steven Spielberg. Perf. Haley Joel Osment, Frances O'Connor, and Sam Robards. Warner, 2001. Film.

"Android." Def.1. *The Free Dictionary. The American Heritage Dictionary of the English Language,* 2000, 2009. Web. 15 Mar. 2012. <http://www.thefreedictionary.com/android>.

Avatar. Dir. James Cameron. Perf. Sam Worthington, Zoe Saldana, and Sigourney Weaver. Twentieth Century–Fox, 2009. Film.

"Avatar." Def. 3. *Merriam-Webster Dictionary.* Encyclopaedia Britannica, n.d. Web. 27 Dec. 2011. <http://www.merriam-webster.com/dictionary/avatar>.

Ayers, Jeff. "Duo Keeps Suspense Building." *Writer* 119 (July 2006): 18–22. EBSCOHost. Web. 23 Dec. 2011.

Barjenbruch, Brian. "Storyline." Rev. of *Law & Order: Criminal Intent.* IMDB, n.d. Web. 26 Dec. 2011. <http://www.imdb.com/title/tt0275140/>.

"Best Sellers." *The New York Times.* 2012. Web. 18 Mar. 2012. <http://www.nytimes.com/best-sellers-books/2012-03-04/overview.html>.

"Best-selling Books." *USA Today.* 2012. Web. 18 Mar. 2012. <http://books.usatoday.com/list/index>.

Bradley, C. Alan, and William A.S. Sarjeant. *Ms. Holmes of Baker Street: The Truth About Sherlock.* Edmonton: University of Alberta Press, 2004. Print.

Cawelti, John G. *Adventure, Mystery, and Romance: Formula Stories as Art and Popular Culture.* Chicago: University of Chicago Press, 1976. Print.

_____. "The Adventure of Charles Augustus Milverton." *The Complete Sherlock Holmes.* Garden City, NY: Doubleday, 1930. 572–82. Print.

_____. "The Adventure of the Blue Carbuncle." *The Complete Sherlock Holmes.* Garden City, NY: Doubleday, 1930. 244–57. Print.

_____. "The Adventure of the Bruce-Partington Plans." *The Complete Sherlock Holmes.* Garden City, NY: Doubleday, 1930. 913–31. Print.

_____. "The Adventure of the Cardboard Box." *The Complete Sherlock Holmes.* Garden City, NY: Doubleday, 1930. 888–901. Print.

_____. "The Adventure of the Copper Beeches." *The Complete Sherlock Holmes.* Garden City, NY: Doubleday, 1930. 316–32. Print.

_____. "The Adventure of the Dying Detective." *The Complete Sherlock Holmes.* Garden City, NY: Doubleday, 1930. 932–41. Print.

_____. "The Adventure of the Illustrious Client." *The Complete Sherlock Holmes.* Garden City, NY: Doubleday, 1930. 984–99. Print.

_____. "The Adventure of the Priory School." *The Complete Sherlock Holmes*. Garden City, NY: Doubleday, 1930. 538–58. Print.

_____. "The Adventure of the Six Napoleons." *The Complete Sherlock Holmes*. Garden City, NY: Doubleday, 1930. 582–96. Print.

_____. "The Adventure of the Solitary Cyclist." *The Complete Sherlock Holmes*. Garden City, NY: Doubleday, 1930. 526–38. Print.

_____. "The Adventure of the Sussex Vampire." *The Complete Sherlock Holmes*. Garden City, NY: Doubleday, 1930. 1033–44. Print.

_____. "The Final Problem." *The Complete Sherlock Holmes*. Garden City, NY: Doubleday, 1930. 469–80. Print.

_____. "The Five Orange Pips." *The Complete Sherlock Holmes*. Garden City, NY: Doubleday, 1930. 217–29. Print.

_____. "The 'Gloria Scott.'" *The Complete Sherlock Holmes*. Garden City, NY: Doubleday, 1930. 373–81. Print.

_____. "The Greek Interpreter." *The Complete Sherlock Holmes*. Garden City, NY: Doubleday, 1930. 435–46. Print.

_____. "A Scandal in Bohemia." *The Complete Sherlock Holmes*. Garden City, NY: Doubleday, 1930. 161–75. Print.

_____. "A Study in Scarlet." *The Complete Sherlock Holmes*. Garden City, NY: Doubleday, 1930. 15–86. Print.

Corrie Swanson's Journal. Hachette Book Group, 2012. Web. 29 Dec. 2011 <http://www.agent pendergast.com/>.

Dalrymple, Theodore. "The Eternal Detective." *National Review* 24 (31 Dec. 2009): 47+. Print.

"Dead." *Law & Order: Criminal Intent*. Season 2. NBC. 29 Sep. 2002. Television.

De Waal, Ronald B. "Introduction." *The Universal Sherlock Holmes*. Toronto: Metropolitan, 1994. Web. 30 Dec. 2011. <http://special.lib.umn.edu/rare/ush/ush.html#Introduction>.

"Enemy Within." *Law & Order: Criminal Intent*. Season 1. NBC. 9 Dec. 2001. Television.

"Frame." *Law & Order: Criminal Intent*. Season 7. USA. 24 Aug. 2008. Television.

Hockensmith, Steve. "The Eternal Detective: The Undying Appeal of Sherlock Holmes." *Mystery Scene* 93 (Winter 2006): 26–30. Print.

Horowitz, Anthony. *The House of Silk*. New York: Little, Brown, 2011. Print.

"In the Wee Small Hours (Part 2)." *Law & Order: Criminal Intent*. Season 7. USA. 24 Aug. 2008. Television.

Jann, Rosemary. *The Adventures of Sherlock Holmes: Detecting Social Order*. New York: Twayne, 1995. Print.

Kingsnorth, Gary. "Sherlock Holmes Coat." *The Style King*. 19 Feb. 2012. Web. 16 Mar. 2012. <http://www.thestyleking.com/fashion/shop-the-look/sherlock-holmes-coat/>.

Kirkpatrick, Marshall. "Google CEO Schmidt: 'People Aren't Ready for the Technology Revolution.'" *ReadWriteWeb*. 4 Aug. 2010. Web. 16 Mar. 2012. <http://www.readwriteweb.com/archives/google_ceo_schmidt_people_arent_ready_for_the_tech.php>.

Knight, Stephen. *Form and Ideology in Crime Fiction*. Bloomington: Indiana University Press, 1980. Print.

Madden, Mary, et al. "Digital Footprints." *Pew Internet*. Pew Research Center, 16 Dec. 2007. Web. 29 Dec. 2011. <http://www.pewinternet.org/Reports/2007/Digital-Footprints.aspx>.

"Magnificat." *Law & Order: Criminal Intent*. Season 4. NBC. 11 Nov. 2004. Television.

Malmgren, Carl D. *Anatomy of Murder: Mystery, Detective, and Crime Fiction*. Bowling Green, OH: Bowling Green State University Popular Press, 2001. Print.

McLaughlin, Joseph. *Writing the Urban Jungle: Reading Empire in London from Doyle to Eliot*. Charlottesville: University Press of Virginia, 2000. Print.

Metress, Christopher. "Thinking the Unthinkable: Reopening Conan Doyle's 'Cardboard Box.'" *The Midwest Quarterly* 42.2 (Winter 2001): 183–198. Print.

Meyer, Karl E. "The Curious Incident of the Sleuth in the Meantime." *The New York Times* late ed. 19 Jan. 2000. E1. EBSCOHost. Web. 4 Feb. 2008.

Microsoft Online. *Search*. Microsoft, 2012. Web. 27 Dec. 2011. <http://office.microsoft.com/clip art/default.aspx?lc=en-us>.

Mitchell, Gladys. *Watson's Choice.* New York: McKay, 1976. Print.

Moorman, Charles. "The Appeal of Sherlock Holmes." *The Southern Quarterly* 14 (1976): 71–82. Print.

Morley, Christopher. "In Memoriam Sherlock Holmes." *The Standard Doyle Company: Christopher Morley on Sherlock Holmes.* Ed. Steven Rothman. New York: Fordham University Press, 1990. 27–36. Print.

Neary, Lynn. "The Enduring Popularity of Sherlock Holmes." *NPR Books.* 19 Dec. 2011. Web. 31 Dec. 2011. <http://www.npr.org/2011/12/19/143954262/the-enduring-popularity-of-sherlock-holmes>.

Nebbett, Adrian. *Sherlock Holmes Pastiche Characters.* Nebbett, n.d. Web. 28 Dec. 2011. <http://www.schoolandholmes.com>.

"One." *Law & Order: Criminal Intent.* Season 1. NBC. 30 Sep. 2001. Television.

Petridis, Alexis. "No Chic, Sherlock." 3 Sep. 2010. Web. 14 Mar. 2012. <http://www.guardian.co.uk/lifeandstyle/2010/sep/04/sherlock-fashion-mens-coats>.

Porter, Dennis. *The Pursuit of Crime: Art and Ideology in Detective Fiction.* New Haven, CT: Yale University Press, 1981. Print.

Preston, Douglas, and Lincoln Child. "Authors Preston & Child Interview Special Agent Pendergast." *The Authors.* Hachette Book Group, 31 Aug. 2004. Web. 30 Dec. 2011. <http://www.hachettebookgroup.com/Douglas_Preston_(1014132)_ Article(1).aspx>.

_____. *The Book of the Dead.* New York: Warner, 2006. Print.

_____. *Brimstone.* New York: Warner, 2005. Print.

_____. *The Cabinet of Curiosities.* New York: Warner, 2003. Print.

_____. *Cold Vengeance.* New York: Grand Central, 2011. Print.

_____. *Dance of Death.* New York: Warner, 2006. Print.

_____. *Fever Dream.* New York: Grand Central, 2010. Print.

_____. *The Relic.* New York: Tor, 1995. Print.

_____. *Reliquary.* New York: Forge, 1997. Print.

_____. *Still Life with Crows.* New York: Warner, 2004. Print.

_____. *The Wheel of Darkness.* New York: Warner, 2007. Print.

"PW Forecasts." Rev. of *Brimstone,* Douglas Preston and Lincoln Child. *Publishers Weekly* (5 July 2004): 36. Print.

Rauber, D.F. "Sherlock Holmes and Nero Wolfe: The Role of the 'Great Detective' in Intellectual History." *Journal of Popular Culture* 6.3 (Spring 1973): 483–95. Print.

Real Steel. Dir. Shawn Levy. Perf. Hugh Jackman, Evangeline Lilly, and Dakota Goyo. Dreamworks, 2011. Film.

"Reviews." Rev. of *The Dance of Death,* by Douglas Preston and Lincoln Child. *Publishers Weekly.* 23 May 2005: 59. Print.

Roberts, Nancy. "Aloysius Pendergast, the Modern Sherlock Holmes." *When in Doubt, Read!* 19 Aug. 2006. Web. 19 Mar. 2012.

Roth, Marty. *Foul & Fair Play: Reading Genre in Classic Detective Fiction.* Athens: University of Georgia Press, 1995. Print.

Sabreanimal4180. "We Are Seeing the Very Death of Creativity." *Law & Order: Criminal Intent Fan Reviews.* TV.com. 13 Dec. 2011. Web. 18 Mar. 2012 <http://www.tv.com/shows/law-order-criminal-intent/reviews/>.

"Second Life." Linden Research, n.d. Web. 29 Dec. 2011. <http://secondlife.com>.

Sherlock. Writ. Mark Gatiss and Steven Moffat. BBC, 2010, 2012. Television.

Sherlock Holmes. Dir. Guy Ritchie. Perfs. Robert Downey, Jr., Jude Law, and Rachel McAdams. Warner, 2009. Film.

Sherlock Holmes: A Game of Shadows. Dir. Guy Ritchie. Perf. Robert Downey, Jr., Jude Law, and Noomi Rapace. Warner, 2011. Film.

Sherlockian Who's Who.com. *Sherlockian Who's Who.* 2002–2008. Web. 29 Dec. 2011. <http://www.sh-whoswho.com/ index.php?refsociety=332>.

Stout, Rex. "Watson Was a Woman?" *The Wolfe Pack.* 4 June 2005. Web. 27 Dec. 2011. <http://www.nerowolfe.org/htm/stout/ Watson_was_a_woman.htm>.

Strebeigh, Fred. "To His Modern Fans, Sherlock Is Still Worth a Close Look." *Smithsonian* 17.9 (Dec. 1986): 60–68. Print.

"Surrogate." Def. 1. *The Free Dictionary. The American Heritage Dictionary of the English Language,* 2000, 2009. Web. 15 Mar. 2012. <http://www.thefreedictionary.com/surrogate>.

Symons, Julian. *Bloody Murder: From the Detective Story to the Crime Novel: A History.* Rev. updated ed. New York: Viking, 1985. Print.

Twilight. Dir. Catherine Hardwicke. Perf. Kristen Stewart and Robert Pattinson. Summit, 2008. Film.

The Twilight Saga: Breaking Dawn, Part 1. Dir. Bill Condon. Perf. Kristen Stewart and Robert Pattinson. Summit, 2011. Film.

The Twilight Saga: Eclipse. Dir. David Slade. Perf. Kristen Stewart and Robert Pattinson. Summit, 2010. Film.

The Twilight Saga: New Moon. Dir. Chris Weitz. Perf. Kristen Stewart and Robert Pattinson. Summit, 2009. Film.

"Untethered." *Law & Order: Criminal Intent.* Season 7. USA. 6 Dec. 2007. Television.

USA. "Law & Order: Criminal Intent." *NBC Universal,* 2011. Web. 28 Dec. 2011. <http://www.usanetwork.com/series/criminalintent/>.

USA. "Law & Order: Criminal Intent [Mash-ups]." *NBC Universal,* 2006. Web. 28 Dec. 2011. <http://mashups.usanetwork.com/ci/>.

"Want." *Law & Order: Criminal Intent.* Season 4. NBC. 10 Oct. 2004. Television.

Whitenack, Susan C. "Law & Order: CI, Season One — One of the Best Series Ever." *Customer Reviews Law & Order Criminal Intent—The First Year.* Amazon.com. 4 Oct. 2011. Web. 18 Mar. 2012. <http://www.amazon.com/Law-Order-Criminal-Intent-First/product-reviews/B0000AVHCD/ref=cm_cr_dp_all_helpful?ie= UTF8&showViewpoints=1&sortBy=bySubmissionDateDescending>.

Wilson, Frances. "A Case of Identity: Tracking Down Sherlock Holmes." *Weber Studies* 12.2 (Spr.-Sum. 1995): 29–46. Print.

Wolf, Dick. "Dick Wolf. Chapter 7." *Archive of American Television.* Television Academy Foundation, 2003. Web. 28 Dec. 2011. <http://www.emmytvlegends.org/interviews/people-/dick-wolf>.

Young, Alex. "Video: Patti Smith's Appearance on *Law & Order: CI. Consequence of Sound.*" Complex Media Network. 20 June 2011. Web. 31 Dec. 2011. <http://consequenceofsound.net/2011/06/video-patti-smiths-appearance-on-law-and-order-ci/>.

Zakheim, Dov S. "What 9/11 Has Wrought." *Middle East Quarterly* 18.4 (Fall 2011): 3–13. *EBSCOhost.* Web. 29 Dec. 2011.

8

The Process of Elimination
The Americanization of Sherlock Holmes

LYNNETTE PORTER

> "Once you eliminate the impossible, whatever remains, however improbable, must be the truth."
> — *Sherlock Holmes*

Perhaps the editors who prepared the BBC's *Sherlock* episodes for U.S. broadcast on PBS misread (or edited) this famous quotation. They may not have eliminated the impossible, but they did remove or change some scenes that illuminate character relationships and allow audiences a more complete, or truthful, understanding of this adaptation's Sherlock Holmes and John Watson. Whatever remains in the U.S.-broadcast episodes offers one version of the "truth," but, alas, it is not the whole story broadcast by the BBC.

When *Sherlock* debuted in the U.S., American audiences were introduced to a slightly different Sherlock Holmes than the one who made himself at home in living rooms across the U.K. Although he was undoubtedly welcomed on both sides of the pond, as evidenced by numerous awards and a plethora of new fan sites on both continents, British Sherlock and John talk and sometimes behave a bit differently on U.K. television screens than they do in the U.S. Although devoted fans buy the series' DVDs, Blu-ray discs, or digital copies of full episodes as they were broadcast in the U.K., American audiences who only watch the PBS-broadcast versions see an abbreviated *Sherlock*, one in which nuances of Sherlock Holmes' or John Watson's character — as well as that of secondary characters Mrs. Hudson and Inspector Sally Donovan — are lost in the translation from BBC to PBS, Britain to America.

Hartswood Films produces *Sherlock,* and Sue Vertue oversees the edits made for the PBS version for time, not, PBS assures viewers, to censor or Americanize episodes. U.S. fans worry that Sherlock's Britishness may be watered down when he loses British vocabulary as well as when his deductive methods are simplified in order to make plots shorter. Actor Benedict Cumberbatch even stated at a PBS event that he wants U.S. fans to see the complete episodes.

Editors who trimmed *Sherlock* episodes for U.S. viewers are not the only ones who have been "Americanizing" the great detective in the past few years. With the success of the BBC's television series, U.S. network CBS apparently decided it wanted to clone Sherlock Holmes for U.S. audiences. After approaching the executive producers of *Sherlock* about remaking the series in the U.S. and having their request turned down, CBS went forward with its own version — recovering addict and former Scotland Yard consultant Sherlock Holmes moves to New York. Whether in a U.S. television series or one edited to fit the needs of PBS, Holmes is becoming a different man via his "Americanization," leading to some cultural concerns — by American and British audiences — about the transatlantic transformation of Sherlock Holmes.

Making a Literary Character Accessible to Fans Old and New

Sherlock's creators, Steven Moffat and Mark Gatiss, anticipated an international audience of newcomers as well as a homegrown Holmes fanbase. The first episode in the new series, "A Study in Pink," provides a comfort zone for Sherlock Holmes fans familiar with the original stories and later adaptations as well as viewers new both to this television series or Holmes. The first episode's title is a variation of *A Study in Scarlet*, Conan Doyle's 1887 novel that introduced Sherlock Holmes to readers; it is an appropriate choice for the episode that introduces 21st century Sherlock to television audiences. The murdered "pink" lady reflects not only a color and story connection with the original text but twists the tale into a modern commentary about eye-catching colors for women working in the media and the victim's need to be perfectly groomed and color coordinated in order to be acceptable for her job and her lovers. Even her accessories, such as a mobile phone, are in, as Sherlock says, "an alarming shade of pink."

In every version of this episode, whether broadcast in the U.K. or internationally, in edited or full format, the story begins not with Sherlock but with John Watson, who becomes the character with whom the audience is expected to identify and thus is an appropriate entry character to get viewers involved with the story. John's flashback to an Afghani war zone, also appropriate to the original Watson's war record (another plus for traditional Holmes fans), makes him a sympathetic modern character who might be a returned veteran like someone viewers know in real life. The news-style flashback modernizes Watson's pre–Sherlock experiences, as does his visit with his therapist and comments about writing a blog. His final line before the opening credits, "Nothing ever happens to me," may be appropriate for the couch potatoes watching this episode; vicariously, their lives, too, are about to change as they enter the world of Sherlock's adventures. The opening theme immediately follows this line, overlaying the rush of London traffic and pulling John, and the viewers, into the story. They, walking alongside Watson, become pulled into Sherlock's world, learning a lot about the detective's "science of deduction" as well as his personal history within the scope of the first episode.

Beyond the television series, new viewers can also "play Watson" by visiting Sherlock's website, The Science of Deduction, which looks just as it does on television. During "A Study in Pink," John tells his potential flatmate that he has read his website in order to learn more about the detective. Skeptical John has Sherlock verify his methods and explain just what the "science of deduction" means. Again, John asks questions partly on behalf of new viewers who also want to know Sherlock.

Missing Scenes from the PBS Episodes

The PBS broadcasts in October–November 2010 provided specifically American-oriented episodes that differed from the version shown on BBC in the U.K. a few months earlier. In addition to Holmes 101 provided by *Mystery!* host Alan Cumming, the U.S.-broadcast episodes were edited or dialogue changed to fit the PBS program's format, which required some edits for time. What was left out or altered from the British-broadcast version provides some interesting commentary about the way British audiences were expected to perceive this new Sherlock and different expectations of American audiences' knowledge of the original text or recent adaptations. The edited scenes may lead to American audiences (or other international audiences who watch edited versions of the original BBC episodes) to develop a different understanding of the main and secondary characters. More specifically, the edits that reflect different cultural familiarity with everything from regional dialect to vocabulary indicate differences between British and American frames of reference. What may be familiar to U.K. viewers may seem foreign or exotic to Americans, adding another element of "otherness" or perhaps mystique to Sherlock.

Time allowances for episodes vary among networks as well as nations. With the inclusion of an introductory segment, as well as the typical *Masterpiece Mystery!* opening and closing credits and previews, PBS needed to broadcast an edited version of the episodes shown in their entirety on the BBC. To be fair, many scenes, such as Sherlock and John's silent taxi ride in "The Great Game," are unnecessary for audiences to understand the plot. In "The Blind Banker," a scene regarding a murdered woman, Soo Lin, is deleted, perhaps because only the actors-of-the-week playing peripheral characters have dialogue that is not necessary for the audience to understand the mystery.

Some scenes missing from or truncated in the PBS version, however, provide insight into the relationship between Sherlock and John or the development of their individual characters. To serve the plot (and the need for a streamlined story), character moments or elongated scenes without dialogue often are sacrificed. Most casual viewers would never know the difference, but their understanding of Sherlock, in particular, as well as the Holmes-Watson dynamic, is nonetheless different from that of viewers who saw every scene as it was meant to be shown uncut on BBC (or on DVD).

Missing scenes involving Sherlock himself are, understandably, fewer than those involving secondary characters like Sally Donovan or Mrs. Hudson. Even so, Sherlock's intense focus when he tries to solve a forensic puzzle and his painstaking attention to detail are minimized when a few such scenes have been cut. The PBS episode "The Blind Banker" reduces the length of a scene in which Sherlock studiously prepares and then studies slides under a microscope. Although the basic action — Sherlock in the lab — is shown, the shortened scene does not allow U.S. audiences to understand the depth of Holmes' immersion in his work and the breadth of his lab skills.

A more critical difference is a missing scene from "The Great Game" in which Sherlock receives a phone call providing him the clue that a car rental company's name will help him solve a missing person's case. The big hint about the Janus car company's name helps Sherlock understand the owner's duplicity. In the PBS version, however, Sherlock never receives this phone call. The plot skips ahead to John, Inspector Lestrade, and Sherlock discussing the car company and searching for clues. Sherlock comments on the double meaning behind the company's name — Janus is a two-faced god, just like the company's owner has both a legitimate and a shady side. Without the audience's awareness of the clue given to Sherlock in the phone call (although the detective has to make sense of it on his own), the American audience sees Sherlock solving this part of the puzzle without assistance from the mysterious caller.

Whereas Sherlock often seems to jump to brilliant deductions even more quickly in the U.S. than in the U.K. episode, poor John suffers by comparison. A long scene in which he investigates a murder on his own is cut from the U.S. version of "The Great Game"; John's competence in asking questions and gathering information — as well as his expressions during the scene and the way in which he looks for evidence — illustrate aspects of his character not seen in previous scenes or episodes. Again, the scene is unnecessary for plot development, but it does strengthen audience's impression of John as an equal partner. It emphasizes John's independence and his ability to work well out of his normal fields of expertise. Furthermore, it allows viewers to see John as an individual character, not only part of the Sherlock-and-John partnership shown in the majority of scenes in which Watson is involved.

In another scene of secondary importance to the plot but important to the development of John's character, Sally Donovan engages Watson in conversation. The characters' dialogue bookends an important scene in "The Blind Banker" that showcases Sherlock's deductive skills. When Sherlock and John arrive at a crime scene, the detective joins Lestrade to analyze the inside of a missing man's car. Sally detains John for a moment to remind him that Sherlock will be bad for him, a follow-up bit of dialogue from the first episode, "A Study in Pink," in which she warns John to stay away from Sherlock. She suggests several possible hobbies John might take up in lieu of following Sherlock and implies that their relationship has grown too close. John reminds her that he and Sherlock are not a couple but otherwise ignores her comments. At the conclusion of the longer investigative scene, Sally reminds John that he should take up fishing. In the PBS version, Sally is all but eliminated from the longer investigative scene. She only is given a command by Lestrade, and all conversation between Sally and John has been removed.

Once more, the missing dialogue would not move the plot forward and simply reinforces a scene in the first episode. The reinforcement in the second episode reminds viewers that John stays with Sherlock despite such warnings, even though he has had more time to get to know his flatmate and presumably become better acquainted with his personality quirks. John's loyalty and the strength of his friendship with Sherlock are underscored in scenes like these, unlike the U.S. version portraying the friendship as a given, without the stress of social disapproval. That John makes a conscious choice to stay in this friendship and to help Sherlock with his investigations adds depth to the characterization, instead of making John seem to be a mere tagalong who obediently follows wherever Sherlock directs him.

Sally may have two strikes against her, being a secondary character with a strong accent (to American ears), but even Mrs. Hudson, a more familiar character to those who have read the Conan Doyle stories, often finds her scenes edited from the Americanized episodes. During "The Great Game," Lestrade and Mrs. Hudson discuss a murdered television celebrity as they watch an episode of the woman's makeover show. Mrs. Hudson has watched the program many times and, in the PBS version of this episode, merely makes a concluding comment before Sherlock, who has been talking on the phone, re-enters the scene.

The conversation between Lestrade and Mrs. Hudson provides no new clues about the murderer and seems to be filler. The edited dialogue does, however, suggest that Lestrade and Mrs. Hudson have gotten to know each other a bit better and are part of Sherlock's closest circle of acquaintances, if not friends. They certainly seem much more at ease with each other than on the night of Lestrade's drug raid on Sherlock's flat, shown in "A Study in Pink."

The brief scene also solidifies viewers' understanding that Mrs. Hudson generally has time on her hands to watch the program, as John alludes to in an earlier scene. However, in that scene John indicates that he only ends up watching what he later calls "crap telly" with Mrs. Hudson because he has been unemployed. The unedited scene's conversation between Lestrade and Mrs. Hudson helps create an image of her as a homebody, certainly, but one who is astute and discerning. Her comments indicate that she thinks about the programs she watches and is aware of details. Her comfort in talking with Lestrade and Sherlock also helps audiences understand that Sherlock's landlady is very much aware of her tenant's investigation.

When her lines are cut from scenes in the PBS version, Mrs. Hudson truly seems to be only a background character who is no more useful than to make tea or periodically check on her tenants. The BBC version illustrates that she is much more aware of Sherlock's activities and feels comfortable not only in spending time with John or conversing with Lestrade but in being a part of Sherlock's life. This understanding is an important story element to help viewers understand why Mrs. Hudson bothers putting up with Sherlock's rude putdowns (e.g., in the drug raid scene during "A Study in Pink" when he snaps that Mrs. Hudson should go away and take her "herbal soothers") or his mistreatment of her flat (e.g., when Sherlock shoots holes in her wall during "The Great Game"). Although only a few lines have been cut here or there, these conversational "fillers" often make a cumulative great deal of difference to an audience's understanding not only of secondary characters but of the main characters' relationship with them.

Perhaps the most troubling edited scenes are those that help build a more complex understanding of the Sherlock–John dynamic. Scenes in which Sherlock and John squabble — whether over the content of John's case blogs or the choice of information stored on Sherlock's "hard drive" of a brain — have been kept in the PBS version, although they, like edited or missing scenes, often do not advance the plot. Sometimes a scene from the PBS version, such as the previously mentioned silent taxi ride, provides a needed break in the action, during which Sherlock and John seem lost in their own thoughts while London passes by their windows. That the pair could share a comfortable silence helps audiences gain a better understanding of the complexity of their relationship.

When the two do converse about a case, only the most pertinent "clue" scenes have been retained in the PBS version, but the BBC episodes provide several longer scenes in which John and Sherlock discuss a current case, whether they are walking down the street or going over documents in their flat. During these discussions, John is clearly as interested as Sherlock in their investigations and is equally involved in solving the case. The body language in each scene (e.g., John leaning over Sherlock's shoulder to look at a document ["The Blind Banker"]; Sherlock standing next to John, who is seated at the kitchen table, while they sip tea and talk; the pair walking in step as they head to a suspect's home ["The Great Game"]) illustrates how close the two have become and how comfortable they are in each other's personal space — without any sexual overtones. The dialogue provides mutually shared information; John is astute in making conclusions from myriad facts and helps Sherlock link facts to form meaningful hypotheses or deducing the truth. From these scenes audiences understand that the two are equals, which makes their criticism of each other more acceptable and less scathing. Audiences better understand why they put up with each other when clearly they have different social and professional skills and values.

A long scene deleted from the PBS version of "The Blind Banker" is perhaps the best example of different interpretations of a scene solely because of the way the characters' dialogue and actions have been edited for different audiences. The edit does not affect an audience's ultimate understanding of the mystery. However, this scene, more than others edited for U.S. audiences, reveals Sherlock's growing understanding of John's common-sense approach to investigation and the detective's ability to rely on his flatmate — Sherlock does not have to be in control of all evidence but can, in fact, trust John to assist him. The equality between the two characters is strengthened in this scene not only by their dialogue and actions but the way the actors' performances provide subtext to this scene.

In the BBC version, one night Sherlock and John hunt for clues among graffiti painted along tunnels and on buildings in a derelict area. They split up, each searching for specific markings. John finds what they have been looking for — specific symbols painted all along a wall. The limited light throws harsh shadows on John's face, but he is clearly excited by finding this evidence and calls out for Sherlock, who is nowhere to be seen. The scene cuts to Sherlock, busily scanning a tunnel lined with graffiti. When John runs into frame, clearly out of breath, he mentions that he has been searching for Sherlock for the past ten minutes. Sherlock and John quickly return to the graffiti they need to study, but, when they arrive, the wall has been repainted, and the evidence is gone. Naturally, John is dismayed, but a concerned Sherlock explains that someone does not want him to see the graffiti — clearly, it must be important, and John's discovery would have helped him solve the case.

Sherlock suddenly invades John's personal space and clasps his hands around John's face, forcing him to look at the detective and give him his full attention. Sherlock shushes John and commands him to concentrate. John does not seem angry or upset but simply startled. He asks Sherlock what he is doing. "We need to maximize your visual memory," the detective explains, as he walks John through the exercise. Sherlock insistently asks whether John can describe the graffiti, which John assures him he can. Sherlock persists, noting that most people only can accurately recall 62 percent of what they see; he clearly doubts John's memory.

During this exchange, Sherlock turns the two, so that they are revolving, connected by Sherlock's hands on John's face. John finally stops the agitated, skeptical Sherlock so that he can pull his mobile phone from his pocket. Resourceful John snapped a photograph of the wall, clearly revealing the evidence painted on it.

Sherlock's reaction shot provides an "ah ha" moment for the detective — John did not let him down, and he provides the information in an unexpected way. Usually Sherlock is the one who is more comfortable with technology and uses it to solve puzzles; John is usually the one who relies on "human" (e.g., memory) solutions to problems. During this scene, their methods are reversed. Whereas Sherlock assumes John humanly will rely only on memory, John very practically uses the technology at hand — a mobile phone camera — to capture the clues and give Sherlock what he needs. Sherlock's sudden silence and downward glance illustrate his humbled awareness that John is an equal partner in this investigation.

John only seems annoyed when Sherlock fails to listen to him and will not let him reach for his mobile. He does not seem surprised or bothered by Sherlock's invasion of his personal space. John's acceptance of Sherlock's quirks, his failure to be offended when Sherlock takes control of the situation, and his persistence in getting Sherlock to listen to him all indicate his equality in this strange partnership. John is never bullied or cowed; he stands up to Sherlock in big and small ways, as evidenced in this scene. Instead of the louder, more confrontational scenes which are left in the PBS version, these quieter but no less important interactions let audiences come to understand, just as Sherlock does, John's immense value in this partnership.

Fans looking for "slashy" (i.e., same-gender romantic) moments in *Sherlock* are likely to read a sexual subtext into this scene, which may be one reason why it was cut from the PBS version. Americans seem to be titillated by possible homoerotic scenes, even if the scenes do not have an overtly sexual context. Seldom if ever on a U.S. detective series would the primary investigator clasp his partner's face in his hands and dance him in a circle to get his full attention and concentration — in short, to block out all other stimuli but the investigator's presence and questions. American audiences might read far too much into Sherlock's "touching" behavior.

The small edits that further illustrate John and Sherlock's equal partnership and emphasize John's "credentials" began almost immediately in Season Two episodes. Of course, by the time U.S. PBS stations showed the next three *Sherlock* episodes in May 2012, many of the series' fans had already found other ways to watch them. Originally broadcast in the U.K. in January and shown around the world before coming to the U.S., hardcore American fans either had downloaded episodes or found other ways to watch them illegally or had purchased U.K. region DVDs, which became available late in January. Casual viewers who only see the PBS version are most likely to watch only one version and have a limited understanding of the characters' development during Season Two, whereas serious fans either do not watch the PBS version because they already have seen the episodes before they were edited, or they become more aware of changes made to the U.S. broadcast version.

In the months leading to the U.S. debut of Season Two, PBS included a scene from "A Scandal in Belgravia" on their website to tease audiences eager to see the new episodes. The selected scene shows John and Sherlock individually being summoned to Buckingham Palace, a quintessential British setting. Like John, audiences (perhaps particularly non–British viewers) are supposed to be awed by or curious about what goes on inside the palace. Throughout most of the scene, Sherlock is draped only in a sheet; he refuses to get dressed to go to see the Queen, although his clothes have accompanied him. When John arrives and sits down near Sherlock, he cannot help but notice his flatmate's attire. After a closer look, he asks "Are you wearing any pants?" Sherlock admits he is not, and both dissolve into giggles. Although Sherlock is obviously nude under the sheet (a fact that is made apparent when Mycroft neatly steps on it and causes a departing Sherlock to lose his grip on the material), the edited version shows the slipping sheet and a brief glimpse of Sherlock's backside. The dialogue even retains "pants," although not every American viewer might associate "pants" with boxers or briefs but instead think of slacks or trousers. Mycroft's later use of "trousers" as he hands Sherlock his clothes clarifies any difference between U.S. and U.K. definitions of "pants."

However, the edited trailer slights John when Mycroft introduces a high-level official who represents the Queen. Sherlock is rather dubiously introduced by an embarrassed Mycroft, and the PBS version then cuts to the more important information about the case. John's introduction has been deleted. As in the first season's edits, the few missing lines add no meaningful content about the mystery, but they do add depth to John's characterization and, early in the second season, reinforce the established equality between John and Sherlock.

In the BBC version, when Mycroft begins to introduce John to the equerry, the official immediately recognizes John and interrupts Mycroft to let John know that he values the veteran's experience. He notes John is a Captain in the Fifth Northumberland Fusiliers, which pleases John. That the Queen's representative knows who he is and seems pleased to meet him reinforces the audience's understanding that John is an important man beyond his association with Sherlock Holmes and, further, that he is a war veteran recognized for serving Queen and country. The fact that the representative's demeanor changes immediately from commiseration with Mycroft over his socially embarrassing little brother to pride and enthusiasm in meeting John also reminds audiences that John's strengths are very different from Sherlock's but equally useful; the pair balance each other. Understandably, for time constraints, the PBS version emphasizes Sherlock's character and, as soon as possible, returns to the plot and the reason for Sherlock's summons to Buckingham Palace. However, by deleting John's introduction, the PBS trailer makes him seem unworthy of the official's notice — he is not even introduced — and emphasizes only Sherlock's importance in this meeting.

What Did He Say? Sherlock's *Vocabulary*

Although missing or truncated scenes are likely removed for practical purposes, they still alter audiences' interpretation of characters. A more specific cultural change for Americans regards the dialogue changed to ensure that Americans can make sense of a plot point (as in the clarification of "pants" with Mycroft's following use of "trousers"). What Americans are likely to understand about British slang or customs is just as important to consider as what they likely will not understand.

The most blatant dialogue substitution occurs in "The Blind Banker," in a follow-up scene after Sherlock takes John to meet an informant, a graffiti specialist Sherlock needs to identify the style and artist behind a series of spray-painted messages. The informant is spray painting the back of the National Gallery when Sherlock finds him. During their discussion, the police show up and spot the vandalism. Because John is holding a spray-paint can when the police arrive, after Sherlock and the informant run away when they see the police coming, John is detained and faces a court hearing the following week.

In the BBC version, upon arriving home to find an unconcerned Sherlock waiting for him, John explodes in anger. "They gave me an ASBO, Sherlock!" he fumes. An Anti-Social Behavior Order would clearly affect John's ability to find a new job and make him far more legally suspect regarding Sherlock's investigations. It basically gives him a criminal record.

Americans likely are not familiar with the term ASBO or its ramifications. Instead of dubbing the dialogue with a voiceover, the scene apparently was filmed two ways, one with an eye toward international distribution. In the PBS version, John yells, "They gave me community service, Sherlock!" Of course, John would be upset about having to do community service, although it would be legally preferable to jail time. As a former soldier and a doctor, John seems to be all about service, and the Americanized requirement of community service adds insult to perhaps a lesser legal injury.

Surprisingly, other British-isms were not cut or reshot to make sense to Americans. Terms like "bloody" or even "shag" are common enough not to need translation, although the impact of British swear words is probably lost on Americans. When Inspector Dimmock calls Sherlock "an arrogant sod," the context is certainly clear. Similarly, Sherlock's use of "quid" is easily understood in context. Language differences do not seem to be a major issue, either because of context or Americans' assumed familiarity with terms heard in films or on other television shows. Only specific cultural references, such as ASBO, have been filmed differently instead of overdubbed.

Although the occasional term replacement may be necessary for non–British audiences to understand *Sherlock*'s plot, the more subtle, but more serious changes involve editing episodes for time constraints imposed outside the U.K. Through these changes, audiences develop a different understanding of each character and the Sherlock-John dynamic.

The American Audience and the Future of Sherlock

BBC Showcase is an annual event designed to help the BBC brand its programming and sell series to new markets. In early 2010 Benedict Cumberbatch and Martin Freeman helped sell *Sherlock* by being charming during interviews. Potential buyers liked the actors as well as the product. In 2010 *Sherlock* already benefited from good reviews of the first season (and its many awards and nominations), which not only helped further increase *Sherlock*'s sales but buoyed sales of other BBC dramas. Writing that the "all-conquering *Sherlock*" built "a serious buzz among the world's broadcasters," Andrew Laughlin reported that the series was the fourth highest rated drama during 2010 in Australia and France. Marketing research by BBC Worldwide's Helen Kellie helped develop a global strategy for introducing *Sherlock* and other BBC programming to international markets; so far, the plan appears to be working.

The news was even better when BBC Worldwide held its annual showcase in 2012. *Sherlock*'s Mrs. Hudson (Una Stubbs) did the honors of talking with broadcasters; the series' stars Cumberbatch and Freeman were overseas filming movies, a further testament to their and the series' growing international popularity. Worldwide's director of investment and content acquisitions, Caroline Torrance, reported that "crime drama captures the imagination of TV audiences all around the world, and is a perennial best seller for us." By the end of the 2012 sales event, *Sherlock* had been sold to 200 territories (Clarke). *Sherlock* was one of three of Worldwide's best-selling series overseas (*Doctor Who* and *Top Gear* were the other two). The series' global sales is one reason why BBC Worldwide could report "a record underlying profit up 10 percent year on year to £1.16" billion, another record amount (Syal).

Although *Sherlock's* global domination of drama programming might be on the BBC's to-do list, Kellie, who is in charge of branding BBC series, called the U.S. market "far and away the biggest media market" and the one to conquer. Fortunately, *Sherlock* "really worked in this market; we made it a key show and it will work in other markets. The excitement we have had from the buyers is immense" (Costa).

Although other markets in Europe, Asia, and South America also are targeted for BBC programming, the U.S. provides special benefits and challenges. The American market is huge, but U.S. television production also is a massive industry, and a BBC program like *Sherlock* faces a much more competitive U.S. market than it does when it travels to other countries with a less dominant television industry. To attract an older audience more interested in programming that is smart but possibly irreverent — what Kellie has identified as the U.S. audience most likely to watch BBC dramas — involves what the *Marketing Week* article called "culturally contextualizing" a series' format while retaining its basic concept. Kellie was quoted as explaining her job as "build-[ing] global scale and consistency, but ultimately I want a particular consumer in a particular city to love what I am doing. It has to connect with them on the ground in a real way, locally" (Costa).

Variety in cultural interpretations of dialogue and action sequences also is enhanced by what audiences do *not* see, because they watch edited versions of BBC episodes. Whether a word has been changed here or there or entire scenes deleted has a cumulative impact on audiences' understanding of the characters and their relationships. Although viewers' understanding of the plot may not suffer, their developing perspective of the "true" nature of each character lacks some important information contained in even the most ordinary of "filler" scenes.

The resulting "Americanized" Sherlock reflects a slightly different culture via changes designed to make the detective more attractive to a wider audience. His sexuality is emphasized at times (e.g., Alan Cumming's introduction to the series, in which he asks whether Sherlock is straight, gay, or bisexual), going beyond the series' "text" and its sexual commentary and innuendo. Action takes precedence over quiet moments, case discussions, or lab time; Sherlock's methods and the time needed to make deductions are streamlined so that the detective seems to solve cases faster. The changes may be subtle, but they customize Sherlock for the American audience.

Whether looking to the U.S. as a secondary market for its London- or Cardiff-based productions or seeking partners to help shoulder the cost of making high-quality television, the BBC recently has turned to international networks or production companies in order to make some of its most highly anticipated dramas. The well-publicized partnership between U.S. cable network Starz and the BBC to produce *Torchwood: Miracle Day* was successful but not the ratings blockbuster either company had hoped for. Nevertheless, partnerships with foreign investors seem to be business as usual these days. During a British Film Institute screening of *Sherlock*'s "A Scandal in Belgravia" in December 2011, a BBC representative touted not only the highly anticipated new episodes of *Sherlock* but promoted series' star Benedict Cumberbatch's new project for the BBC: a miniseries of Tom Stoppard's *Parade's End*. When the miniseries finished shooting and began post-production a few weeks later, the BBC proudly announced that "*Parade's End* is a flagship drama for BBC and [American cable network] HBO and now in association with ARTE. The digital channel is home to cultural and arts programming and is broadcast across France." The press release ("BBC Worldwide") further notes other partners in the venture: "BBC Worldwide is the international distributor for *Parade's End* and as part of its co-venture with Lookout Point, both companies are co-producers. This is the first project to be co-produced and distributed under the new co-venture between BBC Worldwide and Lookout Point," a London-based business that promotes itself as a "global co-production company."

With the financial climate in the 2010s and the BBC's well-publicized cutbacks, a television series like *Sherlock* stands to make a great deal of money in an international marketplace *if* it first can garner the budget required to produce it. Another consideration for this production is the exponentially increasing popularity not only of stars Benedict Cumberbatch (*War Horse; Tinker, Tailor, Soldier, Spy; Frankenstein; The Hobbit*) and Martin Freeman (Bilbo in Peter Jackson's two *Hobbit* films) but of showrunner Steven Moffat (*Doctor Who; The Adventures of Tintin*). A production like *Sherlock*, even when limited to three 90-minute episodes every two years, may feel obligated to cater to international audiences — particularly those represented by its financial partners — and thus edit or even script episodes with international distribution more clearly in mind. Although *Sherlock* was not required to learn "American" during subsequent episodes, the quintessential British character Sherlock

Holmes was destined to speak American English when he moved to New York City for an American television pilot filmed in spring 2012: *Elementary*.

Cloning Sherlock

When CBS announced a much-hyped pilot of its own modern day Sherlock Holmes series, *Elementary, Sherlock* producer Sue Vertue immediately tweeted her displeasure: "Mmm interesting CBS, I'm surprised no one has thought of making a modern day version of Sherlock before, oh hang on, we have!" In an interview with *The Independent,* Vertue explains that CBS approached the BBC series' creators about developing an American version of the British hit. When the producers declined, CBS went forward with their own series. Vertue responded by telling the media that the *Sherlock* creative team would be watching the CBS pilot very closely for any infringement of copyright. After all, the original CBS description of Sherlock Holmes living in a major metropolis in 2012 sounded terribly familiar. However, by the time casting for the CBS series was completed and details of the pilot announced to the media, *Elementary* began to seem far more like a typical CBS detective procedural series (e.g., *CSI*) or even a possible romantic drama (e.g., *Moonlighting*) than the BBC's *Sherlock*.

Stunt casting took the form of Jonny Lee Miller, who, along with the BBC's Sherlock, Benedict Cumberbatch, alternated roles in the National Theatre's *Frankenstein* a year earlier. Of course, British actor Miller is well known to American audiences who enjoyed his work as the lead character in ABC's *Eli Stone* a few years earlier. Nevertheless, the "rematch" between Miller and Cumberbatch playing the same role seemed designed to garner more publicity for the American series. So did the subsequent casting of Lucy Liu as Joan Watson. Instead of praising the "color blind" casting of this iconic role, some television critics commented that CBS is not being innovative in its Sherlock Holmes adaptation but is merely turning the characters into typical CBS police procedural characters who would inevitably, after a suitable amount of sexual tension, become a romantic couple.

Fans of the BBC's *Sherlock* felt they had been dealt a double blow. Not only were episodes of *Sherlock* increasingly difficult to watch, either because of technical differences between U.S. and U.K. DVDs or because of delayed U.S. broadcasts, but if the PBS series does not receive high enough ratings, then its next episodes, expected to be broadcast in the U.K. in 2013, might never make it to the U.S. Instead, American audiences feared they would be given a highly Americanized CBS version of "Sherlock Holmes" who bears little resemblance to the iconic character or, ironically, his immensely popular modern BBC incarnation.

Americanizing Sherlock Holmes, since 2010, has become an increasingly fraught enterprise, one that involves BBC, PBS, and CBS in American-British broadcast relationships. The decisions of multiple networks about two television series indicate the popularity of Sherlock Holmes but also introduce questions about how "British" Sherlock Holmes must be in order to be accepted or understood by American audiences. With the huge American market playing perhaps a disproportionate role in the way international series are developed and marketed, the significance of the battle between Sherlock and an Americanized Holmes may be far from *Elementary*.

WORKS CITED

"BBC Worldwide and ARTE Ink First Ever Pre-sale Deal." BBC Media Centre. 21 Dec. 2011. Web. 23 Dec. 2011. <http://www.bbc.co.uk/mediacentre/worldwide/211211arte.html>.

"The Blind Banker." *Sherlock*. Writ. Mark Gatiss, Steven Moffat, and Steve Thompson. Dir. Euros Lyn. BBC Worldwide, 2010. DVD.

"The Blind Banker." *Sherlock*. Writ. Mark Gatiss, Steven Moffat, and Steve Thompson. Dir. Euros Lyn. PBS. 31 Oct. 2010. Television.

Clarke, Steve. "Crime Pays at BBC W'wide Showcase." *Chicago Tribune*. Web. 28 Feb. 2012. <http://www.chicagotribune.com/entertainment/sns-201202281202reedbusivarietynvr 1118050803feb28,0,7570920.story>.

Costa, Mary Lou. "British Talent's Platform for International Growth." *Marketing Week*. 10 Feb. 2011. Web. 17 June 2011. <http://www.marketingweek.co.uk/analysis/cover-stories/british-talent%E2%80%99s-platform-for-international-growth/3023228.article>.

"The Great Game." *Sherlock*. Writ. Mark Gatiss and Steven Moffat. Dir. Paul McGuigan. BBC Worldwide, 2010. DVD.

"The Great Game." *Sherlock*. Writ. Mark Gatiss and Steven Moffat. Dir. Paul McGuigan. PBS. 7 Nov. 2010. Television.

Laughlin, Andrew. "UK Drama Making Waves at BBC Showcase." Digital Spy. 2 Mar. 2011. Web. 17 June 2011. <http://www.digitalspy.com/broadcasting/news/a306575/uk-drama-making-waves-at-bbc-showcase.html>.

Lookout Point. 23 Dec. 2011. Web. 23 Dec. 2011. <Lookoutpoint.tv>.

Ocasio, Anthony. "'Sherlock' Producer Warns CBS: We Will Protect Our Series (Legally)." Screenrant. 24 Jan. 2012. Web. 5 Mar. 2012. <http://screenrant.com/bbc-sherlock-cbs-elementary-lawsuit-aco-148206/>.

PBS. "A Scene from Season 2, Episode 1." *Sherlock*. "A Scandal in Belgravia." Web. 5 Mar. 2012. <http://www.pbs.org/wgbh/masterpiece/watch/sherlock_belgravia_scene.html>.

"A Scandal in Belgravia." *Sherlock*. Writ. Steven Moffat. Dir. Paul McGuigan. BBC. 7 Dec. 2011. BFI screening.

"A Study in Pink." *Sherlock*. Writ. Steven Moffat and Mark Gatiss. Dir. Paul McGuigan. BBC Worldwide, 2010. DVD.

"A Study in Pink." *Sherlock*. Writ. Steven Moffat and Mark Gatiss. Dir. Paul McGuigan. PBS. 24 Oct. 2010. Television.

Syal, Rajeev. "BBC Commercial Plans are Unambitious, say MPs." *The Guardian*. Web. 5 Mar. 2012. <http://www.guardian.co.uk/media/2012/mar/06/bbc-must-boost-commercial-income?newsfeed=true>.

9

The "Great Game" of Information
The BBC's Digital Native
RHONDA HARRIS TAYLOR

As the Master Detective, Sherlock Holmes is also a master of information and its use. That aspect of the Victorian Holmes' methods that utilized information resources (such as his scrapbooks of clippings and collections of newspapers), emerging information technologies (such as the telegraph and telephone), and informants (such as the Baker Street Irregulars and the reformed criminal turned informant, Shinwell Johnson) and his critical analysis of information, including the seemingly trivial, have fascinated generations of fans and commentators. The critiques have ranged from Collins' 1944 essay recounting what "Holmes read and wrote" (26) to Nown's 1986 annotations of "Holmes' own published monographs" (67) to Harrington's 2007 comparison of Holmes "collection of trace evidence as well as deduction" (366) to a contemporary forensic science television series.

This facile information usage is such a fundamental aspect of the Holmes persona that in Laurie King's third book in the ongoing pastiche series about the Mary Russell/Sherlock Holmes partnership and marital union, Russell suddenly realizes that "Holmes had not read the newspapers for at least three days" (34). A full page of the novel is then devoted to a description of the importance of this information source to the Great Detective, noting that "Dr. Watson's accounts are as littered with references to the papers as their sitting room was with the actual product, and without the facts and speculations of the reporters and the personal messages of the agony columns, Holmes would have been deprived of a sense as important as touch or smell" (34).

The BBC portrayal of a 21st century Holmes in the television series *Sherlock* introduces a younger, edgier character than the Canonical Holmes, but this contemporary character is also information literate, although he has some very interesting deficiencies.

Information Literacy and the Digital Native

The concept of information literacy is a vital one for library practitioners, whose daily work is focused on information and information seeking to meet the needs of their clienteles. It is also crucial for educators at all academic levels, who must not only convey knowledge to novices but instruct their students in navigating and appropriately utilizing information resources so that they can become lifelong learners. The rationale for developing the lifelong learner has been summarized by the National Education Association:

> When we ask them to write copiously, read large amounts of information, learn to manage their time, work well with others, accept and give feedback and criticism, express ideas in clear, concise ways that can be easily understood by others, listen attentively, defend a position or idea, or find a proper source, we do so because they will have to do these things the rest of their lives if they are to be successful ["Clear Rationale"].

It would not be a challenge to argue that these skills are critical for a consulting detective.

To guide librarians striving to assist clients to become information literate, the Association of College and Research Libraries (ACRL) has promulgated five standards for what the information-literate college student, and others as well, should know and be able to do:

> Standard One. The information-literate student determines the nature and extent of information needed.
> Standard Two. The information-literate student accesses needed information effectively and efficiently.
> Standard Three. The information-literate student evaluates information and its sources critically and incorporates selected information into his or her knowledge base and value system.
> Standard Four. The information-literate student, individually or as a member of a group, uses information effectively to accomplish a specific purpose.
> Standard Five. The information-literate student understands many of the economic, legal, and social issues surrounding the use of information and accesses and uses information ethically and legally [Association, *Information* 8–14].

The content of the ACRL standards is paralleled in standards/guidelines for school libraries and for various school curriculum content areas, such as science, from national to state to the local district level. The American Association for School Librarians, the International Society for Technology in Education, and the National Council of Mathematics, as well as programs such as the Common Core State Standards Initiative, support parallel principles for information literacy skills to be taught in common education, preschool through twelfth grade. The ACRL goal is an "information literate person

[who] must be able to recognize when information is needed and have the ability to locate, evaluate, and use effectively the needed information" (Association, *Information* 2). This outcome is viewed as essential for both the professional and personal development of the individual and also for the well-being of society. In addressing the challenges of an increasingly digital world, a 1989 report from the ACRL summarized these perceived benefits of information literacy:

> the awareness of the rapidly changing requirements for a productive, healthy, and satisfying life. To respond effectively to an ever-changing environment, people need more than just a knowledge base, they also need techniques for exploring it, connecting it to other knowledge bases, and making practical use of it.... Knowledge ... is this country's most precious commodity, and people who are information literate — who know how to acquire knowledge and use it — are America's most valuables resources [Association, *Presidential*].

The emphasis on a satisfying life, linked with the well-being of the whole community, suggests information literacy is essential for the functioning citizen — surely it is also essential for that consulting detective who must delve into the secretive criminal underbelly of that community.

In order to foster information literacy, both librarians and educators must understand the profile of the library user or potential user or the student. In the 21st century, both professions have focused on generational differences as they relate to changing approaches to information. That interest is represented by a steady stream of journal articles about Millennials, Generation Y, Gen X, Nextgens, etc. The terms are not consistent in designating birth years to determine categories, so there is confusion about who gets included in which group. Perhaps the clearest distinction has been the concept of "digital native," first introduced by Prensky in 2001. Rather simplistically, Prensky's label is based on the assumption that people who were born after 1970 or who grew up with 21st century technologies are "native" to a digital world, and everyone who is older is a "digital immigrant," lacking a natural fluency in the digital environment and being ill equipped to teach digital natives. Prensky's solution for instructing digital natives is to use computer *games* [italics added] to deliver their lessons, because all of their interactions, including social, are already utilizing digital tools — it's all a *game* [italics added] to them (Prensky).

Although it has its detractors (e.g., Bennett and Maton), the "digital native" designation is supported by research published in numerous Pew Research Center reports, which have provided longitudinal and comparative findings of age group usage of technology. A 2005 study revealed that "the portion of online teens who were blogging, maintaining their own websites, remixing content, and sharing other artistic creations online far outweighed the portion of online adults who had engaged in the same types of activities" (Pew, "Teen").

A 2010 study comparing results with a 2008 study found that teen usage of Internet virtual worlds had remained consistent: "younger teens continue to be more enthusiastic users of virtual worlds —11 percent of online teens 12–13 use virtual worlds, while 7 percent of teen Internet users 14–17 use them" and "use of virtual worlds is more common among teens than among adults" (Pew, "Part 3"). The same 2010 study also determined that young adults, aged 18 to 29, were more likely than older individuals to be online wirelessly, regardless of whether they were using laptops, cell phones, or other devices. From these studies, it would appear that younger individuals are generally more "connected" technologically (Pew, "Part 2").

A Detective "Born Digital"

Sherlock is the brainchild of co-creators Mark Gatiss and Steven Moffat (Moffat is the showrunner of *Doctor Who,* and he and Gatiss also write scripts for that series). They have often spoken of envisioning a modern Sherlock Holmes. Gatiss has commented that "The technology aspect ... might look sort of, rather jarringly modern," but "Sherlock Holmes is always a man of his time.... He completely embraces technology" (Gatiss). So, in one sense, the BBC *Sherlock* has been "born digital," a term used for materials that were always digital: They were never analog, such as is the case of a paper format that is scanned into a computer. This Holmes was designed as a resident of the digital age. Overt signs of this digital Holmes are the tie-in websites seen in the series that are also on the Internet: Holmes' website, "The Science of Deduction" (http://www.thescienceofdeduction.co.uk/); John Watson's blog (http://www.johnwatsonblog.co.uk/), which replaces the Canonical journals; and the blog of Molly Hooper (http://www.mollyhooper.co.uk/blog/01april), a hospital morgue attendant attracted to Holmes but who winds up dating the archvillain Jim Moriarty. (Holmes' and Watson's blogs were updated for the second season, but Molly's site lacks any entries post–Jim.) Thus the ACRL standards are an appropriate checklist for gauging the information literacy competence of the 21st century Sherlock, who was conceived as a "born digital" character for a television series, and whose characterization of a contemporary Holmes is that of a young digital native.

Standard 1. Defines the Nature and Extent of the Information Needed

The first ACRL standard includes defining and articulating the need for information, and the BBC Holmes fares well here. In "The Blind Banker,"

Sherlock Holmes openly admits to a surprised John Watson that he needs some advice and says that he "needs to talk to an expert" — a graffiti artist. Holmes' willingness to acknowledge that he needs information that he does not have and that he is willing to seek it via unorthodox sources is commendable, particularly for someone who, throughout the series, repeatedly and often irritatingly demonstrates his confidence in his own knowledge and skills. How irritating Holmes' confidence can be is captured in Watson's mocking parody, "'No, I'm Sherlock Holmes. I always work alone because no one else can compete with my massive intellect!'" ("The Blind Banker").

Holmes' skill level is more questionable when compared to one of this standard's performance measures: considering the costs and benefits of acquiring needed information. In the "Blind Banker" episode, Holmes has the police deliver the entire book collections of two victims to his flat, in a quest to find a key to a code. He is oblivious to the cost John Watson pays in assisting in the perusal of a roomful of books, when he should be getting adequate sleep for his new job, which Watson has taken from economic necessity.

Similarly, Holmes accompanies the killer in the "Study in Pink" episode because he is promised the chance to understand how the man enticed his victims to kill themselves. However, seeking information from a serial killer in a private face-to-face meeting is not good cost-benefit analysis. Indeed, Holmes almost loses his life and is saved not by his analytical prowess but by Watson's excellent marksmanship.

Standard 2. Accesses Needed Information Effectively and Efficiently

Holmes generally demonstrates achievement of the second standard, which emphasizes effective and efficient access of information. Part of this standard is "selecting the most appropriate investigative methods or information retrieval systems for accessing the needed information," as well as "retriev[-ing] information online or in person using a variety of methods." Holmes effectively uses both human expert and digital resources.

In the series' first episode, "A Study in Pink," Holmes recruits John Watson, on the spur of the moment, to examine the body of a murder victim. Holmes taps Watson because of his expertise as a battlefield army physician. However, Holmes' ability to rapidly identify qualified experts is offset by the inefficiency of his social interactions. The detective needs forensic information, and the police forensic staff "won't work with him" because he goes out of his way to antagonize them. For instance, at the scene of the murder, he deliberately tweaks forensic specialist Anderson about a liaison with police sergeant

Sally Donovan. In the same episode, Holmes requires Anderson to turn around because facing him disturbs Holmes' thought processes, and he further tells Anderson to stop talking because he is "lower[ing] the IQ of the whole street." Holmes' acrimonious relationship with Anderson and Donovan will encourage them to take a backstage revenge in the "The Reichenbach Fall." Recklessly creating enemies is not an effective strategy for the ultimate "game" when accessing needed information.

At the crime scene of "A Study in Pink," Holmes effectively and efficiently accesses information delivered by technology, including using his cell phone to search for a location that fits the travel radius and weather conditions that he has deduced from the crime scene and the corpse of this murder victim. In all three episodes of the first season, Holmes makes liberal use of those apps on his cell phone and his laptop computer (including visit a fan website to gather information about a television celebrity victim).

Holmes is also adept at effectively and efficiently using human sources of information. In "The Great Game," he draws on his relationship with the homeless population of London (in contrast to the Canon's street children, the Baker Street Irregulars). He even uses the police, who invite him into their cases and share information that they have (e.g., "A Study in Pink," "The Great Game," "A Scandal in Belgravia"). He also makes frequent use of the copious and esoteric information in his own head, including (as in the "Banker" episode) classic Chinese escapology and an ancient Chinese numbering system used by street traders.

Also integral to this second standard is an ability for "managing the information," and Holmes demonstrates this quality in his time-sensitive solving of the crimes posed by his nemesis Moriarty and in conveying the solutions to the archvillain just in time to save bomb-rigged innocents ("The Great Game").

Standard 3. Evaluates Information and Its Sources Critically and Incorporates Selected Information into His or Her Knowledge Base and Value System

Holmes continually demonstrates that he is well able to put into practice the first part of Standard Three: "Evaluating information and its sources critically." Sometimes that critical evaluation can be unorthodox. As he explains to Watson, Holmes does not know if the sun goes around the earth or vice versa, and he does not care. The extraordinarily strict criterion for what is incorporated into his "knowledge base" is because, for Holmes' brain, "it only makes sense to put things in there that are useful" ("The Great Game"). This careful selection is sometimes a disadvantage. Disregard of the potentially extraneous means that because he does not have any knowledge of daytime television shows, he misses an important clue in a murder case. Watson, whose unemployment has meant spending time with the landlady and the "telly," knows the answer this time ("The Great Game"). It also means, as Watson reminds him in the "Game" episode, that Holmes' lack of astronomical knowledge almost meant his missing the essential clue to a forged painting.

As with other good detectives, Holmes understands clearly that people are carriers of valuable information, but he does not restrict his information-gathering activities to questioning them any more than the Canonical Holmes did. The audience's first introduction to Holmes' application of deductive abilities is his "reading" of Watson's background and identity in "A Study in Pink." His explanation of his visual observations of Watson's appearance and his cell phone are highlighted as snapshots of the critical clues. In "A Scandal in Belgravia," Holmes' deductions about the individual sent to bring him to Buckingham Palace and the Equerry, who represents Holmes' royal client, are captured in screen overlays of descriptive words and short phrases. Both techniques emphasize the computer-like analysis of human physical attributes that is employed by this digital native. In "The Great Game," Holmes says of a body found on the shore, "He's been in the river a long while; the water's destroyed most of the *data* [italics added]." A more extreme example of this view of physicality as information occurs in "A Scandal in Belgravia," when Holmes uses Irene Adler's overtures to him as an opportunity to take her pulse and check her pupils to gauge her reaction to him — he is most assuredly a dedicated critical evaluator of information sources. Little wonder that some of his initial interest in Adler should be attributed to his inability to "read" her when he meets her — her screen overlays are a series of question marks. She is an enigma, and information puzzles are irresistible to Holmes.

Standard 4. Individually or as a Member of a Group, Uses Information Effectively to Accomplish a Specific Purpose

Standard Four poses some problems. First, Holmes is not a "group player," regardless of the group. In "A Study in Pink," he texts one curt word, "WRONG," to reporters in the press conference where Detective Inspector Lestrade is attempting to promote suicide as the cause of a number of recent deaths. In the same episode, at the murder scene investigation, Holmes tells Lestrade to stop thinking because it annoys Holmes. These behaviors would not meet Dale Carnegie's recommendations for winning friends! Indeed, Sergeant Donovan tells Watson that Holmes has no friends. In an early conversation with John Watson, even Holmes' brother Mycroft explains that he "is the closest thing to a friend that Sherlock Holmes is capable of having — an enemy" ("A Study in Pink"). In one emotionally charged scene, even Holmes blurts out that he has no friends, although he later tells Watson that he has one ("The Hounds of Baskerville").

Holmes is not even tactful with those who might be considered closest to him. In "A Study in Pink," when Watson asks how he could have missed a clue that is essential information, Holmes responds: "Because you're an idiot. No, no, no, don't be like that. Practically everyone is." In "The Blind Banker," a former schoolmate-turned-client tells John Watson that Sherlock Holmes was an "arrogant sod." In this episode, that same assessment is offered by police officer Dimmock.

On the other hand, there are occasions when Holmes bothers, for his own information-gathering and problem-solving goals, to cater to the feelings of others. In "A Study in Pink," Holmes, in order to gain access to a corpse, makes token efforts at complimenting Molly Hooper's looks. He repeats that strategy for a similar reason in "The Blind Banker." At the end of that episode, Holmes tells police inspector Dimmock, who has reluctantly worked with him, that there is "no need to mention us in your report." He adds that "I have high hopes for you, Inspector, a glittering career." But Holmes then provides a caveat to this praise by agreeing with Dimmock's assessment that "I go where you point me."

Also on the positive side, Holmes is obviously very successful as the lone detective. He explains to John Watson that he is the world's only consulting detective, which means "when the police are out of their depth, which is always, they consult me" ("A Study in Pink"). At least from Holmes' perspective, he is able to function effectively as an individual information user.

Standard 5. Understands Many of the Economic, Legal, and Social Issues Surrounding the Use of Information and Accesses and Uses Information Ethically and Legally

Standard Five's emphasis on the ethical and legal is where Holmes gets into trouble. In accessing the Internet in "A Study in Pink," Holmes hacks into John Watson's laptop simply for convenience, because his own is in the other room. He has also breached Watson's password. In the same episode, Holmes reveals that he pickpockets Inspector Lestrade's official ID whenever he gets annoying, and then he uses the credential to present himself as Lestrade. Similarly, in "The Hounds of Baskerville," Holmes uses his brother Mycroft's identification to gain entrance to a top-secret government facility.

In the beginning of "The Great Game," Holmes interviews a potential client imprisoned in Russia. As the man tells his story and reveals the details of his guilt, Sherlock repeatedly interrupts by correcting his grammar, and when the man pleads, "Without you ... I'll get hung with this," Holmes merrily departs with the comment "No, no, Mr. Bewick, not at all. Hanged, yes."

Indulging in self-satisfaction at thwarting Lestrade, rejoicing in his own grammatical superiority at the expense of an admittedly guilty accused killer, and accommodating his own convenience by confiscating others' possessions are transgressions somewhat balanced by other incidents in which Holmes would undoubtedly say that he has justifiable reasons for ignoring legal and ethical boundaries as he seeks information. For instance, at the end of "A Study in Pink," Holmes literally stomps on the wounded, dying serial killer in order to get him to reveal the name of the mysterious individual who has been assisting him. In "The Blind Banker," Holmes lies about his identity to cajole a building's tenant into facilitating his entrance into the flat of a missing man, in order to search for information about symbols found at a murder scene. Later he uses a fire escape ladder to break into the flat of a missing woman, so that he can search for information about her disappearance. In "The Great Game," he masquerades as an art gallery guard because he needs to gain access to a painting integral to his investigation. In the same episode, Holmes pretends to be the friend of a presumed murder victim in order to obtain information from his seemingly bereaved wife. In "The Reichenbach Fall," Holmes accosts the distraught house mistress of a school where two children have been kidnapped: "What are you, an idiot, a drunk, or a criminal?" After she tells him what she knows, Holmes says, "I just wanted you to speak quickly."

More difficult to justify is the repeated behavior, across episodes, of Holmes tricking John Watson in various ways, including hiding information from him for what seem rather trivial reasons. For instance, in "A Study in Pink," he summons John Watson with urgent and cryptic text messages, including a suggestion that there is danger, in order to have John send a cell phone message rather than use his own phone, whose number might be known to a potential killer. In "The Great Game," Holmes leads John Watson to believe that he is working alone to solve the case of a missing set of missile plans on a thumb drive, but Holmes is actually working in the background. A more disturbing incident occurs in "The Hounds of Baskerville," when Holmes secretly drugs Watson with a hallucinogenic and then tricks him into entering a lab where his reactions can be accentuated and monitored. This unorthodox experiment, while in quest of the solution to a murder and although later explained to Watson, surpasses the bounds of ethical behavior.

Besides the issue of how ethically Holmes has obtained information, there is the matter of his propensity for his decidedly unkind, if not unethical, use of information that he casually gleans in everyday encounters with the people in his life. In "A Study in Belgravia," Holmes candidly discusses his observations, within the client's hearing, that the man is "morbidly obese," is "an Internet porn addict," has an "untreated heart condition," and has "low self-esteem, tiny IQ, and a limited life expectancy." During a Christmas gathering in the same episode, Holmes publicly reveals that Lestrade's wife is having an affair and that Watson's sister has resumed drinking. He then brutally dissects indicators that Molly Hooper has a boyfriend. In a similar incident with Mrs. Hudson, he tells her that her new romantic interest already has a wife.

As for the economic issues surrounding the use of information, for a self-employed consulting detective, Holmes seems amazingly cavalier about fees. When he is irritated by Sebastian Wilkes, who wants to hire him to solve a break-in, Holmes responds to the offer of a large retainer by declaring "I don't need an incentive" and stalking away ("The Blind Banker"). Holmes wants to play the information game for its own sake rather than its monetary advantages, a trait that Sergeant Donovan characterizes as psychopathic in "A Study in Pink": "You know why he's here? He's not paid or anything. He likes it. He gets off on it. The weirder the crime, the more he gets off." That observation is borne out in "A Scandal in Belgravia" when Holmes curtly dismisses a sequence of presumably potential fee-paying clients because their cases are "boring."

Information Literacy and Beyond: Outsourcing, Ethics, Information Overload, and Gamesmanship

Besides his information literacy achievements, two other aspects of Holmes as digital native reflect ideas about the larger environment of technology and information and their usage in daily activities. The first aspect is Holmes' status as the world's only consulting detective, which, as he tells John Watson in "A Study in Pink," is a job that he has invented. In this respect, Holmes is very much the model worker of the 21st century. He parallels the ideas of Thomas Malone of the Massachusetts Institute of Technology and the author of *The Future of Work* (2004), who describes a revolution similar to the industrial revolution in the way that individuals will work in the 21st century:

> New information technologies make this revolution possible. Dispersed physically but connected by technology, workers are now able, on a scale never before imaginable, to make their own decisions using information gathered from many other

people and places. The real impetus for the transformation in business will not come from the new technologies, however. It will come from our own innate desires — for economic efficiency and flexibility, certainly, but also for noneconomic goals like freedom, personal satisfaction, and fulfillment [4].

The freedom, personal satisfaction, and fulfillment aspects evoke the Association of College and Research Libraries' assertion that information literacy is necessary for a "productive, healthy, and satisfying life" (Association, *Information*), and Holmes is most definitely information literate — does that provide him a productive, healthy, and satisfying life? If such a life is dependent on successful relationships with others, then the answer is quite likely a negative. At the beginning of their relationship, Watson attempts to elicit information about Holmes' personal life by suggesting that people in "real life" don't have archenemies ("A Study in Pink"). When Holmes inquires what "real people" have, Watson responds "friends, people they know, people they like, people they don't like, girlfriends, boyfriends." Holmes' reaction is a succinct "dull," and he announces that he considers himself "married" to his work.

Malone emphasizes the indicators of this new industrial revolution: "empowering workers, outsourcing almost everything, and creating networked, or virtual corporations" (4). Outsourcing is another hallmark of the BBC sagas of Holmes' contemporary adventures. Holmes is the individual to whom the police turn, albeit reluctantly, for assistance in solving crimes — they are accessing Holmes' outsourced brain power. In "A Study in Pink," Lestrade admits to Watson that he "puts up" with Holmes "because I'm desperate, that's why." In "The Great Game," Lestrade tells Holmes that all of the police read Watson's blog. Is it because they hope to get insights into Holmes' methods (in which case they would surely visit Holmes' website) or because they are looking for vulnerabilities in this seemingly perfect thinking machine that they have to use?

In *Sherlock*, as in the Canonical Holmes stories, the outsourcing is applied in two directions. The Victorian Holmes uses the Baker Street Irregulars — boys who live on the London streets — as his outsourced information gatherers. Any potential consequences to the boys of that outsourcing are not articulated in those narratives. However, the practice is viewed through an ethical lens in the 2011 Sherlock Holmes novel authorized by the Arthur Conan Doyle Estate, *The House of Silk* (Horowitz). After the brutal death of a thirteen-year-old Irregular, Holmes reflects that "certainly, I have used my Baker Street Irregulars without much thought or consideration.... Wiggins, Ross and the rest of them were nothing to me, just as they are nothing to the society that has abandoned them to the streets" (97–98).

The 21st century Holmes has apparently not reached this level of self-reflection. In a conversation with Watson, Holmes discusses his use of people living on the London streets as his own information sources:

HOLMES: Homeless network. My eyes and ears all over the city. Absolutely indispensable.
WATSON: Oh! So, you scratch their back, and then...
HOLMES: Yes, and then disinfect myself ["The Great Game"].

That ethical facet of the fifth information literacy standard is still a stumbling block for this contemporary Holmes.

The second aspect of 21st century digital native Holmes that is disconcerting is the melding of Sherlock with the technology, so that he can seem almost mechanical. Of his own creation, Conan Doyle said that "[Holmes] is a calculating machine" (Moore 85). On the PBS *Masterpiece Mystery!* website for the series, Benedict Cumberbatch, who plays Holmes, has four recorded interviews. In one entitled "Sherlock Holmes and Technology," he says of Holmes that "he's got an extraordinary ability to marry technology with instant thought; that's the extraordinary thing about it" (Cumberbatch, "Sherlock"). "A Study in Pink" enhances this thinking machine aspect by overlaying the text accessed by Holmes on his cell phone searches with his crime-scene observations. In "The Great Game," Holmes says that his brain is his "hard drive," and he puts into it only that which is "useful." Such calculation seems distant from regular human consideration because most people do not regularly assess what they will remember. In "The Hounds of Baskerville," Holmes retreats into a mind palace to analyze information. The flashes of text and pictorial images in his memory are interposed over an almost robotic Holmes, whose arm movements woodenly shift the bits of information. Mind, body, and data are part of an overtly integrated information system. In contrast, in the "Hounds" episode, viewers see Holmes, for the first time, openly emotional and distraught. However, the reaction is to what could be characterized as confrontation with illogic, anathema for a machine. As Holmes explains, "something I've not experienced before ... I felt doubt. I've always been able to trust my senses, the evidence of my own eyes. Until last night."

Given his investment in logic and information, it is not surprising that Holmes' interest in Irene Adler, who is an information seeker, gatherer, and broker, is mediated through cell phone text messages. Nor is it surprising that instead of the sovereign (coin) memento of Adler that is kept by the Canonical Holmes, this digital native chooses to retain the cell phone on which, as a shocked Watson queries Adler, "You flirted with Sherlock Holmes?" ("A Scandal in Belgravia"). The retention of the object is not pure sentimentality on the part of a primarily cerebral being who relies heavily on his ability to recall information — it is actually a cerebral act on the part of an individual who will, ironically, soon confront the overwhelmingly disconcerting experience of not trusting his own senses in "The Hounds of Baskerville." Artifact (thing), memory, and senses, as with mind, body, and data, are also integrated in one system:

> What can be lost is not the senses but the memory of the senses.... Memory ... transports, bridges and crosses all the other senses.... Memory and the senses are co-mingled in so far as they are equally involuntary experiences.... As a sensory form in itself, the artifact can provoke the emergence, the awakening of the layered memories, and thus the senses contained within it. The object invested with sensory memory speaks; it provokes re-call [Seremetakis 9–11].

As the thinking machine, Holmes' distance from what are accepted sensibilities can be jarring in other ways as well. In the first episode of the series, Holmes literally rejoices when he learns of multiple deaths:

> HOLMES: Possible suicides. Four of them. There's no point sitting at home when there's finally something fun going on!
> MRS. HUDSON: Look at you, all happy. It's not decent.
> HOLMES: Who cares about decent? The game, Mrs. Hudson, is on! ["A Study in Pink"].

One is reminded not only of the Canonical Holmes' same sense of the "game" but of Prensky's recommendation that digital natives be taught using games because technology is a game to them. When does the "game" stop and life begin, or end? In "The Great Game," Holmes and Watson get into an argument when Watson upbraids Holmes for not caring about lives being at stake in the "game" between Moriarty and him. Holmes responds by asking, "Would caring about them help save them?" When Watson admits that it would not, Holmes says that he will not "make that mistake" of caring and admits to Watson that he finds that approach easy.

In the technologically-centered world of digital natives, however, there is something that all of their potential information skills cannot totally overcome: information overload. The term, according to the *Oxford English Dictionary* ("Information Overload"), was first noted in 1962 in R.L. Meier's book, *Communications Theory of Urban Growth,* but was popularized in Alvin Toffler's 1970 book, *Future Shock.* Information overload can lead to a condition of information fatigue, a term apparently coined in the 1990s (McFedries). Such fatigue would be characterized by doubt, anxiety, inability to think, and more information seeking. Information overload implicitly carries a time limit that cannot be met — for instance, one cannot live long enough to actually sort through, or control, global incremental information generation (chaos), and many feel hard-pressed to handle personal information overload. A 2009 Pew Research Center study on *Internet Typology: The Mobile Difference* found that "10 percent of adults feel overwhelmed by information and inadequate to troubleshoot modern ICTs [information and communications technologies]" — they are the information encumbered (Horrigan).

Information overload is actually an important part of the paradigm for the 21st century Holmes, who is the world's only consulting detective. For that master of information, there is the recurring challenge of facing the world's only "consulting criminal." Jim Moriarty is introduced in the first year of *Sherlock* as a shadowy presence in the background for two episodes and then as a full-fledged antagonist in the third episode, appropriately titled "The Great Game." Conversations in this episode reveal that Holmes sees himself and Moriarty as both engaged in a game because it keeps them distracted from boredom. By introducing strict time limits to Holmes' task of saving numerous bomb-threatened individuals (eventually including Watson), Moriarty embodies the disorder of information overload, of chaos that is almost insurmountable; how insurmountable is demonstrated in "The Great Game." Holmes does not reveal that he has solved the Connie Prince murder ahead of the imposed deadline in an attempt to "have one up" on Moriarty and use the extra time to ultimately thwart him. But this hostage situation results in the deaths of twelve people, so the chaos of Moriarty triumphs. In "The Reichenbach Fall," Moriarty once again imposes time limits on Holmes as he attempts to make sense of many disparate pieces of information. In reference to two small kidnapped children, Moriarty sends a fax: "Hurry up. They're dying."

However, attempting to control this information overload, in various manifestations, forces Holmes to articulate his own values. In a possibly final confrontation with Moriarty in "The Great Game," Holmes upbraids Moriarty for talking about how much he has enjoyed "this little game of ours." Holmes almost verbatim quotes Watson's earlier reproach to him when he reminds Moriarty that "people have died." After Watson tries to save Holmes by prematurely getting himself blown up by Moriarty's bomb, Holmes awkwardly tries to thank him, and viewers sense that there is genuine affection here. Moriarty knows that there is a more human side to the "thinking machine" Holmes. He threatens Holmes that he will "burn the heart out of you." When Holmes responds that he has "been reliably informed that I don't have one," Moriarty retorts, "But we both know that's not quite true." In "The Reichenbach Fall," Moriarty proves this truth when he threatens three people about whom Holmes cares. In that episode, as in "The Great Game," Moriarty once again places a time limit on Holmes' ability to analyze his way out of a standoff with his nemesis.

Moriarty is absolutely necessary for the technologically savvy, brilliant, and consummate user of information that is 21st century Holmes, just as he was necessary for the Victorian detective. His chaos forces Holmes to side with the humans rather than just play the game. Similarly, while 21st century Watson has a blog, he is thwarted by automated check-out. The portrayal of his character demonstrates that, as with his 19th century counterpart, this

Watson is not the technologically expert or intellectual equal of Holmes, but he is the one who repeatedly reminds Holmes that the victims are people. Thirty-five years ago, Moorman's essay on "The Appeal of Sherlock Holmes" concluded that the appeal lay in "the knowledge that in the end, reason, in the form of Sherlock Holmes, and good, in the form of Watson, will indeed triumph" (82). The *Sherlock* series suggests the possibility that the integration of qualities of technological proficiency, cognitive brilliance, information literacy, and concern for fellow humans might actually dwell in one person. Lestrade tells Watson that Holmes "is a great man, and I think one day — if we're very, very lucky — he might even be a good one." Twenty-first century Holmes is a master of powerful technology (and the overwhelming information it brings) that contemporary, ordinary humans attempt to tame and use. However, the potential path to a "productive, healthy, and satisfying" life also has its appeal for viewers. Little wonder that the return of a duo of reason and good is still just as compelling in stories about 21st century characters as in those with 19th century figures.

WORKS CITED

American Association for School Librarians. *Standards for the Twenty-first Century Learner.* AASL. 2007. Web. 29 Dec. 2011. <http://www.ala.org/aasl/sites/ala.org.aasl/files/ content/ guidelinesandstandards/learningstandards/AASL_LearningStandards.pdf>.

Association of College and Research Libraries. *Information Literacy Competency Standards for Higher Education.* Chicago: ACRL, 2000. Print.

Association of College and Research Libraries. *Presidential Committee on Information Literacy: Final Report.* ACRL. 10 Jan. 1989. Web. 29 Dec. 2011. <http://www.ala.org/acrl/publications/ whitepapers/presidential>.

Bennett, Sue, and K. Maton. "Beyond the 'Digital Natives' Debate: Towards a Nuanced Understanding of Students' Technology Experiences." *Journal of Computer Assisted Learning* 26 (2010): 321–31.

"The Blind Banker." *Sherlock: Season One.* Perfs. Benedict Cumberbatch and Martin Freeman. 2 entertain Video, a Hartswood Films Production for BBC, 2010. DVD.

"Clear Rationale." Tools and Ideas. NEA, n.d. Web. 29 Dec. 2011. <http://www.nea.org/home/ 34221.htm>.

Collins, Howard. "Ex Libris Sherlock Holmes." *Profile by Gaslight: An Irregular Reader about the Life of Sherlock Holmes.* Ed. Edgar W. Smith. New York: Simon & Schuster, 1944. 26–39. Print.

Common Core State Standards Initiative. *Common Core Standards for English Language Arts & Literacy in History/Social Studies, Science, and Technical Subjects.* Common Core. 2010. Web. 19 Dec. 2011. <http://www.corestandards.org/assets/CCSSI_ELA%20Standards.pdf>.

Common Core State Standards Initiative. *Common Core Standards for Mathematics.* Common Core. n.d. Web. 19 Dec. 2011. <http://www.corestandards.org/assets/CCSSI_Math%20 Standards.pdf>.

Cumberbatch, Benedict. "Sherlock and Technology." *Masterpiece.* PBS. n.d. Web. 29 Dec. 2011. <http://www.pbs.org/wgbh/masterpiece/sherlock/cumberbatch.html>.

Gatiss, Mark. "Embracing Technology." *Masterpiece.* PBS. n.d. Web. 29 Dec. 2011. <http://www. pbs.org/wgbh/masterpiece/sherlock/producers.html>.

"The Great Game." *Sherlock: Season One.* Perfs. Benedict Cumberbatch and Martin Freeman. 2 entertain Video, a Hartswood Films Production for BBC, 2010. DVD.

Harrington, Ellen Burton. "Nation, Identity and the Fascination with Forensic Science in Sherlock Holmes and *CSI.*" *International Journal of Cultural Studies* 10.3 (2007): 365–82. Print.

Horowitz, Anthony. *The House of Silk.* New York: Little, Brown, 2011. Print.

Horrigan, John. *Internet Typology: The Mobile Difference.* Pew Internet. 25 Mar. 2009. Web. 29 Dec. 2011. <http://pewresearch.org/pubs/1162/internet-typology-users-mobile-communication-devices>.

"The Hounds of Baskerville." *Sherlock: Season Two.* Perfs. Benedict Cumberbatch and Martin Freeman. 2 entertain Video, a Hartswood Films Production for BBC, 2011. DVD.

"Information Overload." *Oxford English Dictionary.* Web. 29 Dec. 2011. <http://www.oed.com>.

International Society for Technology in Education. *National Educational Technology Standards for Students.* ISTE, 2007. Web. 29 Dec. 2011. <http://www.iste.org/standards/nets-for-students/nets-student-standards-2007.aspx>.

King, Laurie. *A Letter of Mary: A Mary Russell Novel.* New York: St. Martin's, 1996. Print.

Malone, Thomas W. *The Future of Work: How the New Order of Business Will Shape Your Organization, Your Management Style, and Your Life.* Boston: Harvard Business School Press, 2004. Print.

McFedries, Paul. "Information Fatigue." *Word Spy: The Word Lover's Guide to New Words.* Logophilia. 17 Oct. 1996. Web. 29 Dec. 2011. <http://www.wordspy.com/words/informationfatiguesyndrome.asp>.

Moore, John Robert. "Sherlock Holmes Borrows a Plot." *Modern Language Quarterly* 8.1 (Mar. 1947): 85–90. Print.

Moorman, Charles. "The Appeal of Sherlock Holmes." *The Southern Quarterly* 14 (1976): 71–82. Print.

National Council of Teachers of Mathematics. *Principles & Standards for School Mathematics.* NCTM. 2000. Web. 29 Dec. 2011. <http://www.nctm.org/standards/default.aspx?id=58>.

National Education Association. "A Clear Rationale for Learner-Centered Teaching." NEA. n.d. Web. 29 Dec. 2011. <http://www.nea.org/home/34221.htm>.

Nown, Graham. *Elementary My Dear Watson: Sherlock Holmes Centenary: His Life & Times.* London: Ward, 1986. Print.

Pew Internet. "Part 2: Gadget Ownership and Wireless Connectivity." *Social Media and Young Adults.* Pew Internet. 3 Feb. 2010. Web. 29 Dec. 2011. <http://www.pewinternet.org/Reports/2010/Social-Media-and-Young-Adults/Part-2/5-Wireless.aspx>.

Pew Internet. "Part 3: Social Media." *Social Media and Young Adults.* Pew Internet. 3 Feb. 2010. Web. 29 Dec. 2011. <http://www.pewinternet.org/Reports/2010/Social-Media-and-Young-Adults/Part-3/5-Adults-teens-and-virtual-worlds.aspx>.

Pew Internet. "Teen Content Creators and Consumers." *Teens and Social Media.* Pew Internet. 29 Dec. 2007. Web. 29 Dec. 2011. <http://www.pewinternet.org/Reports/2007/Teens-and-Social-Media/3-Teens-creating-content.aspx?view=all>.

Prensky, Marc. "Digital Natives, Digital Immigrants." *On the Horizon* 9.5 (Oct. 2001): 1–6. Web. 29 Dec. 2011. <http://www.marcprensky.com/writing/prensky%20-%20digital%20natives,%20digital%20immigrants%20-%20part1.pdf>.

"The Reichenbach Fall." *Sherlock: Season Two.* Perfs. Benedict Cumberbatch and Martin Freeman. 2 entertain Video, a Hartswood Films Production for BBC, 2011. DVD.

"A Scandal in Belgravia." *Sherlock: Season Two.* Perfs. Benedict Cumberbatch and Martin Freeman. 2 entertain Video, a Hartswood Films Production for BBC, 2011. DVD.

Seremetakis, C. Nadia, ed. *The Senses Still.* Boulder, CO: Westview, 1994. Print.

"A Study in Pink." *Sherlock: Season One.* Perfs. Benedict Cumberbatch and Martin Freeman. 2 entertain Video, a Hartswood Films Production for BBC, 2010. DVD.

Toffler, Alvin. *Future Shock.* New York: Random House, 1970. Print.

10

Detecting the Technocratic Detective

SVETLANA BOCHMAN

> "Look — this is my hard drive and it only makes sense for me to put things in there that are useful. Really useful.... All that matters to me is the *work*. Without that, my brain rots. Put that in your blog."
>
> — *Sherlock, addressing John in the BBC's* Sherlock, *"The Great Game"*

> "[S]o many regard him as a machine rather than a man."
>
> — *Watson describing Holmes in "The Memoirs of Sherlock Holmes"*

Sherlock Holmes is probably the most frequently adapted literary character, and many film adaptations of Conan Doyle's stories, from Jeremy Brett's interpretation of the character in the Granada television series to Robert Downey, Jr.'s in Guy Ritchie's recent films, portray Holmes as a Victorian. Conan Doyle, however, usually depicted the character as a thoroughly modern man. The BBC's recent televised adaptation, entitled *Sherlock*, extrapolates on this idea and presents a modern Sherlock Holmes living in contemporary London.[1] One of the most striking aspects of this new adaptation is an updated appropriation of technology for Holmes, including the use of laptops, smartphones, and modern forensic equipment, all of which are brought into play when showcasing the character's unusual intelligence. In both Conan Doyle's stories and the BBC's television series, Sherlock Holmes' intelligence is conveyed through his use of the scientific method, specifically forensic science combined with the latest medical instruments and technology, revealing that popular culture of both eras perceives technocratic ease as a sign of intelligence. A comparison of Conan Doyle's Holmes' and the BBC's Sherlock's use of technology is significant because it points to a shift in popular culture's reception

144

of unusual technocratic intelligence, in particular, a shift from the Victorian audience's technocratic ease towards one of greater discomfort in modern times. *Sherlock's* opening montage flashes the words "based on the works of Sir Arthur Conan Doyle," consciously referencing the original four novels and 56 short stories. The adaptation, consisting of six 90-minute episodes broadcast in 2010 and 2012, with another three episodes planned for a third season, all are in the expected crime drama genre, as written by Mark Gatiss, Steven Moffat, and Stephen Thompson. The series stars Benedict Cumberbatch as Sherlock Holmes and Martin Freeman as John Watson.[2] It is perhaps with the wish to modernize the character that the BBC production chooses to present Cumberbatch as a younger Sherlock, who, at least during the first season's episodes, is shown without the characteristic curved pipe or deerstalker cap of stereotypical fame. Likewise, Freeman, as John, is modernized through his lack of the Victorian mustache and side-whiskers that characterized Sidney Paget's representations in the original stories published in *Strand* magazine. Holmes' famous cap appears in Season Two when Sherlock puts it on to be unrecognizable to paparazzi. He is photographed anyway and, ironically, becomes famous for wearing it, primarily through photographs posted online ("A Scandal in Belgravia").

As in any adaptation, this new version of the canon for television audiences must make choices regarding what nuances of Holmes to express (or suppress). Of the many "Sherlocks" evident in the *Sherlock* series, Sherlock as digital native is one of the most compelling, if most difficult for audiences to accept. Despite astronomical leaps made by technology from the Victorian period to the present, there appears to be a greater discomfort with technology in *Sherlock*, especially with regard to technology bound to intelligence, than in Conan Doyle's texts. Why should Sherlock Holmes' unusual technocratic intelligence cause the characters in *Sherlock* more discomfort than it did the Victorian characters within Conan Doyle's texts? What changes occurred to cause this popular cultural attitude shift? I believe these were twofold, encompassing perceptions of technology and perceptions of persons who behave in highly controlled, mechanical ways.

Characters within Conan Doyle's popular stories were more receptive to a Holmes who was technologically adept and extremely intelligent in a machine-like way. In the Victorian period, his stoic detachment was more acceptable by society's more reserved behavioral standards; in addition, forensics was an emerging field still open to an amateur like Holmes.

The idea of daily life mingled with modern technology, which began in the 19th century during the Industrial Revolution, has reached a fever pitch today. Perhaps audiences, caught up in the present moment's all-consuming, seemingly out-of-control technology (e.g., the "Crackberry" phenomenon), find it threatening to see Sherlock, an unpaid amateur, take on technology, especially forensic technology, with his characteristic mechanical detachment. In the 21st century, new medical diagnoses such as "high-functioning autism," attributed to people exhibiting Sherlock's detached, mechanical behavior and intense focus on one subject, further isolate him from the mere eccentricity that characterized his Victorian predecessor. Alyssa Rosenberg's article in *The Atlantic* comparing 19th century and 21st century Holmes is a good example of cultural criticism in the popular press. The author seems pleased that, as Sherlock, Benedict Cumberbatch comes across as an ideal "Aspergerian, asexual type" for the role. This intense, socially detached intelligence, combined with a lack of friends, is presented as socially unacceptable within the scope of the series, especially because it is not tempered by sexuality (like that of another highly intelligent, socially detached character from popular culture — James Bond).

As Britain's other icon, Bond, like Sherlock Holmes, often solves crimes and is not above breaking the law when the ends justify the means. Bond is comparable to Holmes whenever he gleefully challenges the intelligence of those in power. Whether he proves himself smarter than arch criminals or those who would otherwise have been on his side, Bond makes many enemies. Like Holmes, Bond uses the newest technology to aid in his missions and can keep calm and continue work under emotionally fraught circumstances. Such emotional detachment wins him few friends, while his unorthodox methods often make him an outcast within the British Secret Service.

Although Moffat and Gatiss portray Sherlock as an outcast within the series, they also make him attractive and interesting for viewers to watch. Because Sherlock is not meant to be seen as completely outside society, several new characters show audiences that he is meant to be viewed as more than a deductive engine. Molly Hooper has romantic feelings towards Sherlock. Part of the audience's participatory supplements for the series is her online diary, in which she writes of Sherlock: "He's so intelligent it's like he's burning. And he's so cool but not really. And he's fit." In "A Scandal in Belgravia," Molly dresses up and gives Sherlock a romantic gift in an attempt to reveal her feelings, while in "The Reichenbach Fall," she is willing to do whatever necessary to save him from Moriarty's plot to discredit him.

Sherlock also has an advocate in Angelo, the owner of a restaurant where he seems to be a regular. These characters add their voices to John Watson and Mrs. Hudson regarding Sherlock's human qualities. Neither Molly nor Angelo is present in the original stories, perhaps because Victorian Holmes did not need these qualifying characters to "normalize" him.

Sherlock Holmes as Digital Native

Although much has already been written on *Sherlock* in the popular press, little cultural criticism has been published on this new BBC series. Much has, of course, been written about Sherlock Holmes in popular culture and on television adaptations of Conan Doyle's texts, but there is room for critical engagement with regard to Holmes' relationship to technology and audience reception to this peculiar relationship. Rosemary Jann provides a 100-year overview on the character as a popular cultural phenomenon linking science and technology, one who was built upon England's industrial might and 19th century breakthroughs in biology. In the character of Victorian Holmes, the scientist becomes a heroic figure (3–4). James Maertens goes so far as to call technologically intelligent Holmes a "technician-hero" (296). Because extreme intelligence and extremely intelligent people, specifically those who are highly adept technologically, have usually been shown as "freaks" in popular culture, film, and television, it is not surprising that Sherlock Holmes has even been "played by" an android. *Star Trek: The Next Generation's* Lt. Commander Data played Holmes in the episode "Elementary, Dear Data."

Thus, James Wright (16) rightly calls Holmes and Watson "the very models of the modern Information Age." The BBC's Sherlock displays his intelligence through his ease with the latest modern technologies, just as Victorian Holmes is proficient with the technological advances of the late 19th century. Both use technology as an aid to scientifically solve crimes. Though the BBC adaptation chooses to illustrate this important nuance of Holmes' character in a modern light, many of present-day Sherlock's technological proficiencies have their antecedents in the Victorian era.

Victorian Holmes used state-of-the-art 19th century technology. For example, he sent telegrams so often that he had a stack of blanks at home for his convenience. In addition, Holmes had a thorough understanding of the latest advances in forensics and ballistics. Holmes' use of telegrams is translated in the adaptation into modern Sherlock's constant reliance on his smartphone to send texts. At the beginning of the first BBC episode, "A Study in Pink," when given the suggestion to make a call, Sherlock answers "I prefer to text." The quickness with which modern Sherlock types and retrieves information from his phone and laptop and his proficiency with online sources is meant to express his intelligence. "A Study in Pink" plays off Conan Doyle's first introduction of Holmes in "A Study in Scarlet." At the end of the episode, the adaptation conveys Sherlock's intelligence through his mastery of technology, which he uses to solve the case. In a climactic scene, John, D.I. Lestrade from the New Scotland Yard, forensics expert Anderson, and a team of police attempt to solve a murder, while Sherlock's housekeeper Mrs. Hudson gets in the way. Sherlock discovers the key to the crime through his detailed knowledge of the type of smart-phone owned by the victim. He guesses her password, "RACHEL," which she had partially scratched on the floor before she died. Once Sherlock has her password, he is able to locate the phone itself. He describes the victim as "clever" because she understood technology well enough to purposely plant the phone on her killer, knowing it would lead the police to her murderer.

Sherlock's mastery of the Internet is key to presenting his rationalist intelligence in the BBC series. He uses the Internet to get the latest news and data, just as Conan Doyle's Holmes uses the latest issues of various newspapers to get the most current information. Victorian Holmes also has an extensive collection of files on a range of people. He saves tabloids, collects newspaper clippings, photographs, and guide books and frequently consults all of these sources when he needs to research information. Sherlock utilizes both newspapers and the Internet to gather data, at one point telling John, "you check the papers, I'll go online" ("The Great Game"). Through phone texts and posts on his website, he lures criminals into meeting him, just as Victorian Holmes uses advertisements in the "Agony" columns of newspapers to trap criminals into meetings at Baker Street or other locations.

Another example of Sherlock's technocratic ease is his website, entitled "The Science of Deduction," where he communicates both with clients and criminals. In "A Study in Scarlet," Watson reads an article Holmes published in a local magazine about the science of deduction; Sherlock uses similarly pompous language on his site.

The television series is more self-reflexive than Conan Doyle's original stories. During the first six episodes, it frequently refers to Sherlock's website and John's blog. The Science of Deduction website, along with John's blog, where he describes Sherlock's cases, and, for example, the website of Connie Prince, a victim in "The Great Game," exist on the Internet for the audience to use and are meant to serve as supplements to the program. There are hidden messages to help viewers solve puzzles on Sherlock's website. In this way, the BBC adaptation has chosen to keep the self-referential quality of Conan Doyle's stories. In the original stories, clients sometimes find Holmes because they read about his exploits in *Strand Magazine,* where Watson writes about Holmes' cases. Likewise, Conan Doyle published his stories entitled "The Reminiscences of John H. Watson, MD" in *Strand Magazine.*

Characters from Conan Doyle's stories also have been modernized to reflect their ease with technology. Stamford, a character from Conan Doyle's stories, attended university with John and introduces him to Sherlock. "He's like you," Stamford says to John, "all Internet savvy. He's got a blog" ("Mike Stamford"). Like his Victorian predecessor, John proves to be an engaging writer. Detective Lestrade confides that everyone at the police precinct reads his blog ("The Great Game"), and John and Sherlock's Internet fame spreads across London by the second season. In "The Reichenbach Fall," the roommates are so popular that they are pursued by paparazzi, and both Sherlock's and John's websites have many more hits.

Like his Victorian predecessor, Sherlock chastises John for treating his cases as "some kind of romantic adventure" rather than "exact science" performed through "analytical reasoning"; characteristically, technocratic Sherlock performs his criticism through a comment on John's blog (Sherlock Holmes, "Comments").

On the other hand, by "The Great Game," Sherlock admits, "I'd be lost without my blogger," just as Victorian Holmes confessed "I am lost without my Boswell" (Conan Doyle, "A Scandal in Bohemia" 167).

Sherlock Holmes as Forensics Expert

Many critics have commented on Holmes' knowledge of medicine (or lack thereof). Pasquale Accardo's well-known work asserts that Holmes, and therefore Conan Doyle, lacked medical expertise, even by Victorian standards, whereas Philip Wilson is one of several critics who believe that Holmes is a "model diagnostician." The BBC program chooses to retain a positive portrayal of Victorian Holmes' forensic and medical studies and knowledge of ballistics, in addition to his knowledge of and comfort with technology. Although neither the word "forensic" nor the phrase "scientific method" is used in Conan Doyle's stories, as doctors, both Conan Doyle and Watson were in a unique position to understand and value Holmes' deep amateur mastery of medical science regarding humans and animals and familiarity with the latest medical instruments and technology. Through Watson's narration, the reader appreciates Holmes' medical and forensic knowledge. When Holmes is introduced to Watson, for example, he is shown as having just discovered a forensic chemical method for testing blood stains, which proves to be incredibly useful for solving crime. "Why man, it is the most practical medico-legal discovery for years," Holmes says (Conan Doyle, "A Study in Scarlet" 10).

With regard to ballistics, several of Conan Doyle's stories describe Holmes' understanding of firearm characteristics and the behavior of bullets, especially when murders are arranged to look like suicides. Holmes' knowledge of forensics and ballistics is remarkable, as the forensics field was quite new in Victorian times, when it was usually referred to as Medical Jurisprudence or Legal Medicine (Wagner 3). In 1887, for example, the year "A Study in Scarlet" was written, although great strides were occurring in the emerging field of forensic medicine, according to E.J. Wagner (29), only "a few adventurous physicians versed in anatomy, pharmacy, and microscopy were beginning to use their skills in the study of unexplained sudden death." In fact, no registry for deaths existed in England until the late 19th century.

Holmes' interest in forensics is outlined in the first chapter of "A Study in Scarlet," in which Stamford warns Watson that Holmes is eccentric and takes part in strange experiments, spending much time in medical laboratories even though he is not a medical student. In the second chapter, Watson observes that Holmes "sometimes spent his day at the chemical laboratory, sometimes in the dissecting-rooms, and occasionally in long walks, which appeared to take him into the lowest portions of the city" (20). The BBC adaptation retains Holmes' keen interest in forensics, capitalizing on modern popular cultural interest in the subject. The opening credits of *Sherlock*, meant to set the tone for the series, present it as a program similar to *CSI*, by exhibiting a close-up view of a drop of blood falling from a medicine dropper, followed by a microscopic view of that blood. The adaptation chooses to introduce Sherlock to the audience by showing him unzipping a body bag at the morgue, smelling the corpse, and asking "How fresh?" ("A Study in Pink"). Victorian Holmes' dramatic test of beating a corpse with a riding crop to ascertain the manner in which bruises form after death is also retained in this sense, albeit anachronistically. Modern Sherlock goes further by, for example, keeping a human head from the morgue in his refrigerator at home in order to study the manner in which saliva collects after death ("The Blind Banker").

Sherlock's specialized knowledge of forensics is evident in "The Great Game," when he sets up a criminal investigation lab in his apartment, complete with microscope, chemical apparatus, and the victim's sneakers hanging up in his kitchen for analysis. His understanding of bacteria and knowledge of poisons help to solve the case. Like Victorian Holmes, 21st century Sherlock is ahead of the forensics investigations of his day; he is able to detect a virtually undetectable poison that the victim's autopsy did not reveal. To catch the killer, in this case a bomber, Sherlock uses an updated version of Holmes' agony column posts, posting an update on his website: "FOUND: Pair of trainers ... toxin still present. Apply 221b Baker St." (Science of Deduction). The phone rings immediately after he posts his discovery, proving that the criminal is also techno-savvy and has been checking Sherlock's website to see if the detective has solved the case. Here the series' self-reflexivity again comes strongly into play: once viewers watch Sherlock type his post into his website, they are able to go on his website and see the post.

Sherlock Holmes' Unusual Intelligence

Whereas Victorian Holmes was frequently viewed as an eccentric amateur by Scotland Yard, contemporary Sherlock is perceived as a "freak" by some of his professional colleagues. For example, when Lestrade invites Sherlock to visit the crime scene in "A Study in Pink," he is greeted with "Hello freak" by Sergeant Donovan. "Freak's here," she says, "Bringing him in." The sergeant warns John to stay away from Sherlock, worrying that someday presenting himself at the scene of the crime will not be sufficient for the amateur detective and that he will commit the murder himself. She objects to the detective's presence because he is not paid for his services and seems to obtain pleasure from viewing dead bodies. In "The Reichenbach Fall," Sergeant Donovan is also suspicious of the speed and ease with which Sherlock solves the mystery of the ambassador's kidnapped children, telling Lestrade that she believes Sherlock must have had something to do with the crime. Such ideas would not occur to the official police regarding Victorian Holmes, who is considered a meddler at worst, whereas contemporary Sherlock is called a "psychopath" by one investigator. "I am not a psychopath, Anderson," retorts Sherlock, "I am a high-functioning sociopath. Do your research" ("A Study in Pink"). Sherlock is more aware of his difference than is his Victorian predecessor, who is often puzzled by references to his eccentricities, which are not inconsiderable, including his "incredible untidiness, his addiction to music at strange hours, his occasional revolver practice within doors, his weird and often malodorous scientific experiments, and the atmosphere of violence and danger which hung around him made him the very worst tenant in London" ("Adventure of the Dying Detective" 932). Contemporary Sherlock is more self-aware, understanding his antisocial tendencies, though he defends himself against the comment that he is mentally ill. He is also cognizant of the fact that his feats of deduction sometimes strike others as a manifestation of an abrasive personality. For example, after astounding John with deductions about his personal life simply by examining his cell phone, John exclaims, "That was amazing." The following dialogue from "A Study in Pink" exemplifies Sherlock's awareness of the way most people view him:

SHERLOCK: You think so?
JOHN: Extraordinary. It was quite extraordinary.
SHERLOCK: That's not what people normally say.
JOHN: What do people normally say?
SHERLOCK: "Piss off."

Like that of Conan Doyle's character, Sherlock's antisocial nature often makes him seem cold blooded to his acquaintances.

In Chapter 1 (9) of *A Study in Scarlet*, Stamford tells Watson

Holmes is a little too scientific for my tastes — it approaches to cold-bloodedness. I could imagine his giving a friend a little pinch of the latest vegetable alkaloid, not out of malevolence, you understand, but simply out of a spirit of inquiry in order to have an accurate idea of the effects. To do him justice, I think that he would take it himself with the same readiness. He appears to have a passion for definite and exact knowledge.

This passage is a prime example of Holmes' unusual rationalist intelligence. Conan Doyle implies that Holmes may be too much of a rationalist, often describing him as an intelligent machine. His face is said to possess a "composure which made so many regard him as a machine rather than a man" ("Crooked Man" 492). The BBC adaptation goes further, and Sherlock's rationalist intelligence sometimes serves to dehumanize him until he is almost at one with the technology he so adeptly manipulates. The BBC production chooses to superimpose typed words upon each clue Sherlock identifies, highlighting the machine-like quality of his thought process. The audience hears robotic sound effects meant to represent Sherlock's computational brain working while given a close-up image of the character's face and eyes, followed by a close-up of the dead body Sherlock examines with a small square magnifying lens ("A Study in Pink"). In "The Hounds of Baskerville," Sherlock enters what he terms his "mind palace" in order to solve the linguistic mystery which includes the words "hound" and "liberty." In order to deduce that "hound" is not a word, but an acronym, Sherlock tries out many possible permutations. The audience is able to follow his thought process because the words actually float around his head. Twenty-first century Sherlock self-identifies as a computer, stating that he has "deleted" the fact that the earth goes around the sun, of which John has just informed him. "Look," says Sherlock, pointing to his head, "this is my hard-drive and it only makes sense for me to put things in there that are useful. Really useful" ("The Blind Banker"). In this way, the adaptation re-enacts the famous scene from "A Study in Scarlet" in which Watson is shocked that Holmes does not know this simple fact. "Now that I know do it, I shall do my best to forget it," says Holmes, explaining that he has only so much room in his memory and he does not want to clutter it with information extraneous to his profession (12).

Concluding Remarks

Sherlock Holmes has evolved as technology evolved; from the earliest silent films to radio, movies, television, and computer games, he has been constantly modernized and updated. Any new adaptation of the Sherlockian canon is forced to make choices regarding which parts of the character to build upon and which to gloss over. In recognizing these choices, it is possible for modern readers of Conan Doyle's texts to compare the cultural significance of late–Victorian society's perception of unusual technocratic intelligence with our own and to conclude that although audiences of both eras perceive technocratic ease as a sign of intelligence, Sherlock Holmes' technocratic ease causes more discomfort to those around him in the 21st century than it does in the Victorian period.

Yet in portraying Sherlock as a "freak," Gatiss and Moffat also create a Holmes who is heroic, continuing in the tradition of the Maertens' "technician-hero." On the one hand, he is a social outcast because of his unusual mastery of technology, specifically new media, and others consider him a "freak" because of his unusual interest in forensics, superior problem-solving skills, and inability to maintain most social relationships. On the other hand, unlike stereotypical freaks portrayed in popular culture, Sherlock does not become flustered during social interaction but usually takes the upper hand; he does back down when confronted with opposition but pushes forward to save his friends. He fails to be intimidated by Irene Adler's nudity ("A Scandal in Belgravia") or Moriarty's blustering and threats ("The Great Game," "The Reichenbach Fall"). In fact, Sherlock is portrayed as quite powerful when interacting with others face to face.

In this series, Sherlock reveals his technocratic intelligence through his obsession with obscure technical knowledge; this he enjoys showing off, often incognizant of the fact that non-experts find this type of display uninteresting, annoying, or even threatening. In this respect both Victorian Holmes and modern Sherlock epitomize the definition of "tech-geek." Comparing the changes the character undergoes over time is crucial because these point to a popular cultural reception shift with regard to technocratic intelligences such as Holmes. The shift occurs from Victorian literary audiences' relative ease with the technologically adept detective to modern television audiences' discomfort with the same detective's technological expertise.

There has long been a close connection between "freaks" and new technology, and Sherlock Holmes' status as a cultural icon derives in part from his technological adeptness. The difference is that Victorian Holmes, while technologically savvy, was not considered a "freak" in popular culture; this appellation was bestowed upon him in the modern *Sherlock* series.

WORKS CITED

Accardo, Pasquale. *Diagnosis and Detection: The Medical Iconography of Sherlock Holmes.* London: Associated University Press, 1987.
"The Blind Banker." *Sherlock.* Writ. Stephen Thompson. Dir. Euros Lyn. BBC. 31 Oct. 2010. Television.

Conan Doyle, Sir Arthur. "The Adventure of the Dying Detective." *The New Annotated Sherlock Holmes.* Leslie S. Klinger, ed. 3 vols. New York: Norton, 2005. Print.
_____. "The Crooked Man." *The New Annotated Sherlock Holmes.* Leslie S. Klinger, ed. 3 vols. New York: Norton, 2005. Print.
_____. "A Scandal in Bohemia." *The New Annotated Sherlock Holmes.* Leslie S. Klinger, ed. 3 vols. New York: Norton, 2005. Print.
_____. "A Study in Scarlet." *The New Annotated Sherlock Holmes.* Leslie S. Klinger, ed. 3 vols. New York: Norton, 2005. Print.
Erisman, Fred, and Wendy Erisman. "'Data! Data! Data!': Holmesian Echoes in *Star Trek: The Next Generation.*" *Sherlock Holmes: Victorian Sleuth to Modern Hero.* Charles R. Putney et al., eds. London: Scarecrow, 1996. 90–101. Print.
"The Great Game." *Sherlock.* Writ. Mark Gatiss. Dir. Paul McGuigan. BBC. 7 Nov. 2010. Television.
"The Hounds of Baskerville." *Sherlock.* Writ. Mark Gatiss. Dir. Paul McGuigan. BBC. 8 Jan. 2012. Television.
Jann, Rosemary. *The Adventures of Sherlock Holmes: Detecting Social Order.* New York: Twayne, 1995. Print.
Klinger, Leslie S., ed. *The New Annotated Sherlock Holmes.* 3 vols. New York: Norton, 2005. Print.
Maertens, James W. "Masculine Power and the Ideal Reasoner: Sherlock Holmes, Technician-Hero." *Sherlock Holmes: Victorian Sleuth to Modern Hero.* Charles R. Putney et al., eds. London: Scarecrow, 1996. 296–322. Print.
Molly Hooper. BBC. 2012. <http://www.mollyhooper.co.uk/>.
The Personal Blog of Dr. John H. Watson. BBC. Web. 2011. <http://www.johnwatsonblog.co.uk/>.
"The Reichenbach Fall." *Sherlock.* Writ. Stephen Thompson. Dir. Toby Haynes. BBC. 15 Jan. 2012. Television.
Rosenberg, Alyssa. "Sherlock Holmes Meets the 21st Century." Web. 19 Oct. 2010. <http://www.theatlantic.com/culture/archive/2010/10/sherlock-holmes-meets-the-21st-century/64788/>.
"A Scandal in Belgravia." *Sherlock.* Writ. Steven Moffat. Dir. Paul McGuigan. BBC Worldwide. 2012. DVD.
The Science of Deduction. BBC. Web. 2011. <http://www.thescienceofdeduction.co.uk/>.
"A Study in Pink." *Sherlock.* Writ. Steven Moffat and Mark Gatiss. Dir. Paul McGuigan. BBC Worldwide, 2010. DVD.
Wagner, E.J. *The Science of Sherlock Holmes: From Baskerville Hall to the Valley of Fear, the Real Forensics Behind the Great Detective's Greatest Cases.* Hoboken, NJ: Wiley, 2007. Print.
Wilson, Philip K. "Sherlock Holmes from Model Diagnostician to Medical Icon: The Physician's Changing Perspective." *Sherlock Holmes: Victorian Sleuth to Modern Hero.* Charles R. Putney et al., eds. London: Scarecrow, 1996. Print.
Wright, James R. "They Were the Very Models of the Modern Information Age." *Sherlock Holmes: Victorian Sleuth to Modern Hero.* Charles R. Putney et al., eds. London: Scarecrow, 1996. Print.

Notes

1. The series is not the first to set the character in modern times. There are several fine examples of non–Victorian adaptations, like the films made by Basil Rathbone and Nigel Bruce, most of which are set during the Second World War in the then-contemporary 1940s.

2. For the purpose of clarity I use "Holmes" to refer to Conan Doyle's original creation and "Sherlock" to refer to the BBC's new character, especially because, when addressed as "Mr. Holmes," the character requests "Oh — Sherlock, please" ("A Study in Pink").

11

Investigating Victorian Propriety in Money Matters

Svetlana Bochman

SEBASTIAN: Find it and we'll pay you. Five figures. [Reaches into his pocket, brandishes a check. JOHN clearly impressed by the amount — SHERLOCK not.] This is only an advance. Tell me how he got in — there's a bigger one on its way.
SHERLOCK: I don't need incentives, Sebastian. [SHERLOCK will not even look at it — breezes off to begin work. SEBASTIAN about to put the check away.]
JOHN: He's kidding you, obviously.
> —Sherlock, *"The Blind Banker"*

"Holmes folded up his check and placed it carefully in his notebook. 'I am a poor man,' said he, as he patted it affectionately, and thrust it into the depths of his inner pocket."
> —*Watson describing Holmes accepting a 6000 pound fee in "The Return of Sherlock Holmes"*

The word "money" is mentioned over 100 times in the Holmes stories and novels. Victorian obsession with matters of decorum and propriety in social manners and mores, specifically money matters, are evident in the BBC's recent televised adaptation of the Sherlock Holmes stories. *Sherlock* makes some interesting decisions regarding what nuances of Arthur Conan Doyle's detective either to build upon or gloss over. Set in contemporary London, *Sherlock* is an example of a popular cultural adaptation that tells readers of Conan Doyle's texts much about late–Victorian society, particularly with regard to changing perceptions of remuneration for intellectual labor.

This chapter will address the process, complications, and changing views regarding hiring and paying an amateur consulting detective. For example, in Victorian times, Holmes received remuneration according to his clients' financial capacities. Sometimes he would be approached by clients and sometimes by Scotland Yard. Contemporary Sherlock is not usually paid, as clients typically do not approach him, despite his website's advertisement. Both characters aid the police unofficially, but Sherlock has few private clients.

"The Work Is Its Own Reward": A Victorian Aversion to Doing Business

Most critical discussion on the character's association with money has focused on the canon, as well as on Conan Doyle's own ambivalence towards earning a living from his Sherlock Holmes tales, which he considered beneath his full literary power. Robbie Goh sums up much critical commentary on this subject when he states that "one need not look too deeply into the author's biographical details to see a long-standing anxiety and concern with financial matters.... [Consequently,] the idea of money comes up repeatedly in Conan Doyle's writings" (97). There is room for further investigation of monetary issues in the Holmes legacy, especially in television adaptations such as *Sherlock*. A comparison of Victorian and modern portrayals of the character reveals the counter-intuitive discovery that Sherlock Holmes *not* receiving money for his services seems more odd to those around him in the 21st century than in the 19th. This is evident by the BBC choosing to depict Sherlock's nemesis accepting payment for his "consultations," whereas Sherlock is for the most part unpaid. Why does Sherlock *not* getting paid for his detective work and forensic services cause the characters in the series, representing society at large, more discomfort than it did the Victorian readers of Conan Doyle's texts? What change occurred to make it unacceptable for Sherlock to remain unpaid? The answer lies both with the professionalization of the police and detective forces and in the type of cases 21st century Sherlock attempts to solve.

The process of professionalization of detective and police forces was only beginning during the Victorian period. In the 21st century, there is a shift in audience expectations of the detective genre with regard to payment and professionalization of detectives towards one of greater formality. Perhaps, in our current time of financial instability, it is threatening to see an unpaid amateur with no desire for monetary reward become involved in dangerous situations, not for the sake of performing social good, but because these dangers present interesting puzzles. During the Victorian period, when the British Empire was experiencing great financial stability, an unpaid amateur such as Holmes did not seem as odd. In addition, because there is a shift in the audience's own ease in discussing money in the 21st century, Sherlock, who does not wish to discuss the practicalities of earning a living, seems odd to those around him. Sherlock also focuses on much more violent crime than his Victorian predecessor. Rosemary Jann (71) notices that Holmes' cases for the most part involve thefts, loss, and disorder, not murder. Sherlock's cases are more grisly, generating a greater discomfort regarding his role as an unpaid amateur detective and forensics expert.

Although the character's relationship with the official police is often fraught with tension, both in the original stories and in this adaptation, Victorian Holmes was viewed as merely an eccentric amateur by Scotland Yard. Sherlock, on the other hand, is perceived as a "freak" by some of his professional colleagues. Their main objection is that Sherlock is not a "professional" and therefore does not "belong" at the crime scenes. In the 21st century, acting as an unpaid detective and forensic professional has become "improper."

With regard to his management of money matters, Victorian Holmes is portrayed as "eccentric" but still a "gentleman": though he breaches decorum numerous times in the process of solving cases, Watson hardly ever deems Holmes socially vulgar, crude, or crass. Watson's opinion of Holmes' propriety regarding money is key, for Watson himself represents Victorian propriety. Holmes calls him "the one fixed point in a changing age" (Klinger 491). However, Sherlock in our contemporary era is perceived as a "freak" by those around him precisely because he *does not* accept payment for his services; the BBC's Sherlock is also more self-aware of his difference, referring to himself as an "outcast" and a "sociopath" ("A Study in Pink"). Ironically, modern Sherlock displays a Victorian aversion to "doing business." The adaptation chooses to retain this important nuance of Holmes' character, and many of Sherlock's issues with receiving payment for his "consulting" have its antecedents in the Victorian era.

During the Victorian period, earning money, and especially discussing or enjoying the process of the earning of money from one's work, was looked down upon by the upper classes and consequently by the middle classes that aspired to copy them. Because working for money was considered a bit ungentlemanly and Holmes is often portrayed as a gentleman, he defends his professional activities by reiterating that "The work is its own reward" (Klinger 56). Holmes protests that not only does he not want compensation, but that he does not wish for his name to appear in the newspapers; publicity of this sort was also considered ungentlemanly. But these protests often prove contradictory, as in several instances Holmes almost gleefully accepts payment, praise and media notice. Sherlock, on the other hand, more fully accepts the Victorian idea of shunning remuneration for "amateur" activities.

"Princely Sums" or "Interesting Cases"? Victorian Holmes and Modern Sherlock

In both Conan Doyle's stories and the BBC's adaptation, Sherlock Holmes often displays a negative reaction to earning money for what he considers a higher calling. Goh (105) asserts that "the Holmes stories as a whole are, not surprisingly, coy and also ambiguous about the detective's monetary motivations. By and large, any suggestion of the practical reality that Holmes must depend on his hire for his living, is concealed behind notions of zeal for his work." Watson reinforces this idea when he earnestly asserts that

> I have seldom known him to claim any large reward for his inestimable services. So otherworldly was he or so capricious — that he frequently refused his help to the powerful and wealthy where the problem made no appeal to his sympathies, while he would devote weeks of most intense application to the affairs of some humble client whose case presented those strange and dramatic qualities which appealed to his imagination and challenged his ingenuity [Klinger 97].

Watson does not mention that in the few cases that Holmes does claim a "large reward," the fees are extremely large, allowing him the luxury to choose more interesting cases in the future. Likewise, Sherlock specifies "interesting cases only, please" on his website, "The Science of Deduction," through which he communicates with both potential clients and criminals.

Both detectives begin showing potential at a young age, but only Victorian Holmes sees in his skills "that a profession could be made out of what had been up to that time the merest hobby," and a remunerative profession at that, when a Justice of the Peace said, "Mr. Holmes, it seems to me that all the detectives of fact and fancy would be children in your hands. That's your line in life, sir, and you may take the word of a man who has seen something of the world" (Leavitt 114).

Though both 19th and 21st century detectives seem to possess a Victorian propriety regarding remuneration for intellectual labor, Victorian Holmes at times protests too much. This is evidenced not only by his actions, but by the language the character uses to speak about money. When Holmes introduces himself and his professional activities to Watson in "A Study in Scarlet," Watson has just identified himself as a doctor. "Well, I have a trade of my own," Holmes says. "I'm a consulting detective." Holmes then explains that his clients, aside from other detectives who need assistance, "are all people who are in trouble about something and want a little enlightening. I listen to their story, they listen to my comments, and then I pocket my fee" (Klinger 18).

This he does most literally in "The Adventure of the Priory School." Holmes, at first too busy to take a less than "interesting" case, changes his mind when offered 6,000 pounds, commenting that "It is a princely offer" (74). At the end of the story, Conan Doyle describes how "Holmes folded up his check and placed it carefully in his notebook. 'I am a poor man,' said he, as he patted it affectionately, and thrust it into the depths of his inner pocket" (96).

Victorian Holmes also uses the lure of an all-expense paid trip to Switzerland and a large fee when attempting to persuade Watson to accompany him on a case. "My dear Watson," he says. "First-class tickets and all expenses paid on a princely scale? ... The family is anxious, and as they are exceedingly wealthy no sum will be spared if we can clear the matter up" (Klinger 447).

Whereas modern Sherlock is portrayed as not having enough money to pay for groceries, Victorian Holmes is able to personally raise 3,000 pounds in a few hours in "The Adventure of the Beryl Coronet." Compared to 1886, when the story was set, this would have been worth approximately £150,000 in today's money, funds Holmes is able to raise after only five years in practice. In addition, Holmes receives a £1,000 reward for the case, or approximately £50,000 for one day's work (Hyder 24). By 1895 Watson states that Holmes' "increasing fame had brought with it an immense practice" with many "illustrious clients" ("Adventure of Black Peter" 97). (Holmes eventually earns enough to retire to the country.)

Twenty-first century Sherlock's treatment of a large fee makes for a striking contrast. Sherlock's single private client is Sebastian Wilkes, with whom he attended college. "I heard you're a consulting detective now.... This might be right up your alley," Sebastian tells Sherlock in an email (The Science of Deduction). In the second episode, "The Blind Banker," Sebastian hires Sherlock to investigate a security breach at his bank. He offers an advance on a £20,000 payment if Sherlock can solve the case. At this time, neither Sherlock nor John is gainfully employed. Yet Sherlock refuses the fee, though he takes the case. "I don't need incentives, Sebastian," he says, offended.

In addition, hiring a consulting detective is more difficult in the 21st century than it was in the 19th. When John asks him "Who are you? What do you do?" Sherlock answers "What do you think?"

JOHN: I'd say ... private detective....
SHERLOCK: But?
JOHN: Police don't go to private detectives.
SHERLOCK: I'm a consulting detective. The only one in the world — I invented the job.
JOHN: What does that mean?
SHERLOCK: What it means is that when the police are out of their depth — which is always, they consult me ["A Study in Pink"].

Sherlock has a complex relationship with official police: they desire his help but do not wish for him to tamper with evidence. Victorian Holmes was given more freedom of movement by the official police. "I follow my own methods and tell as much or as little as I choose. That is the advantage of being unofficial," Holmes says (Klinger 411). Holmes was happy to allow the police all the credit for solving a crime, so long as he was allowed to work out what to him was often simply an interesting puzzle: "I have no wish ever to score at their expense," he says regarding the official authorities (*Valley of Fear* 255). Modern Sherlock is different; he relishes proving the official police wrong, as when he taunts them with text messages screaming "Wrong!" during a press conference ("A Study in Pink"). Sherlock seems more involved in the crimes he is asked to consult upon, yet much less tampering is permitted with modern crime scenes. Contemporary Lestrade, like his Victorian predecessor, has a difficult relationship with Sherlock Holmes, as is evident in the following representative exchange:

> LESTRADE: Sherlock, this is our case. I'm letting you in, but you do not go off on your own. Clear?
> SHERLOCK: I'm not your sniffer dog! ["A Study in Pink"].

"A Man Whom I Should Be Proud to Do Business With": Holmes' and Moriarty's Views of Money

The BBC's adaptation transforms Moriarty's role as an evil intelligence working alone into one of a "consulting criminal" hired by clients for unsavory purposes. Victorian Moriarty remains hidden behind the crimes of others and is compared to a spider at the center of a vast criminal network. Contemporary Moriarty is personally hired by private individuals who need criminal assistance for everything from fleeing the country to committing murder (*Sherlock*, "The Blind Banker"). Modern Moriarty views the acquiring of money as a means to gain greater influence; although he is already quite wealthy, he breaks into the Bank of England to broadcast his power (*Sherlock*, "The Reichenbach Fall"). Sherlock is not interested in money, scorning payment, although he is financially insolvent. He is also not impressed by his clients' wealth, behaving with purposeful rudeness at Buckingham Palace (*Sherlock*, "A Scandal in Belgravia").

Though he often claims not to want fame or see his name in the paper, after seeing a reference to "Mr. Sherlock Holmes, the well-known consulting expert" in a news-bill, Victorian Holmes asserts that "The Press, Watson, is a most valuable institution, if you only know how to use it" (Klinger 134). This way of reflecting on fame and fortune, which seems to go against his Victorian propriety when dealing with money matters, carries over to the way in which Holmes speaks of Moriarty and other criminals.

Holmes speaks almost respectfully about Moriarty's chief of staff, who is paid "six thousand a year. That's paying for brains, you see the American business principle.... It's more than the Prime Minister gets. That gives you an idea of Moriarty's gains" (Klinger 243). He sometimes speaks about dealing with criminals in corporate terms, when discussing Jonathan Wild, a precursor of Moriarty, for example. According to Holmes, Wild was "the hidden force of London criminals, to whom he sold his brains and his organization on a fifteen percent commission" (243). In another adventure, Holmes doubts that a culprit would behave in a uniquely intelligent way: "A criminal who was capable of such a thought is a man whom I should be proud to do business with" ("Adventure of the Priory School" 83).

In both the original stories and the adaptation, Moriarty points to similarities between himself and Sherlock Holmes. Modern-day Moriarty tells Sherlock "I'm a specialist, you see. Like you." Sherlock does not see Moriarty this way; in contrast to Holmes' grudging respect for intelligent criminals, Sherlock taunts 21st century Moriarty precisely because he gets paid for a living, and paid by private clients at that. When detective and criminal meet, Sherlock derides Moriarty's employment: "Dear Jim," he mocks, "please will you fix it for me? To get rid of my lover's nasty sister? Dear Jim, please will you fix it for me to disappear to South America?" ("The Great Game"). The BBC adaptation changes Moriarty's role from an evil intelligence amassing wealth by acting behind various criminal elements to one of a consulting criminal that might be hired by clients for unsavory purposes. John is astonished that "people come to him wanting their crimes fixed up like booking a holiday?"

Moriarty proves capable of committing exponentially worse crimes on behalf of others. In "The Reichenbach Fall" he markets himself as the top consulting criminal by committing outlandish crimes, getting himself arrested, then showing himself able to walk away unpunished. His show trial, the fact that Sherlock is called as a witness against him, and the fact that Moriarty is found innocent become an advertisement to those who may wish to employ him. While Moriarty accumulates a great amount of wealth from his various exploits, Sherlock accepts gifts instead of cash, remaining in a state of genteel poverty.

Concluding Remarks

With regard to Sherlock Holmes' significance for literary audiences, Kyle Freeman attempts to explain the detective's enduring popularity. From the Sherlock Holmes stories there is that sense of solidness we get from this world in which logic triumphs over super-stition, and where justice in one form or another is meted out to violators of the social order. The sense of order that runs through this world is one of the great satisfactions of these stories. No matter how bizarre the circumstances, Holmes will tender a rational explanation for everything. Criminals are caught not because they make a fatal error, but because all human actions, good and bad, leave traces behind. If you pay close enough attention to the causative chain of events in every-day life, and you've trained yourself to think logically, you'll be able to follow that chain when someone has committed a crime [xxii].

In "Sherlock Holmes, Order, and the Late-Victorian Mind," Christopher Clausen famously argues that Holmes represented social order to Conan Doyle's literary audience (66). Paula Reitner takes this argument further, positing that Victorian Holmes represented an ideal type professionally (57). Meanwhile, 21st century audience expectations of the detective genre have shifted to one of greater formality regarding a detective's payment and pro-fessionalization: those who work without pay are considered "freaks."

WORKS CITED

Atkinson, Michael. "Small Change: Money and Transformation in 'The Man with the Twisted Lip.'" *The Secret Marriage of Sherlock Holmes and Other Eccentric Readings*. Ann Arbor: University of Michigan Press, 1996. Print.

"The Blind Banker." *Sherlock*. Writ. Mark Gatiss, Steven Moffat. Dir. Euros Lyn. BBC. 31 Oct. 2010. Television.

Clausen, Christopher. "Sherlock Holmes, Order, and the Late-Victorian Mind." *Critical Essays on Sir Arthur Conan Doyle: Critical Essays on British Literature*. Harold Orel, ed. New York: G.K. Hall, 1992. Print.

Conan Doyle, Sir Arthur. "The Adventure of Black Peter." *The New Annotated Sherlock Holmes*. 3 vols. Leslie S. Klinger, ed. New York: Norton, 2005. Print.

_____. "The Adventure of the Norwood Builder." *The New Annotated Sherlock Holmes*. 3 vols. Leslie S. Klinger, ed. New York: Norton, 2005. Print.

_____. "The Adventure of the Priory School." *The New Annotated Sherlock Holmes*. 3 vols. Leslie S. Klinger, ed. New York: Norton, 2005. Print.

_____. "The Adventure of the Six Napoleons." *The New Annotated Sherlock Holmes*. 3 vols. Leslie S. Klinger, ed. New York: Norton, 2005. Print.

_____. "The Disappearance of Lady Frances Carfax." *The New Annotated Sherlock Holmes*. 3 vols. Leslie S. Klinger, ed. New York: Norton, 2005. Print.

_____. "His Last Bow." *The New Annotated Sherlock Holmes*. 3 vols. Leslie S. Klinger, ed. New York: Norton, 2005. Print.

_____. *Memories and Adventures*. Wordsworth Literary Lives. Hertfordshire, UK: Wordsworth Editions, 2007. Print.

_____. "Silver Blaze." *The New Annotated Sherlock Holmes*. 3 vols. Leslie S. Klinger, ed. New York: Norton, 2005. Print.

_____. "A Study in Scarlet." *The New Annotated Sherlock Holmes*. 3 vols. Leslie S. Klinger, ed. New York: Norton, 2005. Print.

_____. *The Valley of Fear*. *The New Annotated Sherlock Holmes*. 3 vols. Leslie S. Klinger, ed. New York: Norton, 2005. Print.

Freeman, Kyle. "Introduction." *The Complete Works of Sherlock Holmes*. Vol. 1. 2 vols. New York: Barnes and Noble Classics, 2003. Print.

Goh, Robbie. "Reading Holmes: Capital and the Sign of the Market in 'The Hound of the Baskervilles.'" *Semiotica* 160, 1–4 (2006): 95–113. Print.

"The Great Game." *Sherlock.* Writ. Stephen Thompson. Dir. Paul McGuigan. BBC. 7 Nov. 2010. Television.

"The Hounds of Baskerville." *Sherlock.* Writ. Mark Gatiss. Dir. Paul McGuigan. BBC. 8 Jan. 2012. Television.

Hyder, William. "Holmes' Busy Day." *Baker Street Journal* 51 (2001): 23–29. Print.

Jann, Rosemary. *The Adventures of Sherlock Holmes: Detecting Social Order.* New York: Twayne, 1995. Print.

Klinger, Leslie S., ed. *The New Annotated Sherlock Holmes.* 3 vols. New York: Norton, 2005. Print.

Leavitt, R.K. Shreffler, "Nummi in Arca, or the Fiscal Holmes." *The Baker Street Reader: Cornerstone Writings About Sherlock Holmes.* Contributions to the Study of Popular Culture. No. 8. Philip A. Shreffler, ed. London: Greenwood, 1984. Print.

McQueen, Ian. "First Interval: Financial Problems." *Sherlock Holmes Detected: The Problems of the Long Stories.* New York: Drake, 1974. Print.

"The Reichenbach Fall." *Sherlock.* Writ. Stephen Thompson. Dir. Toby Haynes. BBC. 15 Jan. 2012. Television.

Reitner, Paula J. "Doctors, Detectives, and the Professional Ideal: The Trial of Thomas Neil Cream and the Mastery of Sherlock Holmes." *College Literature* 35.3 (Summer 2008): 57–95. Print.

Rye, Marilyn. "Profession and Performance: The Work Ethic of Sherlock Holmes." *Sherlock Holmes: Victorian Sleuth to Modern Hero.* Charles R. Putney et al., eds. London: Scarecrow, 1996. Print.

"A Scandal in Belgravia." *Sherlock.* BBC. 1 Jan. 2012. Television. *The Science of Deduction.* BBC. Web. 2011. <http://www.thescienceofdeduction.co.uk/>.

"A Study in Pink." *Sherlock.* BBC. 24 Oct. 2010. Television.

Sweeney, Susan Elizabeth. "The Other Side of the Coin in Arthur Conan Doyle's 'The Red-Headed League.'" *Sherlock Holmes: Victorian Sleuth to Modern Hero.* Charles R. Putney et al., eds. London: Scarecrow, 1996. Print.

NOTE: I thank Sue Vertue, *Sherlock*'s producer, for allowing me to quote from the shooting scripts for the series.

12

Welcome to London
The Role of the Cinematic Tourist
LYNNETTE PORTER

When Sherlock and John mistake an American tourist, fresh from Heathrow, as their murder suspect, the detective is momentarily at a loss for words. After all, he has just accosted an innocent man in the backseat of a taxi. "Welcome to London," Sherlock finally tells him, much to John's amusement ("A Study in Pink"). That also could be series' creators Steven Moffat and Mark Gatiss' message to viewers. When they collaborated to bring Holmes back to life on television as *Sherlock*, they deliberately created a visual love letter to London. As Gatiss explains, modern London "is just as exciting as a London full of fog and hackney carriages. We have tried to fetishise the modern era. There are ways of shooting even the most familiar place that refreshes everything about it" (Higgins). *Sherlock* visually introduces London to a potentially large international tourist market by showcasing familiar iconic images while presenting London as a clean, efficient modern metropolis — in short, the ideal holiday destination.

The opening credits feature the London Eye, the Thames, and Big Ben in the background, a virtual tour that satisfies potential visitors' expectations. A time-lapse shot speeds the traffic through a modern city center and portrays the hustle of a time-conscious, technology-driven society. Sherlock, who relies on laptops and smartphones, thrives in the bustling city. Nevertheless, Sherlock's and John's[1] quiet, leisurely taxi rides through London not only provide time for some earnest discussions between the leads but also provide glimpses into London life. Storefronts are reflected in the windows as John stares through the glass; St. Paul's Cathedral or other landmarks drift by the audience's (and the characters') bridgetop view as the taxi crosses the Thames.

Like Sherlock and John, or Holmes and Watson, audiences see different Londons in the post–2000 adaptations. Fans who want a glimpse of Holmes' Victorian London need look no farther than a nearby movie poster for either

Sherlock Holmes (2009) or *Sherlock Holmes: A Game of Shadows* (2011). Promotional posters, viewed the world over, feature Big Ben or Westminster Abbey in the background, identifying Holmes as British, but the posters' background also suggests a foggy, mysterious London, with narrow streets illuminated by gas lamps. Former filming locations representing Holmes' Victorian landmarks include the easy-to-find Somerset House, which became a prison for *Sherlock Holmes,* and St. Paul's Cathedral, where a circular staircase led to Lord Blackwood's lair. A re-creation of Piccadilly Circus, most easily identified by its central statue of Eros, also provides a familiar backdrop for scenes in the first film. Because so many iconic places mentioned in the Conan Doyle canon and featured in films mimicking Victorian London still are prominent tourist destinations in 21st century London, cinematic tourists on the trail of Sherlock Holmes can deduce just where their particular Holmes — from books, television series, or films — may have traveled.

Although London's landmarks provide visual references for audiences, *Sherlock Holmes* (2009) filming also took place in Manchester and Liverpool, and former filming locations in these and other cities are listed at the film's Internet Movie Database (IMDB) site ("Filming Locations"). Promoters of national tourism, such as VisitBritain, also assist cinematic tourists by providing itineraries and maps of filming locations across the U.K. and share information provided by studios wanting to promote their films. Because many former filming sites are near typical tourist destinations and are easy to find without resorting to matching shots from the film against the location's everyday appearance, fans often take advantage of such websites as they plan their vacations. These websites turn fans into experts about the movies they enjoy and encourage them to become cinematic tourists.

The role of the cinematic tourist in Sherlock Holmes fandom has become increasingly important to the British government and businesses, who use their web sites to encourage visitors to learn more about the country as well as its entertainment connection. A 2008 U.K. report commissioned by VisitBritain and the Tourism Alliance estimated that the British tourism industry was worth £114 billion. That astounding amount equaled 8 percent of the Gross Domestic Product (Kuhn). A late 2010 article in *The Telegraph* estimated that film-related tourism is responsible for £1.9 billion tourist dollars annually and added that high-profile films attract an international clientele (Davidson, "Film Locations"). Even in the aftermath of economic downturns that caused potential tourists to re-evaluate their travel plans, the British tourism industry still plays an important role in the nation's economy.

Certainly not every visitor is a cinematic tourist, but an increasing number of international travelers visiting the U.K. are interested in taking tours or even planning an entire vacation around locations filmed for television or movies. As the *Telegraph* reports, "From Alnwick Castle in Northumberland, which doubles for Hogwart's School of Witchcraft and Wizardry in the Harry Potter films, to Chatsworth House in Derbyshire, where *The Duchess* was filmed, the stately homes of England have acquired a new lease of life as places of cultural pilgrimage" (Davidson, "Film Locations"). U.K. beaches, for example, are becoming popular tourist destinations not only for their rugged natural beauty but the number of films made there. Freshwater West Beach became a backdrop for both *Robin Hood* (2010) and *Harry Potter and the Deathly Hallows* (2010/11) (Davidson, "Britain's"), and VisitBritain helped promote the films as part of their promotion of British tourism.

Cinematic tourism usually takes two forms: the real-life locations associated with a non-fiction story (e.g., the subject matter of a film — the house where a murder really took place, a battlefield, an author's or a filmmaker's home) or the filming locations used within fiction (e.g., the platform where Harry Potter boards the Hogwarts train). Not all locations are stately or naturally beautiful. Street corners or everyday businesses like restaurants or banks also are typical filming locations that are far from glamorous but hold special meaning to fans. In the U.K., tour companies often blend the two types of cinetourism, showing, for example, the locations of real-world events (e.g., the cinema where film premieres took place, the studio where a film was made) as well as the locations where scenes were shot for a television series or film (e.g., a "fictionalized" setting, such as real-world Somerset House becoming fictionalized as a Victorian prison).

In his analysis of the impact of cinematic tourism in specific countries (e.g., Thailand as a result of the movie, *The Beach*), Rodanthi Tzanelli discusses the power of signs and their significance to viewers/audiences/tourists. Research indicates that "simulations" — what appears to be real but is not — is often more important to cinematic tourists than what is real. Tourists may actually prefer the simulated experience instead of the purely realistic.

One example of simulation is the Wizarding World of Harry Potter section of the Universal theme park in Orlando, Florida, where visitors might "live" at Hogwarts (at least for the day), drink butterbeer in the nearby village, and buy their first wand. These visitors' experiences are real, but they take place within an environment simulated to look like the places described in literary and cinematic fiction.

Tzanelli uses the term *global sign industries* to define the intersection of filmmaking, tourism, and tourists' consumption of images and experiences. According to Tzanelli, these sign industries "generate, manipulate, and market cultural signs" and play "a game of endless hermeneutics: by filmmakers (of novels on which films are based), by audiences (of films) and by holiday providers (of audiences' film readings)" (Tzanelli 7). Television, like film, also fits into this analysis. The images created, manipulated, and distributed to consumers (i.e., cinematic tourists) help them create what is real and meaningful to them. These tourists consume culture, but only those aspects that are real to them and which may or may not have any bearing on a country's or city's real culture.

Fans of the BBC's television series *Sherlock* often visit, for example, the real-world address of 185 North Gower Street in London, where exterior shots are filmed to represent Sherlock and John's residence at 221B Baker Street. The doorstep is easily recognizable in both realities by its proximity to sandwich shop Speedy's next door; the shop is a real business and its distinctive red awning clearly identifies the location to fans who watch the television series. (During the second season, the interior of Speedy's also became a *Sherlock* filming location and now receives even more visits from cinematic tourists.)

As appropriate to television fiction, alterations have been made to the real location of "221B Baker." Not only has the production gained permission for filming but to cover the blue English heritage plaque by the door. The building's door and street number have been temporarily replaced with the 221B door seen on television. Nevertheless, the location is easily recognizable even when filming is not taking place, and fans (who share photographs and maps online) often are seen having their photograph taken standing on "Sherlock Holmes' front doorstep" or visiting Speedy's, just like John and Mycroft do in "A Scandal in Belgravia." Although such fans realize that this location is "fake" (i.e., Sherlock and John do not really live here), their knowledge of the filming location becomes part of their experience of visiting London and exploring residential areas like North Gower Street. The fact that this doorstep has been filmed for a television series adds another layer of meaning to their visit to this part of the city.

Helping fans mix reality and fiction is often the job of tourism directors, who market filming locations on behalf of a nation. VisitBritain certainly understands the power of cinematic tourism and, in recent years, has partnered with film companies to help promote their product (a movie) while the filmmakers promote Britain's product (culture). The national tourism board developed such partnerships for *Robin Hood* (2008), James Bond film *Quantum of Solace* (2008), and the Guy Ritchie–directed *Sherlock Holmes*. The latter's 2009 partnership with Warner Bros. Pictures invited tourists to "discover Sherlock Holmes' Britain — Past and Present" in the campaign to link the film's locations with those made famous by Sir Arthur Conan Doyle.

The resulting movie (and other products') promotional website includes links to maps of filming locations across the U.K. and specific tourist destinations (e.g., London's Sherlock Holmes Museum at 221B Baker Street). Sample itineraries (VisitBritain, "Sherlock Holmes") help tourists discover filming locations in London, Manchester, Liverpool, and Dartmoor (home to the Hound of the Baskervilles and, in May 2011, a filming location for the latest adaptation of this story as a *Sherlock* episode).

VisitBritain ("Brand Partnerships") describes such campaigns as part of a program to market British tourism internationally. Their business is "to profile the destination alongside the release of a major movie. This can either be a movie which profiles British locations (e.g., *Pride and Prejudice*), or a movie that is quintessentially British but not really shot on location in the U.K. (e.g., James Bond)." They estimate that 40 percent of potential tourists would like to visit television or filming locations.

National tourism interests like VisitBritain work with film productions to help market both the locations and the films; they also generate interest among potential tourists to visit the U.K. and spend their travel dollars there. Upon arrival in the U.K., however, these cinematic tourists can choose whether to find locations on their own, possibly aided by other fans or Internet information, or to take an established tour with a company that knows the local culture, history, and locations as well as the cinematic history of specific film-related destinations. Most tour companies specializing in television, film, or book locations offer additional value — clips of a scene, shown before guests visit the location; photographs matching a location with a scene; re-enactments of scenes filmed at a location; and guides well prepared to answer tourists' questions. Tour companies make it easy for cinematic tourists to customize their destinations, learn more about film or television production, and even travel to and find precise filming spots.

With several powerhouse cinematic franchises built around iconic British characters like Harry Potter, James Bond, and Sherlock Holmes, independent tour companies like London-based Brit Movie Tours cater to a variety of fans with highly specific interests. Cinematic tourism surrounding Sherlock Holmes covers both real and fictional locations associated with the Conan Doyle original texts as well as numerous adaptations. Travel itineraries may include locations in and around London as well as sites several hours' drive away.

Fans who spend money on film- or television-themed tours often want a more inclusive experience than they would receive on typical city or country orientation tours. Brit Movie Tours invites role play on some tours, such as their *Doctor Who* day tour, and entire scenes may be acted out on location. Cinematic tourism can allow fans not only to see where scenes were filmed but to experience what it is like to "live" the role of an actor or a character in that location. Not only does the tour allow fans to vicariously experience what filming or being part of a story might be like, but it also rewards fans for knowing dialogue and characters so well. Although re-enactments might look strange to passersby who happen to see tourists role playing a scene in public, cinematic tours provide hardcore fans with a safe space in which to share fan experiences with like-minded participants who understand exactly why they love a movie or television series.

During Brit Movie Tours' walking, bus, or car tours of London and Cardiff, tourists can visit former shooting locations for the Guy Ritchie films (*Sherlock Holmes,* 2009; *Sherlock Holmes: A Game of Shadows,* 2011) and the BBC television series *Sherlock* (2010–present). Among the many tours his company offers, director Lewis Swan lists the Sherlock Holmes tour as more specialized instead of the top choice among tourists, but, in summer 2011, it was one of the newest offerings. It had been running only a few months and was not expected to reach the "commercially mature stage" for at least a year.

Tour guide Val Sturgess specializes in Brit Movie Tours' Sherlock Holmes tours, where she observes three categories of fans. Most knowledgeable about Holmes before they take the tour, Sherlockians (or Holmesians) make up about 1 percent of tour participants. Sturgess describes these avid fans as knowing every book and adaptation very well. Next on the hierarchy are the majority of tourists, who are mild Holmes fans looking for something different to do in London. This group makes up about 80 percent of clientele. The third group includes people who stumble onto the tour and think it looks interesting or simply tag along with friends who are Holmes fans.

Sturgess explains that, especially for Sherlock Holmes fans unfamiliar with London, "these books and films are all they know about London, [and they] enjoy comparing their knowledge with the real locations. They are also interested in exploring the same places that their literary and onscreen heroes would have known."

Bearing the "Sherlock Holmes" Brand Name

In addition to professional tour companies, other commercial or civic interests encourage cinematic tourists to visit specific locations. Companies branded with the Holmes name or likeness shrewdly market themselves to attract cinematic or literary tourists. Public locations or markers, such as monuments, that commemorate the link between a character/story and a locality often outlast commercial ventures and become part of the historic landscape of a city. Locations once used by production companies to film a movie or television series often become a mecca for fans, even without the assistance of tour companies. Nearby businesses may benefit by their proximity to sites where filming took place, although they do not cater to tourists.

Baker Street is one of the most likely places for cinematic tourists to begin their journey, and businesses near the 221B Baker Street museum benefit most from casual tourists who head for the most obvious address related to Holmes. In Sir Arthur Conan Doyle's day, Baker Street addresses did not go above 100; the road north of Marylebone, instead of being North Baker Street, was called Upper Baker Street. In an early manuscript, Conan Doyle did use that designation, indicating that Sherlock Holmes would live in the section closest to Regent's Park. In the 1930s, Baker Street was numbered to include the road north of Marylebone, but 221 became part of the address of a bank building (numbered 219–229). The address currently known as 221B Baker Street belongs to the Sherlock Holmes Museum, although its true mailing address is 239 Baker Street. Nevertheless, Holmes' fans have written to the detective at the 221B Baker Street address for decades, and the correspondence now is delivered to the museum ("Baker Street").

Inside the museum is a faithfully re-created Victorian sitting room with Holmes' adjoining bedroom and, upstairs, Dr. Watson's bedroom. The sitting room, like several similar re-creations throughout London, is filled with memorabilia appropriate to the Conan Doyle stories. Great care has been taken to include only authentic items from the Victorian era, although some photographs of Irene Adler and the Prince of Bohemia, for example, are far more recently taken of actors playing a role. The sitting room and bedrooms provide the appropriate atmosphere for fans of the novels, as well as films and television series set in this time period, to experience what living at 221B might have been like. Fans eager to record their visit for posterity sign the guest book, which documents visitors from around the world.

As appropriate for a small museum, next door is a gift shop, also appropriately Victorian themed. Fans can buy all sorts of merchandise bearing the Holmes logo, including novels, DVDs, maps with a walking tour of Holmes' London (in several languages), deerstalkers, and t-shirts. Sometimes "Mrs. Hudson" even greets visitors, while clerks attired in Victorian-style dresses and aprons assist customers.

Next to the gift shop is Mrs. Hudson's Restaurant. Across the street at 224-226 Baker is Bar Linda, best known for the Sherlock Holmes photographs from film and television that adorn the walls. Across Marylebone, on South Baker Street, is the Sherlock Holmes Hotel, which offers its own collection of photographs, paintings, and prints commemorating the great detective. These addresses have no legitimate connection with Conan Doyle or the Sherlock Holmes stories, but they attract tourists because they showcase memorabilia from the Victorian era, novels, television series, or films. The name alone brings in visitors, and although this section of London was well known to Conan Doyle and is the location of many of Holmes and Watson's adventures, the trail of businesses branded with the name Sherlock Holmes is the primary way that casual fans would know they are in the right place. Most visitors taking a tour of the sites mentioned in Conan Doyle's stories begin with this section of Baker Street, whether they are taking a Brit Movie Tours guided tour or an independent walking tour, perhaps guided by a copy of *The Sherlock Holmes Walk,* a booklet sold at the Sherlock Holmes Museum that outlines the important London locations mentioned in Conan Doyle's stories that are still apparent to visitors of modern London (Garner).

Farther away, but at another iconic location for the original stories, is the Sherlock Holmes Pub, situated on the late 1800s' site of the Northumberland Hotel. An earlier pub, known as the Northumberland Arms, was replaced with the Sherlock Holmes Pub in the 1950s. Holmes fans typically dine upstairs. A section of the dining room has been set aside as Holmes and Watson's sitting room, complete with fireplace, lab equipment, overflowing bookcases, and the unfortunate wax mannequin who took a bullet for Holmes. Although in the past half century other versions of Holmes' sitting room have been opened around London, the Sherlock Holmes Pub is "not only the first, but also the most important collection in the world to be based on the famous detective" (Sherlock Holmes Pub). It also received the blessing of— as well as several donations of memorabilia from — the Conan Doyle family.

For many years the menu played up the Sherlock Holmes connection with entrées preferred by specific characters: Sherlock's Own Favourite (sirloin steak), Dr. Watson's Favourite (Cumberland sausages), Mrs. Hudson's Steak and Mushroom in Ale Pie, and Mycroft's Favourite (lamb). Some dishes reflected famous stories, such as The Hound of the Baskervilles (toad in the hole) or A Scandal in Bohemia (duck). Although, after a 2011 renovation and re-opening, the pub has downplayed character-menu word associations, some characters are still featured in the revamped listing.

Television fans recently found new ways to connect their favorite characters to the pub. *Sherlock* co-creator Steven Moffat attended the pub's re-opening celebration, and star Benedict Cumberbatch's fans excitedly tweeted after they spotted the actor having dinner upstairs and enthusiastically looking at the pub's renowned re-creation of the Holmes' study (Waggers1245).

Not only does the pub combine a legitimate story-related connection through its location and association with the Conan Doyle estate, but it provides an appropriate Victorian home-like atmosphere where fans can "role play" while they dine. As they depart the pub, tourists might also look at the ceramic tiles across the alley on an adjacent building that once housed the women's Turkish baths. The colorful tiles are the only remaining marker of the baths' entrance. Although the men's facility which, in the stories, Holmes and Watson frequented, is long gone, fans can see what the entrance would have looked like a century or more ago.

Because of the many cinematic adaptations of the Conan Doyle stories over the years, another appropriate location for yet another Holmes-Watson sitting room is the London Film Museum. A timeline of the cinematic adaptations crosses the exhibit in front of the re-created sitting room. This one, however, features memorabilia specifically from television series or films and attracts a different group of cinematic tourists — those more interested in the filmed stories than actual history or authentic connection to Conan Doyle.

Whereas film locations offer the excitement of being where the actors stood or seeing a setting from a different perspective, businesses affiliated with the Sherlock Holmes "brand" provide historic artifacts that represent a time or place associated with British, Conan Doyle's, or cinematic history. The best collections of memorabilia, such as the various sitting rooms, can provide a role-playing experience for visitors who not only can see items from another era but can be surrounded with artifacts representing a specific time and place. They can feel what it would be like, even briefly, to visit Holmes and Watson and see firsthand the items about which they have read.

The idea that Holmes and Watson memorabilia are documented and displayed also makes the characters seem real, with their own address and home that can be visited. Such documentation also places them within a historic context. The London Film Museum's exhibit is updated as new adaptations, such as the recent *Sherlock Holmes* movies, add another layer to the ongoing documentation and entrenchment of Holmes and Watson into modern popular culture. The Sherlock Holmes brand name helps businesses broaden their marketability by attracting a specific clientele in addition to "regular" tourists or local guests.

Community Creation of Tourist Hot Spots

Down the street from 221B Baker Street is the Baker Street underground station. What makes this station different from other London tube stops is the Sherlock Holmes artwork adorning the walls. Travelers who arrive here immediately know they are at Baker Street because of the familiar silhouette of Holmes, whether enlarged on the station walls or adorning a series of small tiles on columns.

Outside the Baker Street station, which is featured in several Conan Doyle stories, is the Sherlock Holmes statue, an easily identified landmark that attracts even casual tourists' attention. A 1999 article published by the nearby Sherlock Holmes Museum emphasizes the statue's importance: "The landmark statue is destined to become a major tourist attraction in its own right and will complement the Sherlock Holmes Museum's services to London's overseas tourists — many of whom come to London especially to see the lodging rooms of Sherlock Holmes at 221b Baker Street." The nine-foot statue by John Doubleday presents a vibrant Holmes wearing deerstalker and overcoat ("New Statue").

In its history of the London statue's creation, the Sherlock Holmes Society of London also notes the statue's implications for tourism (Horrocks). The Society describes the statue as "a London landmark in its own right and ... one of the first major sights to greet visitors to London as they approach the center of town along Marylebone Road. There is only one other statue in London of an allegedly fictitious character, that of Peter Pan in Kensington Gardens. Both are among the most popular of all London's monuments" (and literary/cinematic icons).

Public markers of popular culture often outlive commercial investments, and the statue of Holmes, after being discussed and proposed for three quarters of a century before finally becoming part of the Marylebone/Baker landscape, likely will outlast the restaurants and hotels catering to Sherlock Holmes cinematic tourists. Such monuments not only document international popular culture icons but become a tourist destination. The historic (literary history associated with Conan Doyle's characters and stories) and the popular (modern Sherlock Holmes fandom) are merged in these public markers of cinematic or literary tourism.

Fan-Popularized Tourist Destinations and the Power of Internet Fandom

Sherlock Holmes fans gather a great deal of information about filming locations via the Internet. Through virtual travel (e.g., street-level camera views provided by Mapquest or Google Maps), actual travel to a filming location, and acquisition of information about the story and filming of it, fans make stories and locations personally meaningful. *Sherlock* scenes in which the detective travels by taxi past famous landmarks or discovers clues at famous tourist destinations also allow audiences to vicariously visit London. Tzanelli explains that this process "matches actual with virtual cosmopolitanism, knowledge and experience of otherness with simulation of this experience, turning film viewing and Internet surfing into a project of personal development" (Tzanelli 17). *Sherlock* fans, for example, conduct research related to their personal interests, along the way learning more about Sherlock Holmes, television stories and the literary works from which they have been adapted, the series' actors, television production, or London's history and landscape. Even if these fans never visit London in person, they have become familiar with the real and televisionary locations associated with Sherlock Holmes and ascribe personal meaning to them.

With the recent trend in more high-profile dramas being produced by BBC Wales, several fan-favorite (especially in the U.K.) television series, including *Doctor Who* and *Sherlock,* often use the same locations to create vastly different settings. Swansea's historic Central Library (now the Institute for Sustainable Design) not only provided the right atmosphere for *Doctor Who's* futuristic but appropriately titled "Silence in the Library" episode but also was featured in *Sherlock* a few years later (Turner). A few blocks from the buzz of Cardiff's frequently filmed city center, *Sherlock's* Holmes and Watson strolled down a residential street while discussing a case, the location obvious to residents familiar with Cardiff.[2] A cinematic tourist's *Sherlock* itinerary might include sites familiar to fans of several series being filmed during the past few years in South Wales, and fan sites like Sherlockology point fans toward current filming locations as well as archive information about former filming sites.

Sherlock also ventures beyond London or Cardiff to film in remote locations rooted in the Conan Doyle stories and far more difficult for fans to visit during production. Over time, however, even these isolated spots are likely to become just as popular as the easier-to-reach locations. Perhaps because some locations are so remote, people officially working with the production — such as *Sherlock* co-creator Mark Gatiss — may feel more comfortable in sharing with fans a travel diary of high points in production. Tweets or Facebook posts, whether from fan sites like Sherlockology or actors, writers, and directors affiliated with the production, generate an even greater fan desire to see the locations and be updated about what is happening on set.

While filming the much anticipated episode "The Hounds of Baskerville" near Dartmoor in late May and early June 2011, Gatiss frequently tweeted updates about the location and filming, even posting twitpics that fans eagerly scanned for details of the production's exact location. Some highlights included the introductory message, "On my way to Cardiff for start of #Sherlock shoot tomorrow. Very excited!" (May 15, 2011), a post–BAFTA awards update: "Well that was a fantastic night by any standards! We're all chuffed to bits. Back to Cardiff now for more frolics on the moor..." (May 23), and, later that day, the even more spoilerish "As you value your life and your reason, stay away from the MOOR...," accompanied by a twitpic of a silhouetted character walking toward a cloudy sunset. This photograph led fans to share information about probable places near Dartmoor where it might have been taken. Additional Gatiss tweets referenced Dartmoor as the location of several night shoots, along with such tidbits as "Passed a Barrormore Farm. Delightful to think that perhaps Conan Doyle went by in a pony & trap a hundred odd years ago & the name lodged..." (June 4) and "Another 8–5 nightshoot. Only four days to go and 'The Hounds of Baskerville' will be in the can!" (June 6). Another twitpic, this time of the Cardiff studio's 17 steps to 221B (June 10), alerted fans to the shift in location and production schedule.

As a result, Sherlock Holmes fan fiction sites and fan forums (especially those dedicated to Benedict Cumberbatch, who plays Sherlock) retweeted the information and instigated discussion about where and when filming was taking place. After the identifying details have been mapped once fans see the completed episode, these locations become hot spots on a tour of *Sherlock* filming locations, in addition to Dartmoor's perennial importance as the story's setting of the original Conan Doyle story.

By carefully following Gatiss on Twitter, fans immediately gathered information about *Sherlock,* learned more about specific locations to visit, and gained a sense of ownership of the television series. Because Gatiss and Moffat interact with fans via social media, their followers feel that they are part of the network supporting the series and have insider information appropriate to their dedication to the series. Highly motivated fans who follow the series' every development are far more likely to become cinematic tourists.

Some lucky fans even found themselves on location while they were going about their everyday business. During the filming of a first season episode in central London's Trafalgar Square, passersby stopped to watch a scene being shot. Most people merely enjoyed the novelty of filming taking place in a very public location (or they discreetly took photographs), but a few fans caused a problem for the director, who needed to ensure getting and matching shots (*Alan Carr*). These fans insisted on following the actors as the scene was shot. Because they stayed in frame behind the actors, they destroyed the illusion of Sherlock and John unobtrusively discussing a case while walking toward the National Gallery.

Filming in London is becoming increasingly difficult. Although Cumberbatch commented in a *Wales Online* interview that "some of this [production] is really in London in Piccadilly Square," he added that he preferred the ease of filming the Baker Street scenes in studio at the BBC studios at Treforest Industrial Estate, Pontypridd. Gatiss added that filming could not take place on Baker Street, although they filmed nearby (on North Gower Street), because "it is too busy to look like Baker Street now" (Gaskell). The presence of series' fans or cinematic tourists who track down productions has become a distraction that *Sherlock's* cast and crew hope to avoid — without alienating their audience.

The use of a more remote location, however much its whereabouts are teased via tweets, ensures far fewer fans showing up. The Cardiff studios also are off limits to fans; BBC studio tours notoriously stay far away from the set. Through social media, Gatiss and Moffat can entice *Sherlock's* fanbase, and presumably ensure future cinematic tourism for out-of-the-way sites used primarily within one episode, while being able to film without interference.

Whether filming was taking place in a city or remote countryside, during the filming of *Sherlock's* second season episodes from May through August 2011, Sherlockology frequently updated fans through its website, Facebook and Tumblr pages, and frequent tweets. In a tweet on June 22, it established a special code (#shsr: Sherlock Holmes set reports) to alert fans of the latest filming locations, and on June 24 tweeted "Today's #Sherlock filming in Cardiff apparently consisted of interior scenes in Scotland Yard." Such an up-to-the-minute grassroots campaign to share filming information creates a vast network of eyes and flying fingers as information is gathered, evidence photographed, and messages sent through an interconnected web of social media sites. Whether fans use this information to keep up with filming on a favorite series, try to visit the locations during filming, or make reference of documented locations for a later trip, the increasing use of Facebook, Twitter, YouTube, Tumblr, and personal websites to document filming locations makes social media yet another aspect of cinematic tourism.

Travel databases also often include trivia that provide fans with greater knowledge and enjoyment of specific scenes as they view episodes or movies more than once and gain personal meaning from seeing what casual viewers might miss or regular tourists would not know about a specific location. Websites like The Worldwide Guide to Movie Locations, Filmaps, and U.K. Onscreen list easy-to-find London sites shown in the 2009 *Sherlock Holmes* movie. Although the Internet primarily guides Holmes fans to the most recent filming locations, even the Granada television series has a list of locations from the region surrounding Manchester, where the series was primarily shot 1984–1994 (*England, Scotland, and Wales*).

Travel sites catering to fans document filming trivia that add value to fans' knowledge of a location. *Sherlock* provides an excellent example of one unimportant-to-the-plot detail that enhanced a scene for Holmes fans and linked cinematic tourists to two London locations. In "A Study in Pink," John Watson sits on a park bench, sipping coffee, while he talks with old friend Mike Stamford. In the original Conan Doyle story, *A Study in Scarlet*, on which this episode is based, Watson and Stamford have dinner at the Criterion, a restaurant on Piccadilly Circus. In *Sherlock*, John's coffee cup displays the name Criterion, a nod to the original story and a link to a Sherlock Holmes–related tourist site. Because the *Sherlock* scene was filmed in Russell Square, easily identified by buildings surrounding the square and in frame during this scene, cinematic tourists have another location to visit. Fan-scholars who see the Criterion cup and understand its significance gain a deeper appreciation of this scene. Cinematic tourists thus make the link between original story and new adaptation and may add two locations — one literary, one cinematic — to their itinerary.

With knowledge from official travel or production sites and information accumulated by fan sites, cinematic tourists often like to meet with others, from the local area or abroad, to share their common interest and, in the process, gain greater credibility within fandom. Because experience (e.g., attending a premiere or screening, getting an autograph, talking with an actor, watching filming) and knowledge (e.g., an actor's filmography, history of filming locations, anecdotes about filming) help fans build status within their community, meet-ups are a way of sharing information, making new friends, and establishing a status-based hierarchy. These meet-ups may seem more like pilgrimages in which fans visit sites having great personal meaning or participate in special events.

In summer 2011, notices about Sherlock Holmes fan meet-ups in Europe and North America appeared several times a week on fan websites. The London meet-up notice asked participants to list places they would like to visit and clearly became a gathering of cinematic tourists. Other fans met up before the December 7, 2011, preview screening of *Sherlock*'s "A Scandal in Belgravia," and Twitter once again became a forum for providing the latest information about the BFI event, Cumberbatch sightings, and details about the venue and episode. The following evening provided yet another fan-gathering opportunity at the red carpet premiere of *A Game of Shadows,* held at the Empire theatre on Leicester Square. Not only are these locations now part of Sherlock Holmes fandom because of the events themselves, but their venues (i.e., BFI, Empire theatre) also are added to the list of event locations and actor sightings and, as such, have become noteworthy to cinematic tourists.

Why the Interest in Holmes-Related Tourism?

Cinematic tourism blurs the lines between reality and fiction. It makes fictional characters seem real when they live at an address fans can visit. It adds value to historic or popular tourist destinations that also have served as on-screen sets. Particularly in a culture that values celebrity and the ability to acquire the most up-to-date information, cinematic tourism provides a way for fans to gain insider knowledge about film or television production and to be where the famous once worked. It forges a link between the audience and the story and makes that story personal to each fan.

Sherlock Holmes continues to be an important part of British literary and cinematic history, but the detective's international fame only increases with the promotion and popularity of new films and television series that generate new fans (and thus has the potential to add to the GNP). As Brit Movie Tours guide Sturgess points out,

> Sherlock has a lasting appeal because he is so well written, believable, and likeable, coupled with an equally well-written sidekick Watson. (The fact that [Holmes is] written from Watson's point of view goes a long way toward making him likeable.) Sherlock is also the forerunner to other series' characters, such as James Bond. When he was first written, readers got to know him over months and years through his many adventures. The stories are very easy to read, [and] the language isn't too flowery or alienating and doesn't appear outdated, so audiences/readers now still find [the stories] accessible.
>
> Sherlock has become a part of Britain's culture and heritage which we're quite proud of. Sherlock has never disappeared over the last 120 years. First the stories were written, then there were stage adaptations, then film adaptations. Sherlock is a formula that can work in any era, and many others have continued to write about Sherlock Holmes and created their own adaptations even after Conan Doyle's death.

With the prevalence of Internet usage in fandom, knowledge about filming locations is a commodity shared among fans and used to increase cinematic tourism at a grassroots, independent-traveler level. Although businesses and even the government also provide similar information to potential cinematic tourists, they do not offer the immediacy of retweeted insider information or twitpics or the shared exuberance of meeting an actor or watching a scene being filmed. National tourism boards may work at a different, and more official, level with studios and production companies, but the information shared with fans is carefully manipulated and presented after the film or episode has been completed and is ready for mass consumption.

In the 21st century, Sherlock Holmes has increased the likelihood of cinematic tourism simply because of the number of new, popular productions that visually entice audiences at home or in theaters to visit the U.K. Public infatuation with celebrities, also on the increase in the 21st century, further encourages fans to visit the U.K. for premieres or special events, or even in the hope of seeing a film or television series being made. Although Sherlock Holmes is likely to remain a literary icon for years to come, new film and television adaptations are doing their part to encourage cinematic tourists to visit London — and maybe Sherlock and John — now.

Works Cited

Alan Carr: Chatty Man. Interview with Benedict Cumberbatch. Channel 4. 24 Jan. 2011. Television.

"Baker Street — London." London Travel Tips. n.d. Web. 12 June 2011. <http://www.london-traveltips.com/baker-street.htm>.

Davidson, Max. "Britain's Best Destinations for Film Lovers." *The Telegraph.* 4 Sep. 2010. n.d. Web. 12 June 2011. <http://www.telegraph.co.uk/travel/picturegalleries/7979506/Britains-best-destinations-for-film-lovers.html>.

_____. "Film Locations in Britain: Tamara Drewe and the Lure and Illusion of Cinematic Tourism." *The Telegraph.* 4 Sep. 2010. Web. 12 June 2011. <http://www.telegraph.co.uk/travel/artsandculture/7977226/Film-locations-in-Britain-Tamara-Drewe-and-the-lure-and-illusion-of-cinema-tourism.html>.

England, Scotland, and Wales: A Travel Guide. The Tourist's Sherlock Holmes: A Not So Elementary List of Filming Locations. n.d. Web. 12 June 2011. <http://my.core.com/~jcnash/sherlock_places.html>.

Filmaps. *Sherlock Holmes Film Locations.* n.d. Web. 12 June 2011. <http://www.filmaps.com/films/sherlock-holmes-ref-1454/>.

"Filming Locations for *Sherlock Holmes.*" IMDB. n.d. Web. 12 June 2011. <http://www.imdb.com/title/tt0988045/locations>.

Garner, Paul. *The Sherlock Holmes Walk.* London: Louis' London Walks, 2008. Print.

Gaskell, Simon. "Sherlock Finds that Cardiff Is a Real Home for Holmes." *South Wales Echo.* 24 July 2010. Web. 12 June 2011. <http://www.walesonline.co.uk/cardiffonline/cardiff-news/2010/07/24/sherlock-finds-that-cardiff-is-a-real-home-from-holmes-91466-26920743/>.

Gatiss, Mark. Twitter. 23 May 2011. Web. 23 May 2011. <http://twitpic.com/5lo8eg>.

Higgins, Charlotte. "London Gets Star Billing in New Sherlock Holmes Series." *The Guardian.* 25 July 2010. Web. 12 June 2011. <http://www.guardian.co.uk/culture/charlottehigginsblog/2010/jul/25/london-star-billing-sherlock-holmes>.

Horrocks, Peter. "The Statue of Sherlock Holmes at Baker Street Station." The Sherlock Holmes Society of London. n.d. Web. 12 June 2011. <http://www.sherlock-holmes.org.uk/press_cutting.php?id=136>.

Kuhn, Kerstin. "UK Tourism Industry Worth £114b." CatererSearch.com. 11 Nov. 2008. Web. 12 June 2011. <http://www.caterersearch.com/Articles/2008/11/11/324581/UK-tourism-industry-worth-163114b.htm>.

"New Statue of Sherlock Holmes in London." Sherlock Holmes Museum. 1999. Web. 12 June 2011. <http://www.sherlock-holmes.co.uk/news/statue.html>.

"A Scandal in Belgravia." *Sherlock.* Writ. Steven Moffat. Dir. Paul McGuigan. BBC. 7 Dec. 2011. BFI screening.

Sherlock Holmes (2009). The Worldwide Guide to Movie Locations. n.d. Web. 12 June 2011. <http://www.movie-locations.com/movies/s/SherlockHolmes2009.html>.

Sherlockology. "Myth, Rumour, and Hearsay." May 2011. Web. May 2011. <http://sherlockology.tumblr.com/post/6564815721/sherlocks2filming#disqus_thread>.

"A Study in Pink." *Sherlock.* Writ. Steven Moffat and Mark Gatiss. Dir. Paul McGuigan. BBC Worldwide, 2010. DVD.

Sturgess, Val. Brit Movie Tours. Email. 24 May 2011.

Swan, Lewis. Brit Movie Tours. Email. 27 May 2011.

Turner, Robin. "New Role for Swansea's Former Central Library." *Wales Online.* 10 June 2011. Web. 10 June 2011. <http://www.walesonline.co.uk/news/wales-news/2011/06/10/new-role-for-swansea-s-former-central-library-91466-28853401/>.

Tzanelli, Rodanthi. *The Cinematic Tourist.* London: Routledge, 2007. Print.

UK Onscreen. *Sherlock Holmes* (2009). n.d. Web. 12 June 2011. <http://www.ukonscreen.com/gfbjjkb-Sherlock-Holmes-%282009%29.html>.

VisitBritain. "Brand Partnerships: Film." n.d. Web. 12 June 2011. <http://www.visitbritain.org/aboutus/marketing/brandpartnerships/film.aspx>.

_____. Sherlock Holmes microsite. n.d. Web. 12 June 2011. <http://www2.visitbritain.com/en/campaigns/sherlock-holmes/index.aspx>.

Waggers1245. Twitter. 27 Oct. 2011. Web. 27 Oct. 2011.

NOTES

1. As Gatiss is quick to correct fans, "Sherlock" and "John" are preferred over "Holmes" and "Watson" in this adaptation, all part of the modernization. When an audience member asked about Holmes and Watson at the December 7, 2011, *Sherlock* screening at the BFI, Gatiss smiled and gently corrected the fan, "Sherlock and John, please." Keeping everything in this series current and casual is yet another way to entice virtual or real tourists to enjoy London.

2. On May 25, 2011, I took Brit Movie Tours' Cardiff-based *Doctor Who* tour that also included some *Sherlock* locations. Neighborhoods that once hosted production crews for a few days are now hot spots on cinematic tourists' maps. In this case, I walked down the same street as the actors/characters and could match trees or houses to the filmed scenes in order to learn how and where the scene was shot.

13

True to Their Victorian Roots

The House of Silk

LYNNETTE PORTER

It's good to be Sherlock Holmes in the 21st century. CNN touts the "recent Holmes renaissance" (DuChateau), and *The Telegraph* announces that "we are living in a golden age of Sherlockiana" (Spencer). Not only are television series and films making his name internationally known to an ever wider audience, but, for the first time in 125 years, Sherlock Holmes is the subject of a novel receiving the Arthur Conan Doyle Estate's approval. The Estate specifically selected scriptwriter and crime novelist Anthony Horowitz to write this tale in which John Watson, as an old man, writes of one last case and closes the book on his longtime friendship with Sherlock Holmes.

Although Horowitz's writing style in *The House of Silk* is meant to approximate Conan Doyle's — and in many ways succeeds — the book also differs from Conan Doyle's approach to storytelling by serving as a 21st century apology to some characters. During one last meeting with the now-retired George Lestrade, Watson confesses a "need to apologize to Lestrade on two counts. First, I had never described him in perhaps the most glowing terms.... But where I perhaps did Lestrade an injustice was in suggesting that he had no intelligence or investigative skill whatsoever" (64–5). Horowitz-as-Watson then recounts Lestrade's work as a "capable man" who deserved more credit, even if his reputation was primarily built on cases Sherlock Holmes solved. At time, Horowitz seems to make amends for Conan Doyle's characters, or for the author himself.

The book's greater purpose, however, one more important than entertainment, is to memorialize one of literature's greatest friendships. With this novel, Horowitz concurs with every other writer of recent, globally popular adaptations: Sherlock Holmes "was the first, the father of all modern detectives. But I think what makes him so unforgettable is his relationship with Watson.

He is austere, irritating, aloof. Watson is warm, loyal, affable. Together, they have the greatest friendship in literature" (DuChateau).

The House of Silk explores the world of the British male, whether he is rich and powerful or young and impoverished. The novel encapsulates the concept of power and the extent to which those who wield it will go to protect it. However, the common thread between two cases that become interwoven, even as their individual mysteries are unraveled, is the underlying (and probably more intriguing to Holmes fans) story of Sherlock Holmes and John Watson.

Horowitz-writing-as-Watson necessarily presents two perspectives: a 21st century writer and Holmes fan and the elder John Watson who recalls details of a case long past, one too controversial to be written until late in his life and, even then, sealed for a hundred years. In many ways, Horowitz "unseals" the original Conan Doyle manuscripts with this book and looks at them with a critical eye more than a hundred years after they were written. He cannot help but infuse his novel with modern interpretations of the original texts, even as he strives to imitate their style. His understanding of the world of Victorian men at the heart of this novel thus brings to light an interesting way to interpret the Holmes-Watson relationship, one that fans of the BBC television series or Guy Ritchie film franchise may not like nearly so well.

Love Is All Around

Horowitz is hampered, in some ways, by the popularity of television and film adaptations that may color many readers' (especially those new to the Sherlock Holmes stories) interpretation of his book. As discussed in previous chapters, the Holmes-Watson relationship is the subject of a great deal of speculation by 21st century fans. Many fan fiction writers base their romantic or sexually explicit stories on their assumptions about what they have seen or heard on screen: the characters' shared smiles, isolated dialogue, or lack of personal space. Slash fiction (i.e., in this case, stories about male-male sexual activities) glorifies the duo's personal relationship and assumes that two men living together in modern London (*Sherlock*) or former flatmates dealing with their impending separation due to Watson's marriage (*Sherlock Holmes, Sherlock Holmes: A Game of Shadows*) are probably both emotionally and sexually involved. Although *Sherlock's* Season Two episodes, most notably, "A Scandal in Belgravia," clarify Sherlock and John's relationship (i.e., Sherlock is asexual, John is heterosexual), the friends also obviously love each other and maintain a very Victorian male friendship that is far more difficult for modern audiences to accept than would their 19th or 20th century counterparts. The Sherlock

Holmes film franchise suggests that Holmes and Watson off screen may be bisexual or homosexual, but on screen they are simply shown having an extremely close friendship still acceptable within the parameters of Victorian society.

The BBC television series' co-creators agree that love and sex should not be confused. Mark Gatiss explains that *Sherlock* is a love story. Steven Moffat emphasizes that the relationship, rather than individuals, is paramount: "people fall in love, not with Sherlock Holmes or Dr. Watson, but with their friendship. I think it is the most famous friendship in fiction, without a doubt. It is a moving and affecting one, and best of all, it's a great portrait, as in the original stories, of a male friendship" (Bernstein). Although Gatiss and Moffat may try to present a very Victorian male friendship true to Conan Doyle's stories, they nonetheless have to deal with a passionate fandom, many who want to see Sherlock and John together as a couple in every sense. Their scriptwriting in the second season especially teases the audience along that very thin line between Victorian appropriateness and modern obsession with sexuality. "Love" does not have to equate "sex," but many fans or fan fiction writers pick up on dialogue using the word "love" and interpret it in the way they prefer.

In a *Total Film* interview published shortly before the second season's episodes were broadcast in the U.K., Martin Freeman (John Watson) notes that the more recent episodes illustrate growth in the friends' relationship: "I guess like any friendship, marriage or whatever it is, familiarity breeds more contempt, and more love" (Dibdin 89). In "A Scandal in Belgravia," the first episode of the second season, John vents his frustration about people's inability to believe that he and Sherlock have a non-sexual relationship. "Doesn't anyone care that I'm *not gay?*" he asks Irene Adler, who admits that, although she is lesbian and Sherlock is asexual, they are still fascinated by each other, what viewers might interpret as a narcissistic love between damaged people who recognize each other's brilliance and are attracted to that. Nevertheless, Adler reminds John that he is very much part of a couple and questions whether he is jealous of Sherlock's twisted relationship with her. Freeman explains his character's reaction to Irene Adler: "John thinks it would be much healthier that Sherlock did have a relationship with a human being, as opposed to with a book or a theory or something. It's just that Holmes happens to be falling in love with someone who is as insane as he is!" (Mumford). Such analysis highlights what Benedict Cumberbatch (who plays Sherlock) calls "Sherlock *and* love," rather than Sherlock *in* love, and indicates whatever Sherlock's "heart" may be ("Benedict Cumberbatch").

The Guy Ritchie films do not help to straighten out Sherlock's sexuality. The first in what is promised to become at least a three-film franchise explains through dialogue that Holmes sometimes steals Watson's clothes (specifically a waistcoat is mentioned in dialogue). Holmes and Watson bicker over going away together to Mycroft Holmes' estate for a holiday and dispute the true ownership of pet dog Gladstone. When Watson is gravely wounded, Holmes, in disguise as a doctor, checks on his friend's condition. When Watson's fiancée, Mary Morstan, arrives for a visit, Holmes swiftly departs, but not before Morstan orders him to solve the case that led to her beloved's injury and explains she knows that Holmes also cares deeply about Watson (*Sherlock Holmes*). Although both Holmes and Watson have love interests in the first film, their bromance is a key reason why that film was successful. As director Guy Ritchie enthuses, "the bread and butter of [sequel *A Game of Shadows*] is always going to be the relationship between Sherlock and Watson and you can't really have enough of those two and their camp banter" (Crowther 83).

The second film's early trailers stirred controversy when they showed Holmes in drag standing very close to Watson. Robert Downey, Jr., (Sherlock Holmes) explains that he wanted Holmes' disguise to be a woman, which could lead to all sorts of innuendo and hilarity on screen, especially when he turns up in drag during Watson's honeymoon (Warner). Although Watson finally marries Morstan, Holmes quickly dumps her off a moving train (to save her, of course) and proceeds to have one last adventure with Watson. During Holmes' encounters with Professor Moriarty, the detective asks that Watson and his bride be left alone, a request that Moriarty denies. When Holmes and Moriarty finally face off at the Reichenbach Falls, Holmes is given one last opportunity to lock eyes with Watson, who arrives too late to save his friend from plunging apparently to his death (*Sherlock Holmes: A Game of Shadows*).

Nothing is ever shown explicitly in the first two seasons of *Sherlock* or the first two Ritchie films, but innuendo and, especially in *Sherlock*, the running joke that everyone thinks John and Sherlock are a couple — but they are not — makes the Holmes-Watson relationship titillating to modern audiences, especially those looking for a same-gender relationship that is more than a friendship. The word most often used to describe the Downey-Law version of Holmes and Watson is "bromance," and the romantic subtext is hardly subtle, as shown in the pair's final conversation in the second film. To discuss clues with Watson during a ball that likely will involve an assassination attempt, Holmes takes Watson onto the dance floor. Holmes compliments Watson on his dancing before innocently asking, "Who taught you to dance?" "You did," smiles Watson. Whether in this case dancing is a metaphor remains up to audience interpretation.

New audiences may become fans of Holmes and Watson not because of the way in which Arthur Conan Doyle originally wrote the characters, but because of the recent adaptations' sexual subtext in scenes like this. Whether in defiance of this trend or simply in adherence with canon, Horowitz takes the famous friendship back to its origins and, in the primary plot, illustrates that not all male-male sexual relationships in Victorian times are so titillating or bromantic. Readers who enjoy the recent television or film adaptations because they read "slash" relationships into the story may be dismayed or shocked at Horowitz's depictions of male-male sex limited to pedophilia and sexual slavery.

The Separate Worlds of Friendship and Sex

After dissecting Sherlock Holmes' relationship with Victor Trevor, one fan analyst discussing the *Gloria Scott* case reminds other fans that "The Victorians were a very repressed people, and yet they often communicated their desires and lust through thinly veiled wording, as it would have been considered quite improper to display these emotions through action" ("Decoding the Subtext"). Asking fans to "decode" canon or modern texts by paying close attention to word choice invites reading a sexual subtext.

Another reading of Holmes' friendship with Victor Trevor, for example, could rely on Victorians' acceptance of male-male friendships developed during public school or university. As Carolyn Oulton writes in *Romantic Friendship in Victorian Literature*, "the idealization of love between male friends, on which the public school tradition was based, could lay claim to two distinct traditions, both of which were accessible to young men with a genteel education. One was based on platonic ideals ... but upholders of love between friends could also invoke biblical and religious precedent" (41). Although Holmes and Watson are not schoolboys or university mates, they are well-educated gentlemen who would have matured during a time when male friendships were unquestioned and acceptable, long before Freud's 1905 definitions of sexual identity.

After a chapter in which many scholars analyze the Holmes-Watson relationship in light of English social mores and Victorian fiction, Christopher Redmond concludes that "homosexuality between Watson and Holmes is not to be taken as a described fact, and as a threat or a promise below the surface it is hypothetical at best ... one need only note that Holmes can be involved with murderers and prostitutes without being accused of murder or prostitution" (131).

Plenty of textual and sociocultural analyses conclude the same point about the non-sexual nature of the Holmes-Watson relationship — yet few fiction readers or television or film audiences likely read such textual analyses. They draw their conclusions based on popular interest in innuendo-laden Sherlock Holmes adaptations.

Thus, Horowitz's novel may be read by two very different potential audiences: readers who will take his novel in the spirit of Victorian society in which it was intended and those who will try to read a sexual subtext into the Holmes-Watson relationship. Although I doubt very much that Horowitz intended to provide a bromantic subtext for his novel, but instead is mimicking Conan Doyle's style in discussing a Victorian male friendship, such a sexual decoding is as likely to occur with his text as with the "texts" of recent television or film adaptations. It may be difficult for readers who want Holmes and Watson to be partners in every sense to read the descriptions of homosexual activity in Horowitz's novel. The House of Silk is a "house of ill repute" in which men pay for the sexual services of adolescent boys, making homosexuality and pedophilia text, not subtext, in his novel. Male-male sex acts are not only illegal but immoral in this novel — a far cry from the way that many fans prefer to view "slash" in Sherlock Holmes adaptations.

The Male-Male Sexual Relationship in The House of Silk

Evildoers in the novel go beyond murderers or thieves. They rape young boys. This crime is so horrendous and pervasive among affluent, influential men that it is covered up even by government officials, with the implication that this corruption has infiltrated every level of British society. Of course, non-consensual sexual relations with minors, male or female, was and is a crime in London. Homosexual relationships were not only illegal (and would remain so until 1967) but carried a serious social stigma as being "unnatural" and amoral. For the pillars of British society — gentried landowners, wealthy businessmen, politicians, judges — to be wantonly involved in sex crimes would indeed have been a scandal that had to be sealed for a century, until long after everyone who could squelch the story was dead.

Horowitz also shows, through descriptions of the poverty facing the homeless young people haunting London's streets, that the rich and powerful figuratively "screwed" the lowest socioeconomic class. In this novel, the impoverished boys who would grow up to become men enslaved by their social class are victimized by ruthless upper class men, whether they overtly rape them or covertly use them as low-paid workers and thus ensure their limited future by enforcing rigid class distinctions. Horowitz-as-Watson comments early in the novel that "childhood, after all, is the first precious coin that poverty steals from a child" (52); innocence, in every sense, is lost early. Unlike more romantic visions of Victorian London inherent in other adaptations, Horowitz presents a brutal social reality.

During a case revolving around the House of Silk, in which Holmes is drawn deeper into a murder mystery, a boy working with the Baker Street Irregulars ends up dead. Even stoic, pragmatic Holmes begins to question the way he treats the ragtag youths who keep him informed of London's seedier activities. He pays the boys for their information and somewhat keeps an eye on them, but he also puts them in harm's way without really thinking about the potentially dangerous consequences they may suffer. Not really thinking about class distinctions is about as "immoral" as the detective gets — and he surpasses most of his peers' sense of social responsibility by paying the Irregulars well, and frequently, for being his eyes and ears on the street. Nevertheless, Holmes considers that his actions may be representative of a larger societal problem (97–8).

Holmes and Watson become horrified by what they discover as they solve a murder mystery. Long before Watson figures out the House of Silk's importance, Holmes realizes what is taking place at the secret meeting place. He warns Watson that what the doctor may see upon entering the "house of ill repute" may sicken him. Whether that is because the perpetrators are pedophiles or because the crime is non-consensual sex — or even just same-gender sex — is never made clear. The whole situation is depicted as depraved.

Most, if not all, readers will agree with Holmes that pedophiles need to be caught and punished for their actions. However, in this novel, girls are not the focus of men's sexual appetites — boys are. Readers "decoding" Horowitz's text thus may interpret the source of Holmes' and Watson's horror in several ways — pedophilia, sexual slavery, illicit sex, abuse of power by the privileged classes, and/or prevalence of social corruption/lack of willingness to report or stop the illegal acts — but also the shock or shame of same-gender sex. Although no adult homosexual relationships are indicated in this story, which likely would make the novel more controversial by creating a then-versus-now comparison of social acceptance of same-gender relationships, readers may question whether Horowitz/Watson is subtly condemning not only pedophilia but same-sex relationships, because only boys are sex slaves in this story.

Clearly, the sexual relationships are depicted as forced — innocent, wide-eyed boys have no choice but to accept their fate or, in one case, run away and possibly die on London's streets rather than be subjected to further abuse. Readers may question how they should interpret male-male relationships in light of this plot. Are the pedophiles who use these boys evil because they are pedophiles — or are they especially evil because they prey upon their own gender? Are they evil because they have hidden homosexual desires that are met by secret societies hidden away outside London? Are the perpetrators corrupt because they cover up a lucrative sex trade involving young boys, or are they representative of the larger society's corruption? Is the pervasive corruption within the wealthy classes, illustrated by the cover-up of the House of Silk, possibly a result of homosexuality itself?

Whether too much may be read into Horowitz's choice of criminals and victims depends on readers'/Holmes fans' decoding of the text and their expectations of the way same-gender sexual relationships "should" be decoded in a modern Sherlock Holmes adaptation. However readers otherwise interpret this text, the novel's sexual undercurrent clearly reminds readers that Holmes and Watson, despite their obvious fondness for each other and extremely close friendship, are not lovers and are not homosexual or bisexual. In fact, Watson's marriage and his children and grandchildren are mentioned as a way of providing closure to Watson's life, as well as Holmes, by the end of the novel.

The House of Silk becomes a significant modern text because it is sanctioned by the Estate, which gives it far more weight than any other of the many Sherlock Holmes adventures published in the past decade. That the novel's inclusion of homosexuality in this crime story differs significantly from the ways that innuendo-laden male-male relationships have been depicted in recent live-action adaptations further increases the novel's importance as a text to be analyzed.

What Is the Real Holmes-Watson Relationship?

If Horowitz's plot clearly shows what the Holmes-Watson relationship is *not,* Watson's comments, especially the sentimental closing to the book — and quite possibly to canon, if this is the last officially sanctioned book — just as clearly indicate what that relationship *is.* The cases forming the novel's plot take place during Watson's marriage to Mary Morstan, who is conveniently away from home during this story. During Mary's absence, John Watson returns to 221B Baker. By setting the story in this way, Horowitz has the best of both relationship worlds to emphasize Watson's heterosexuality. First, Watson is married and in love with his wife, and his later explanation of his children's and grandchildren's role in his elder years emphasizes his commitment to marriage and family. Even if Conan Doyle's stories did not discuss Watson's marriage(s) in great detail, Horowitz reasonably fills in the gaps by alluding to Watson's congenial and loving relationship with successive generations of Watsons. Second, Watson loves Holmes and, as the chronicler of this most controversial of Holmes' cases, often sentimentalizes the detective far more than the Conan Doyle stories have done. The resulting picture is a balance between the canon depictions of Holmes and Watson individually and together and a modern emotional attachment to the depth of Holmes and Watson's partnership.

According to Horowitz, although Watson remains at home with his wife once her illness becomes apparent, he never abandons Holmes. When Mary is away visiting friends, or when she is well enough for her husband to leave her side, Watson returns to Baker Street to check on Holmes. They often spend the day together, simply enjoying each other's company, if Holmes is not working on a case. Much later in life, Watson writes that one of his grandchildren is named Sherlock as the doctor's daughter's way of paying homage to her father's friendship (289). Watson's family apparently understands his need of Holmes' friendship and respects their partnership. The novel does not mention whether Holmes tries to intrude in Watson's marriage or compete for Watson's attention, as the recent television and film adaptations have done. Instead, this novel, told from Watson's point of view, shows the doctor's devotion to his friend and his interest in Holmes' work, but it also indicates that Watson is aware of his friend's social shortcomings.

Watson may be more charitable and apologetic toward Inspector Lestrade, but he still notes Holmes' own weaknesses of personality. Although the detective may think of himself as a machine, Watson suggests an outing to the Royal Academy because "perhaps an appreciation of art is what you need to humanize you" (56). Watson gently takes Holmes to task for his personality, but he also is unfailingly supportive and shows concern when Holmes is endangered.

While Holmes is incarcerated after an investigation goes horribly awry, Watson receives an invitation to visit an anonymous informant who, in hindsight, sounds suspiciously like Moriarty. To receive the information he desires, Watson must promise not to reveal the man's identity and to agree to his terms before he provides details that could save Holmes' life. Watson swears on his marriage to honor the agreement. "Not good enough," the informant replies, to which Watson then amends the agreement to swear "on my friendship with Holmes" (196). Watson's depth of commitment to his friendship, not his marriage, convinces the man that the doctor will keep his word. Readers cannot help but understand that, for all Watson loves his wife, his bond with Holmes is even more inviolate.

For his part, Holmes shows concern for Watson in a section reminiscent of "The Three Garridebs," when the detective shows his fear that Watson is seriously injured. In *The House of Silk,* Watson is attacked, and Horowitz reminds readers of the canon incident: "I remember that there would be another occasion, ten years later, when I would be hurt while in the company of Sherlock Holmes ... I felt almost a sense of gratitude toward both my attackers who demonstrated that my physical well-being did at least mean something to the great man" (93). This time Watson is not seriously hurt, and

Holmes insists on getting a carriage to take them back to Baker Street, where they can relax by the fire and contemplate the latest turn in the case.

Perhaps even more important, the Holmes described in *The House of Silk* has a moral center which is disturbed by the sexual abuse and murders revealed by his recent investigations. Instead of solving puzzles for their own sake, Holmes seems disturbed or possibly depressed by the lack of justice for the boys whose lives were destroyed by the House of Silk. The powerful men behind the operation get away, possibly to start again somewhere else, and the corruption within the highest levels of British society remains hidden. Watson suggests that Holmes' conscience should be somewhat eased because the detective ensured the demise of the House of Silk, but Holmes does not seem convinced. The novel emphasizes Holmes' conscience and suggests that the detective's "socialization" is complete now that he has recognized the lack of justice and tried to do something about it. Of course, Holmes does not always work within the law himself, but in this story he seems to be as interested in avenging an impoverished, murdered boy as in solving a complicated case.

Holmes-Watson fans looking for romantic same-gender relationships may question why, out of all possible plots, Horowitz chose to write about pedophiles and non-consensual homosexual sex in a Sherlock Holmes novel given added significance from its association with the Conan Doyle Estate. They may wonder if Horowitz, or Horowitz-as-Watson, or Horowitz as representative of Conan Doyle wanted to clarify the nature of the Holmes-Watson relationship by contrasting it with a very negative depiction of homosexual sex. That the Holmes-Watson friendship is as deeply binding a love relationship as a marriage is not in question, but Horowitz's plot reinforces reader awareness of Victorian acceptance only of platonic male friendships; love, but not sex, is legally, socially, and morally permissible between men.

Horowitz ends his novel with Watson's summary of the importance of this last case and the way Holmes deals with its aftermath. The last lines describe Holmes playing his violin, music that Watson cannot forget and even seems to hear calling him years after Holmes has died. Horowitz writes a fitting romantic, if platonic, conclusion: "The style is unmistakable. It is Sherlock Holmes who is playing ... I hope with all my heart that he is playing for me..." (294; author's ellipsis, indicating the continuing story, perhaps even after both characters' deaths).

Although Moffat was discussing his own television series, perhaps he best summarizes all recent adaptations of the Sherlock Holmes-John Watson relationship, including the one described in *The House of Silk*: "It doesn't actually have to be as mundane as a love story — it's much more interesting than that" (Frost).

Works Cited

"Benedict Cumberbatch on the Return of Sherlock." SeenIt. 9 Dec. 2011. Web. 26 Dec. 2011. <http://www.seenit.co.uk/benedict-cumberbatch-on-the-return-of-sherlock/1216712/>.

Bernstein, Abbie. "The Ax Interview: Showrunners Steven Moffat and Mark Gatiss on 'Sherlock' and 'Doctor Who.'" Assignment X. 12 Nov. 2010. Web. 26 Dec. 2011. <http://www.assign mentx.com/2010/the-ax-interview-showrunners-steven-moffat-and-mark-gatiss-on-sherlock-and-doctor-who/>.

Crowther, Jane. "A Fine Bromance." *Total Film* 187 (Dec. 2011): 80–4, 86. Print.

"Decoding the Subtext: The Gloria Scott." The Gloria Scott — With Love, S.H. n.d. Web. 26 Dec. 2011. <http://www.nekosmuse.com/sherlockholmes/subtext/gloriascott.htm>.

Dibdin, Emma. "Holmes Improvement?" *Total Film* 187 (Dec. 2011): 88–9. Print.

DuChateau, Christian. "Inside the New Sherlock Holmes Book." CNN. 4 Nov. 2011. Web. 26 Dec. 2011. <http://www.cnn.com/2011/11/04/living/anthony-horowitz-author-interview/index.html>.

Frost, Vicky. "Sherlock Returns for Second BBC Series." *The Guardian.* 8 Dec. 2011. Web. 26 Dec. 2011. <http://www.guardian.co.uk/tv-and-radio/2011/dec/08/sherlock-returns-bbc?newsfeed=true>.

Horowitz, Anthony. *The House of Silk.* New York: Mulholland, 2011. Print.

Mumford, Gwilym. "Sherlock Returns to the BBC: 'He's Definitely Devilish.'" *The Guardian.* 16 Dec. 2011. Web. 26 Dec. 2011. <http://www.guardian.co.uk/tv-and-radio/2011/dec/17/sherlock-bbc-cumberbatch-freeman-interview?newsfeed=true>.

Oulton, Carolyn. *Romantic Friendship in Victorian Literature.* London: Ashgate, 2007. Print.

Redmond, Christopher. *In Bed with Sherlock Holmes: Sexual Elements in Arthur Conan Doyle's Stories of the Great Detective.* Toronto: Dundurn, 2002. Print.

"A Scandal in Belgravia." *Sherlock.* Writ. Steven Moffat. Dir. Paul McGuigan. BBC Worldwide. 2011. DVD.

Sherlock Holmes. Writ. Michael Robert Johnson, Anthony Peckham, and Simon Kinberg. Dir. Guy Ritchie. Warner Bros. 2009.

Sherlock Holmes: A Game of Shadows. Writ. Michele Mulroney, and Kieran Mulroney. Dir. Guy Ritchie. Warner Bros. 2011.

Spencer, Charles. "Sherlock Holmes: We Are Living in a Golden Age of Sherlockiana." *The Telegraph.* 19 Dec. 2011. Web. 26 Dec. 2011. <http://www.telegraph.co.uk/culture/film-/film-blog/8966559/Sherlock-Holmes-we-are-living-in-a-golden-age-of-Sherlock iana.html>.

Warner, Kara. "Robert Downey, Jr., Drags on 'Sherlock Holmes.'" MTV. 15 Dec. 2011. Web. 26 Dec. 2011. <http://moviesblog.mtv.com/2011/12/15/robert-downey-jr-sherlock-holmes-drag/>.

14

Bookends of the Great Detective's Life
Neil Gaiman's Award-Winning Pastiches
LYNNETTE PORTER

Within a decade, Neil Gaiman has bookended Sherlock Holmes' vaunted career with two award-nominated or winning pastiches: "A Study in Emerald" (2004 Hugo Award-winning best story) and "The Case of Death and Honey" (2012 Mystery Writers of America's Edgar Award nominee). The former story inserts Holmes and Watson in an alternate reality and blends Arthur Conan Doyle with a dose of H.P. Lovecraft, although readers do not need to be familiar with these authors' mystery or science fiction canon in order to enjoy and understand Gaiman's science fiction/mystery stories. The latter follows Holmes overseas during the great detective's retirement as he solves a last, but most important crime. These well-designed pastiches capture Sherlock Holmes' personality and clever aspects of the Conan Doyle canon, but they also quite effectively place Sherlock Holmes in the science fiction genre. Although they simulate Conan Doyle's writing style, they also cleverly reflect the plot twists and style of one of the world's best known and loved fantasy/science fiction writers, Neil Gaiman.

Holmes, as characterized by Gaiman, is appropriately British, whether fighting aliens with Watson by his side or conducting experiments with mutant bees in China. Gaiman's skewed vision of the Victorian age is revealed first in "A Study in Emerald"'s alternate universe that introduces sci-fi horrors into the typically Holmesian setting of foggy London near the turn of the 20th century. The alternate universe mirrors the Victorian society that readers know from the Conan Doyle texts, and Gaiman deftly works into his alternative London the elements that will seem most comforting or common to readers. Gaiman's London, for example, still has hansom cabs, back alleys, dodgy sections of the city, and itinerant theater troupes, as well as plot devices familiar to Holmes fans: a mysterious murder (this time, of foreign royalty), a detective working undercover, and a trail of clues that gradually reveal the truths surrounding the murder.

Even the later story, "The Case of Death and Honey," which is set after Holmes' retirement, reflects expected elements of Victorian culture that reinforce Holmes' personality. As a man of science and one interested in logical deduction, Holmes well represents Victorian interest in science and technology. A modern Victorian scientist quite rightly might believe that, if man could only uncover Science's (or Nature's) secrets, he could, in effect, be as knowledgeable as God. He is confident in his potential to logically, scientifically analyze cause-effect relationships and understand the natural world as logical and law driven, not as part of a religious paradigm. Gaiman simply exchanges "Victorian man" for a man — Sherlock Holmes — who quite methodically narrows his study of bees until he finds the right hive and, under the right experimental conditions, achieves the result he theorized was possible.

That Holmes' final puzzle is the nature of Death — and by understanding it, how to reverse physical decay — is appropriate not only as a coda to Holmes' retirement but as a commentary (appropriate for this book's final chapter) on the everlasting appeal of Sherlock Holmes as a character and Holmesian detective stories as an eternal source of entertainment. Death is also one of Gaiman's favorite themes (or characters, as in the Sandman series). Through this story, Sherlock Holmes and Neil Gaiman share a common interest.

Holmes' travels into a land where he is the foreigner also emphasize the "traditional" aspects of the character's personality. Because Holmes' actions and manner of speaking reflect different cultural norms than those of rural China, the detective's differences from Chinese villagers is even more striking than his differences from other Englishmen. In physical appearance, the old man who enters the village is markedly different from local citizens. He is much taller and paler than anyone in the village, and he carries a strange leather satchel. He shares the locals' love of tea, but he is much more forthright in his tea-time conversation. Holmes is looking for a particular type of bee and someone who will allow him to study hives — quite a strange request. When Holmes leases a hive from Old Gao and then lives for the better part of a year in isolation that is only relieved by Gao's intermittent visits, he truly seems foreign to the more social villagers. Only Gao, who is himself a loner, understands Holmes' solitude, even if he does not comprehend the strange experiments involving his hives. Even Holmes' departure is mysterious, and the villagers eventually tear up the floor boards in the hut where he lived in order to determine if Holmes was murdered. They find remnants of his strange notes regarding his experiment — nothing more. Holmes' extreme focus on his work, general lack of sociability, and use of people to gain what he needs for his work are well illustrated in this short story, and his physical appearance and personality should be familiar to readers of Conan Doyle's Sherlock

Holmes stories. In both "A Study in Emerald" and "The Case of Death and Honey," Gaiman shows that, no matter in which genre or setting the detective is placed, he is quintessentially Sherlock Holmes, London citizen and genius.

Although Gaiman's stories are, to a great extent, true to Victorian Holmes' personality and modus operandi, they also cast him in the more familiar modern realm of sentimentalism, especially regarding his relationship with John Watson. These pastiches are not as emotional as fan fiction or as sexual orientation-questioning as, for example, Guy Ritchie's films, but they still illustrate a 21st century fondness for making Sherlock Holmes more intentionally heroic as well as more human than he seems in the original stories. Holmes the hero is better represented in "A Study in Emerald," set earlier in the detective's life, when he and Watson are fighting a corrupt society and, quite appropriately, James Moriarty. Sentimental Holmes is better represented in "The Case of Death and Honey," set after the detective's retirement. This story emphasizes Holmes' closest personal relationships — those with his brother Mycroft and his old friend Watson.

The Avenging Hero of "A Study in Emerald"

What if Victorian London regularly called upon the world's only consulting criminal instead of detective — and that "criminal" worked on behalf of the monarchy and police? In a world in which vice is virtuous and aliens literally rule, Sherlock Holmes becomes an avenging hero, working outside society not to solve puzzles or avert crime, but to commit crimes — including murder. Such is the Conan Doyle-Lovecraft mashup presented by Gaiman in "A Study in Emerald."

Like Conan Doyle's "A Study in Scarlet," from which Gaiman freely borrows his murder plot, a consultant is brought in to deduce what exactly happened to the victim. Because he was a visiting royal and a distant relative of Queen Victoria, solving his murder is a top priority. The story quickly moves from deduction to deduction, leading the consultant and his assistant to a theatrical troupe presenting a historical re-enactment among its evening entertainments. In this section of the story, Gaiman drops far more hints about Holmes' world and its history; he also describes the political unrest between those who accept the current regime in power and the anarchists working to undermine it. The persons who murdered the royal visitor are probably anarchists, and the consultant on the case deduces that two men involved in the plot are part of the theatrical troupe.

Although the consultant determines that an actor, Sherry Vernet, is the murderer, the culprit manages to escape. However, he is cheeky enough to correspond with the consultant and vows to continue their rivalry. At this point in the story, readers seduced by Gaiman's mimicry of Conan Doyle's style realize that they, like the consultant, have been duped. The detective encouraged by Queen Victoria herself to take on the murder investigation is none other than Professor Moriarty. What readers expect from a traditional Sherlock Holmes story — that Moriarty and Sebastian Moran are the bad guys — is inverted in this alternate universe. Gaiman relies on readers' knowledge of Conan Doyle's Moriarty and Moran to create the story's twist.

Even in a world in which Moriarty represents government/authority/law, Holmes must still be Moriarty's equal and opponent. Readers familiar with the Conan Doyle stories, or their adaptations, assume that Sherlock Holmes and John Watson will be the "good guys" in any story, but in "A Study in Emerald," Gaiman makes them murderers and criminals working far outside society's laws. Gaiman's characters reverse their traditional roles in order to fool readers about the roles of Moriarty and Holmes in Gaiman's London. In the same way, the Victorian world portrayed in "A Study in Emerald" mimics and mocks the Victorian world portrayed in "A Study in Scarlet." This story succeeds in large part because readers already familiar with Sherlock Holmes automatically base their initial understanding of Gaiman's story on the assumption that it follows the structure and point of view presented in Conan Doyle's stories. Only as they read further do they begin to question the true identity of Gaiman's narrator and realize that the familiar characters live in a very different London.

If the "good" characters are those trying to solve the crime involving the murder of visiting royalty, then Holmes and Watson (who, in Holmes' letter to Moriarty, admit they committed the murder) are the story's villains. They deserve to be caught and punished. That they escape and are probably living somewhere in inner London is a travesty of the law.

However, Gaiman also leads readers into understanding the difference between legal justice and human justice. In this Holmes' London, aliens have subjugated humanity, and those in charge are defined as corrupt because they literally and figuratively prey upon humanity. Humans who work on behalf of their alien masters are, to Holmes' moral reckoning, the villains who must be stopped. Thus, in a more positive interpretation of Holmes' and Watson's disregard for life and law, they can be perceived as freedom fighters who kill the invaders feasting upon humans. In essence, Holmes and Watson avenge enslaved humanity.

Readers familiar with Conan Doyle's stories undoubtedly pick up more clues about the identities of the detective and the criminal long before the revelation of the plot's twist at the story's end. "Sherry Vernet" is an apt alias for Holmes. This tribute to the Conan Doyle canon comes from Holmes' one-time comment that he is distantly related to the French artist Vernet ("The Adventure of the Greek Interpreter").

The accomplice that Moran calls the Limping Doctor, based on evidence from the crime scene, is Dr. Watson, whose war wound (although Conan Doyle often seemed to forget exactly where Watson had been shot) has become an important characteristic of the BBC's latest John Watson, who has a "psychosomatic limp" that periodically returns ("A Study in Pink").

When Moriarty visits the theater troupe after their performance and, as part of his trap, tries to learn more about the playwright, Holmes-as-Vernet notes that "the playwright is a good friend of mine," an indirect reference to Watson's role as Holmes' chronicler in the Conan Doyle stories. These clues alert readers that the way they initially read the story—from the perspective of Holmes as he solves a murder—is incorrect. Holmes, as revealed later in the letter to Moriarty, lures an alien (truly a foreign dignitary) to the location where he will die, but Watson, with his medical knowledge as well as soldier's skill, does the killing.

Watson-as-healer is ignored in this story, but Watson-as-soldier, who also has the medical knowledge to become an efficient executioner, is nonetheless a "war hero" fighting on behalf of humanity. Just as Mycroft Holmes, in the BBC's *Sherlock,* tells John Watson that London is a battlefield ("A Study in Pink"), so does Neil Gaiman describe the alternate Victorian London as a battlefield. In both adaptations, Watson is valued more as a soldier with medical knowledge than as a doctor who can fire a gun. Both adaptations invite audiences to consider the nature of heroes and villains in time of war; these war-themed interpretations of John Watson also reflect the moral ambiguity of protagonists in many 21st century stories, whether told in print or on television.

In "A Study in Emerald," Holmes and Watson have taken on the moral duty to free humanity from invading overlords. Gaiman's Holmes and Watson are cunning and have many of the same traits ascribed to the original characters, but they are motivated not by solving puzzles or fighting for Queen and country—they are avenging heroes working on behalf of humanity. Their immoral acts—such as killing another—are deemed "moral" because they take place in a time of "war" and are conducted to save human lives. In this battle, Holmes has clearly chosen a side. Instead of being Conan Doyle's logical machine, Gaiman's Holmes thus is incredibly human.

Sentimentalism and "The Case of Death and Honey"

From the first sentence in this story, Death surrounds Holmes. Gaiman initially describes the retired detective as "the old white ghost man" considered a "barbarian" by the Chinese in the village he visits (167). Indeed, Holmes in this story is far from being a "civilized Christian" as the Chinese might expect of a visitor from England. He rather sacrilegiously intends to divine the god-like power of life over death, and he alone chooses who should receive the benefits of his knowledge. Because his experiments with bees give him a super-natural power over life, Holmes effectively begins a second life (or an after-life) as a much younger man as the result of his research.

Holmes' identification as a ghost also is practical as much as symbolic. By this point in his life, he suffers from ennui, the feeling that there are no great mysteries left to solve and thus no further purpose to his life. He realizes that "I am only alive when I perceive a challenge" (168). His mind is dying, a fact underscored during Mycroft's final days and last discussion with his brother. Unlike Sherlock, who seems ready for death because he is so bored with life, Mycroft laments his impending death because he will no longer be able to guide the Empire; he sees all that is left unaccomplished and wishes for more time. Quite likely, he also sees that his brother is deteriorating men-tally, just as Mycroft is physically debilitated. Therefore, he sets one last chal-lenge for his younger brother — the mystery of Death.

Of course, manipulative, unsentimental Mycroft saves his brother through the clever suggestion that he solve a heinous crime. Mycroft denigrates Sher-lock's profession by describing the crime as being as "monstrous as any of the penny-dreadful massacres you have investigated" (173). Mycroft views his own death as a crime, "one that might keep your attention for longer than it will take you to establish that the poor fellow who used to conduct the brass band in Hyde Park was murdered by the third cornet using a preparation of strychnine" (174). Although Sherlock seems unimpressed with Mycroft's sug-gestion, he eventually begins keeping bees in Sussex and then travels the world in search of the perfect bees to suit his purpose — to help him detect a flaw in Death's plan and to solve the crime. By understanding the nature of death, he can deduce the secret to long life, or possibly immortality. Sherlock could not save the "murdered" Mycroft, but he can unravel the nature of the crime and solve the puzzle.

However, solving the puzzle — even one as potentially satisfying as immortality — is not enough for Gaiman's Sherlock Holmes. Conan Doyle's great detective seems to care little for victims and is interested only in solving the crime — justice is not his motive. Gaiman's Holmes, however, deduces the nature of the "crime" for selfish interests that go beyond the satisfaction of puzzle solving. He wants to use his new knowledge to return himself and his friend Watson to their former youth.

Holmes might have trod other paths than the one eventually leading him back to England and Watson. He could have only chosen to save himself. He could have profited from the "honey of youth" or even wielded this knowledge to save the world's best and brightest from decay and death. He could achieve even greater, longer lasting fame or accumulate great wealth. Instead, Sherlock Holmes carefully packs a few jars of honey and destroys all evidence of his research. He keeps the secret of immortality to himself.

In a letter to Watson regarding one of Holmes' cases being written for posterity, the detective adds a paragraph about the danger of living forever and his belief that, if everyone could become immortal, the world would become a "cesspool" as people prolonged their "worthless lives" (178). Clearly, Holmes has no such fears about his or Watson's lives or the choices they would make as immortals.

In a roundabout way, Holmes makes one other exception; he grants youth and longevity to the beekeeper whose hive he leases, but instead of telling Old Gao his secret, Holmes leaves enough clues that the shrewd old man can solve the puzzle of Holmes' research and benefit from the results — if he is clever enough. Perhaps this is Holmes' way of thanking the old man for the opportunity to conduct his experiments and reap the rewards. An even more sentimental interpretation is that Holmes sees in Gao another old man who loves his work, has become isolated from society by choice because of that work, and has no successor to continue his work. Giving Gao the opportunity for another life thus may be a bit narcissistic, even if it is an extraordinary farewell present.

In contrast to his limited interaction with Gao, Holmes plans to ensure that Watson partakes of the life-restoring honey. He will not give Watson the opportunity to decide whether he becomes young again. Holmes confides to readers that "I shall invite my old friend over for tea. There will be honey on buttered toast served for tea that afternoon, I fancy" (186). True to Conan Doyle's "The Empty House," Gaiman's Holmes plans to disguise himself as an old man in order not to spook his friend after his long absence. His disguise will help ensure that Watson trusts him and can be "dosed" with the honey. Thus, Watson will grow young with him and live a long, possibly immortal life, even if that may not be what Watson would choose for himself.

This sentimental, if selfish, decision near the story's end is not the only time that Gaiman uses more emotional language to discuss Holmes' thoughts regarding his friend. Whereas the Holmes brothers' final conversation at Mycroft's death bed is unemotional in tone (although Mycroft clearly wants his brother to survive and even thrive, because he sets one final challenge for him), Sherlock's letter to Watson and his thoughts while they are separated clearly paint a more emotional portrait of the pair's friendship.

As Holmes plans his return trip to England, taking only enough honey for himself and Watson, he envisions their reunion. "I shall seek out Watson, if he still lives — and I fancy he does. It is irrational, I know, and yet I am certain I would know, somehow, had Watson passed beyond the veil" (186). This description is uncharacteristic of unemotional, logical Sherlock Holmes as depicted through his dialogue with Mycroft or Old Gao. Even Sherlock's interior monologues are straightforward and logic based. Only when Watson is considered does Holmes become anything but rational. The statement "It is irrational, I know" becomes more than a comment that he recognizes his lack of objectivity when it comes to his old friend. It introduces Holmes as something of a romantic — he would know if Watson died thousands of miles away. Mycroft's death is discussed in coldly efficient terms, such as how his rotund body will be removed from his death bed. Watson's demise is more emotionally, and less scientifically precisely, described as passing "beyond the veil."

Although "The Case of Death and Honey" concludes with the resolution to Old Gao's story, Gaiman's words about Sherlock Holmes reveal the detective's intention to invite Watson to tea and inoculate him against Death with a dose of honey, literally a sweet ending to Gaiman's Holmes' saga.

Gaiman's Pastiches and Modern Adaptations of Sherlock Holmes

Gaiman's stories, especially "A Study in Emerald," are remarkably true to the style, tone, and setting established by Conan Doyle. They illustrate Gaiman's knowledge of canon and familiarity with Conan Doyle's style. For all that these pastiches are intriguing stories that reflect Victorian society, they also succeed as modern stories compatible with other adaptations' depictions of Sherlock Holmes created for 21st century audiences.

Gaiman, especially in the more recent "The Case of Death and Honey," celebrates the Holmes-Watson friendship, but the character of Sherlock Holmes always takes center stage, whether he is disguised as an actor or is in his element as a scientist-detective. Despite Watson's presence being keenly felt in both stories, he never is directly seen or is given dialogue — he is created through other characters' (primarily Holmes') words or thoughts about him. He is a crucial part of both stories, but his character is filtered through the words, recollections, and even feelings of Sherlock Holmes. Unlike other adaptations of John Watson in print, on film, and on television, Gaiman's Watson exists only through Sherlock Holmes.

In "A Study in Emerald," Sherlock Holmes/Sherry Vernet exists because of James Moriarty and his ilk, who thrive in a society managed by an alien monarchy and a corrupt legal system. Holmes provides the necessary balance by opposing Moriarty. Many recent adaptations question Holmes' morality and give him the opportunity to join, rather than oppose, Moriarty. They ask what if Sherlock Holmes had become a "consulting criminal" rather than a consulting detective whose work — no matter what motivates him — results in criminals being caught and crimes solved. Gaiman's answer to the "what if" regarding Holmes' decision to oppose or collaborate with Moriarty is forcefully and cleverly illustrated in "A Study in Emerald." Although Holmes is society's criminal, he is no villain to humanity. Moriarty, although the government's or law enforcement's "good guy," only achieves this designation by supporting the powerful, corrupt aliens in charge.

In "The Case of Death and Honey," Holmes may or may not be working for the greater good by keeping the life-restoring honey a secret from the rest of the world. Readers may infer, by the end of the story, that once-again youthful Holmes and Watson will continue their crime-solving ways, but Gaiman gives no indication that this will happen. Perhaps Holmes merely wants to spend more time with his no-longer-old friend and will forego crime solving in favor of other pursuits. Whether that choice is a moral or purely selfish one is not important. Instead, in this story, Sherlock Holmes exists — or continues to live — because of Watson. Of course, the thrill of such an intriguing new "case" as solving Mycroft's "murder" undoubtedly motivates Holmes to travel the world in search of a solution, but the underlying sentimentality of Gaiman's story hints that, without Watson as a possible beneficiary of his research, Holmes might not be nearly so dedicated to this pursuit, or he might have stayed in China to conduct further experiments. Gaiman's stories require someone to balance and motivate Sherlock Holmes. Moriarty does so in the first, but Watson is given this role in the second.

Like other popular adaptations, including Guy Ritchie's *Sherlock Holmes: A Game of Shadows* and the BBC's *Sherlock*, Gaiman's stories help audiences understand and define Sherlock Holmes by comparing him with James Moriarty. One of Gaiman's two Sherlock Holmes stories significantly involves Moriarty, giving this character a great deal of importance in Gaiman's Holmes-themed writing. Perhaps not coincidentally, given Holmes' fans' fascination with this character, both the recent film franchise and BBC television series featured Moriarty in 2011–12. Ritchie's and the BBC's decision to adapt Conan Doyle's "The Final Problem" cannot be coincidental.

In *A Game of Shadows,* Sherlock Holmes' decision to destroy Moriarty, even if it requires self-sacrifice, is heroic in large part because it is a moral decision — Holmes wants to avert a world war being instigated by Moriarty's political and economic manipulations. In *Sherlock*'s "The Reichenbach Fall," the modern version of the title character turns down Moriarty's offer of a partnership and continues to disrupt the consulting criminal's lucrative business. During a final showdown, Sherlock's "moral" decision to take down

Moriarty seems to backfire: not only Jim Moriarty but Sherlock Holmes must die, or Moriarty's henchmen will kill others. Sherlock's decision is more personal and less global — he is more concerned with his own little world than with Moriarty's plans for global domination. Sherlock chooses to end his life only because, by doing so, he immediately saves the lives of the three people closest to him. His fascination with amoral, if successful characters during the second season's episodes — including Irene Adler and Jim Moriarty — renders him a morally ambiguous character. However, his "humanization" during the second season makes his final confrontation with Moriarty, in which both are meant to be destroyed, a personal decision instead of one for the greater good.

Gaiman's Sherlock Holmes in "The Case of Death and Honey" is more akin to the BBC's Sherlock, whose emotional attachment to John Watson is key to his actions. Gaiman's younger Holmes, as described in "A Study in Emerald," is the one who, like Ritchie's Holmes, takes a definitive moral stance regarding Moriarty. Thus, through both stories, Gaiman's Holmes not only accurately reflects Conan Doyle's original creation but also the most popular recent adaptations.

As the many adaptations discussed in this book illustrate, Gaiman is on the right track with the conclusion of "The Case of Death and Honey." Sherlock Holmes and John Watson will never grow old in our imagination or their ability to entertain us. No matter in which time period, or even universe; no matter if they are portrayed as young, middle-aged, or old men; Holmes needs Watson, and readers/audiences the world over need Sherlock Holmes.

WORKS CITED

Conan Doyle, Arthur. "The Adventures of the Greek Interpreter." *The Mysterious Adventures of Sherlock Holmes.* London: Puffin Books, 1995. Print.
_____. "The Empty House." *The Return of Sherlock Holmes.* Mineola, NY: Dover, 2010. Print.
Gaiman, Neil. "The Case of Death and Honey." *A Study in Sherlock: Stories Inspired by the Holmes Canon.* Laurie R. King and Leslie S. Klinger, eds. 167–189. New York: Bantam, 2011.
_____. "A Study in Emerald." Web. 2004. <http://www.neilgaiman.com/mediafiles/exclusive/shortstories/emerald.pdf>.
"The Reichenbach Fall." *Sherlock.* Writ. Steve Thompson. Dir. Toby Haynes. BBC Worldwide. 2012. DVD.
Sherlock Holmes: A Game of Shadows. Dir. Guy Ritchie. Warner Bros., 2011. Film.
"A Study in Pink." *Sherlock.* Writ. Steven Moffat and Mark Gatiss. Dir. Paul McGuigan. BBC Worldwide, 2010. DVD.

About the Contributors

Svetlana **Bochman** holds a Ph.D. in Victorian studies and teaches at the City University of New York, where her specialties are 19th century British literature and first-year composition. She has written not only about Conan Doyle but also Jane Austen and Oscar Wilde.

Jennifer C. **Garlen** teaches English as a visiting assistant professor at the University of Alabama in Huntsville. She is a graduate of Agnes Scott College and Georgia Southern University, with a doctoral degree from Auburn University. She writes an online column on classic movies and is the co-editor with Anissa M. Graham of *Kermit Culture: Critical Perspectives on Jim Henson's Muppets* (McFarland, 2009).

Anissa M. **Graham** is an instructor of English at the University of North Alabama, where she teaches composition and introduction to literature courses. Her work as a scholar includes examinations of 18th and 19th century Gothic literature and popular culture.

Ana E. **La Paz** teaches at Chemeketa Community College in Salem, Oregon, and is planning to earn a Ph.D. Although the focus for her dissertation will not be Holmes, she does teach Conan Doyle's stories in her Chemeketa classrooms.

Carlen **Lavigne** is a professor of communications at Red Deer College in Alberta, Canada. She holds a Ph.D. in communications studies and is the co-editor of *American Remakes of British Television: Transformations and Mistranslations* (Lexington, 2011).

Francesca M. **Marinaro** is a Ph.D. candidate in Victorian studies at the University of Florida and teaches in the English department. Her major research interests include feminist/gender studies and embodiment studies. Her dissertation is on political and sociological shifts in conceptions of motherhood in the Victorian novel.

Lynnette **Porter** is a professor in the Humanities and Social Sciences Department at Embry-Riddle University in Daytona Beach, Florida. She holds a Ph.D. in English from Bowling Green State University with specializations in technical communication and Victorian literature. A contributor to the popular culture magazine *PopMatters* and an editorial board member of *Studies in Popular Culture*, she has written more than a dozen books.

Rhonda Harris **Taylor** is an associate professor in the University of Oklahoma School of Library and Information Studies, where she teaches graduate courses in administration, popular culture and libraries, and the organization of information; her publications reflect these interests. She is the 2011 recipient of her university's College of Arts and Sciences Longmire Prize for Teaching.

Kayley **Thomas** is an English Ph.D. candidate at the University of Florida. Specializing in Victorian literature and culture and film and media studies, her research interests include adaptation, intertextuality, genre fiction and film, masculinities, and queer theory. Her dissertation examines the intersections of art with 19th century crime and detective fiction.

April **Toadvine** is an associate professor of English at Saint Joseph's College in Rensselaer, Indiana. A Victorianist, she has previously published on Anthony Trollope.

Index